STRAYED

STORY BY // **CARLOS GIFFONI**   ART AND COLORS BY // **JUAN DOE**

STRA

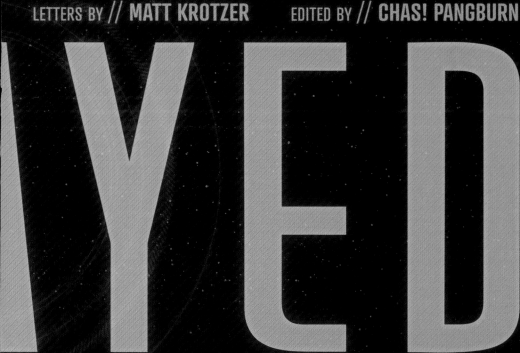

LETTERS BY // **MATT KROTZER**   EDITED BY // **CHAS! PANGBURN**

Publisher // **MIKE RICHARDSON**

Dark Horse Editor // **SPENCER CUSHING**   Dark Horse Assistant Editor // **KONNER KNUDSEN**

Designer // **SARAH TERRY** · Digital Art Technician // **JOSIE CHRISTENSEN**

Special Thanks to Trinity Bartel.

This volume collects issues #1 through #5 of the Dark Horse comic-book series *Strayed*.

Published by Dark Horse Books
A division of Dark Horse Comics LLC.
10956 SE Main Street // Milwaukie, OR 97222

DarkHorse.com
First edition: April 2020 // ISBN 978-1-50671-428-8

1 3 5 7 9 10 8 6 4 2
Printed in China

To find a comics shop in your area, visit comicshoplocator.com

NEIL HANKERSON Executive Vice President // TOM WEDDLE Chief Financial Officer // RANDY STRADLEY Vice President of Publishing // NICK McWHORTER Chief Business Development Officer // DALE LAFOUNTAIN Chief Information Officer // MATT PARKINSON Vice President of Marketing // CARA NIECE Vice President of Production and Scheduling // MARK BERNARDI Vice President of Book Trade and Digital Sales // KEN LIZZI General Counsel // DAVE MARSHALL Editor in Chief // DAVEY ESTRADA Editorial Director // CHRIS WARNER Senior Books Editor // CARY GRAZZINI Director of Specialty Projects // LIA RIBACCHI Art Director // VANESSA TODD-HOLMES Director of Print Purchasing // MATT DRYER Director of Digital Art and Prepress // MICHAEL GOMBOS Senior Director of Licensed Publications // KARI YADRO Director of Custom Programs // KARI TORSON Director of International Licensing // SEAN BRICE Director of Trade Sales

Library of Congress Cataloging-in-Publication Data

Names: Giffoni, Carlos, 1978- author. | Doe, Juan, artist. | Krotzer, Matt, letterer.
Title: Strayed / story by Carlos Giffoni ; art and colors by Juan Doe ; letters by Matt Krotzer.
Description: First edition. | Milwaukie, OR : Dark Horse Books, 2020. | "This volume collects issues #1 through #5 of the Dark Horse comic-book series Strayed." | Summary: "In the far future, a military-industrial complex reigns over all humanity and actively destroys distant alien worlds. The galaxy's only hope can be found through an unlikely pair: an astral-projecting cat named Lou and his loving owner Kiara"-- Provided by publisher.
Identifiers: LCCN 2019049094 | ISBN 9781506714288 (trade paperback)
Subjects: LCSH: Comic books, strips, etc.
Classification: LCC PN6728.S779 G54 2020 | DDC 741.5/973--dc23
LC record available at https://lccn.loc.gov/2019049094

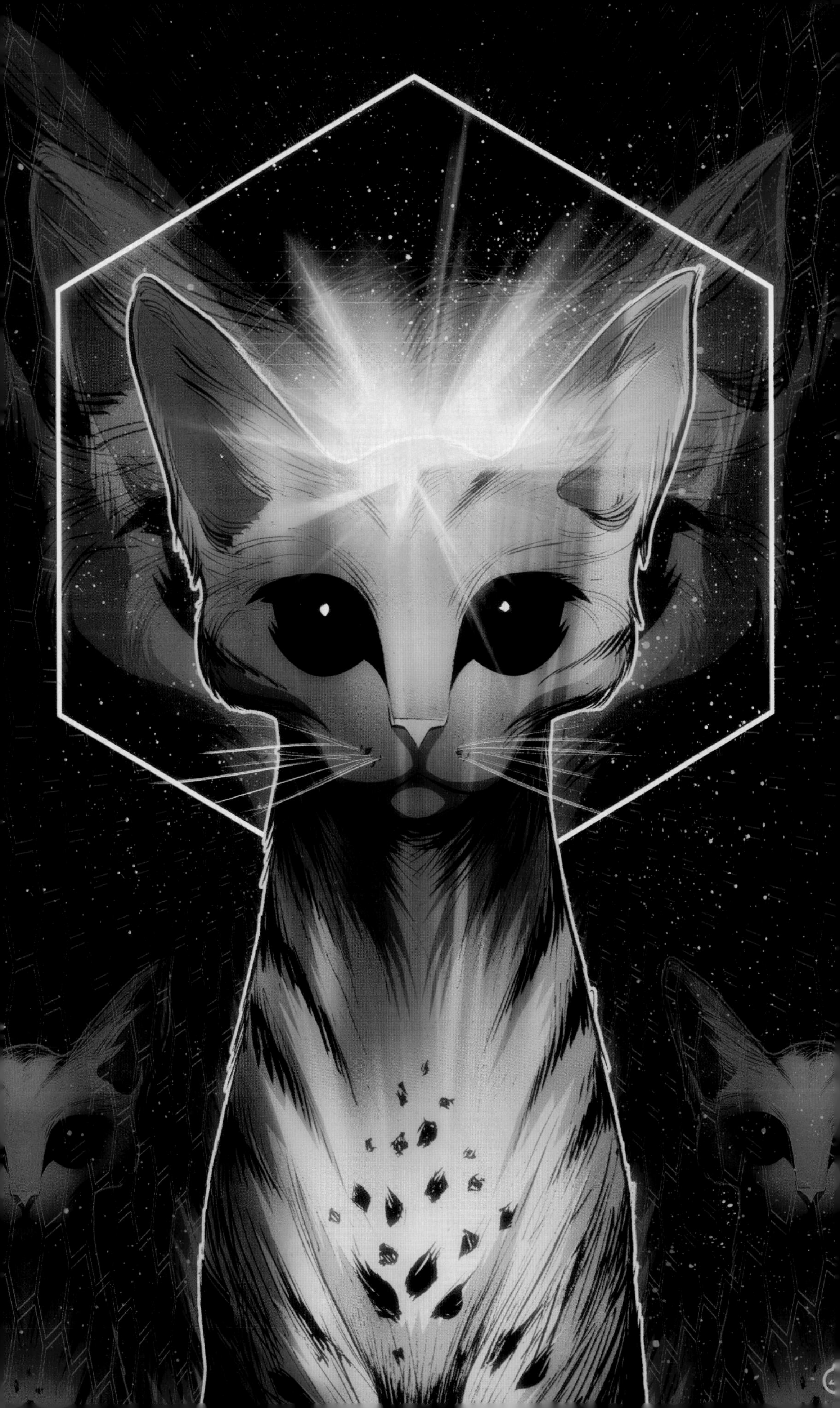

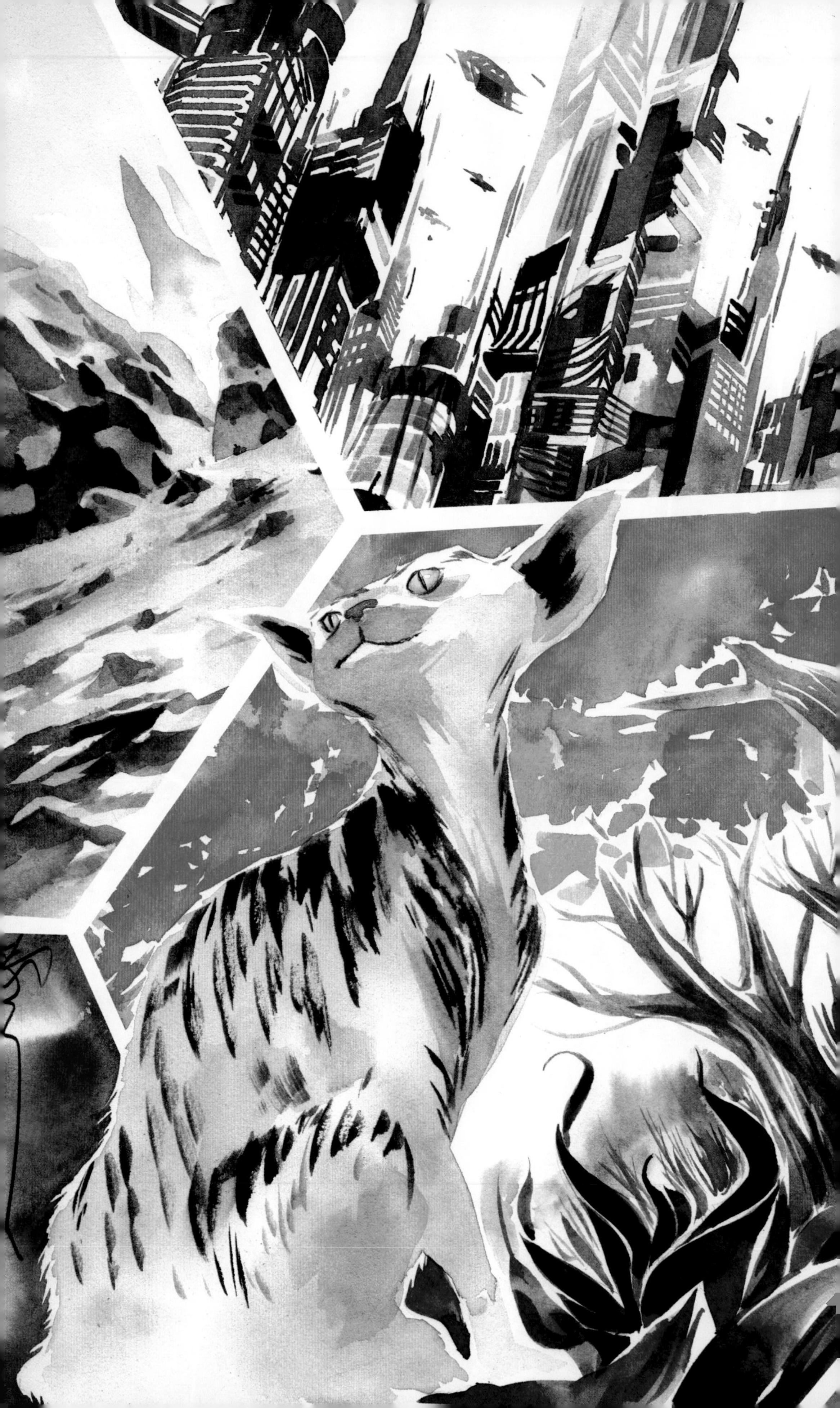

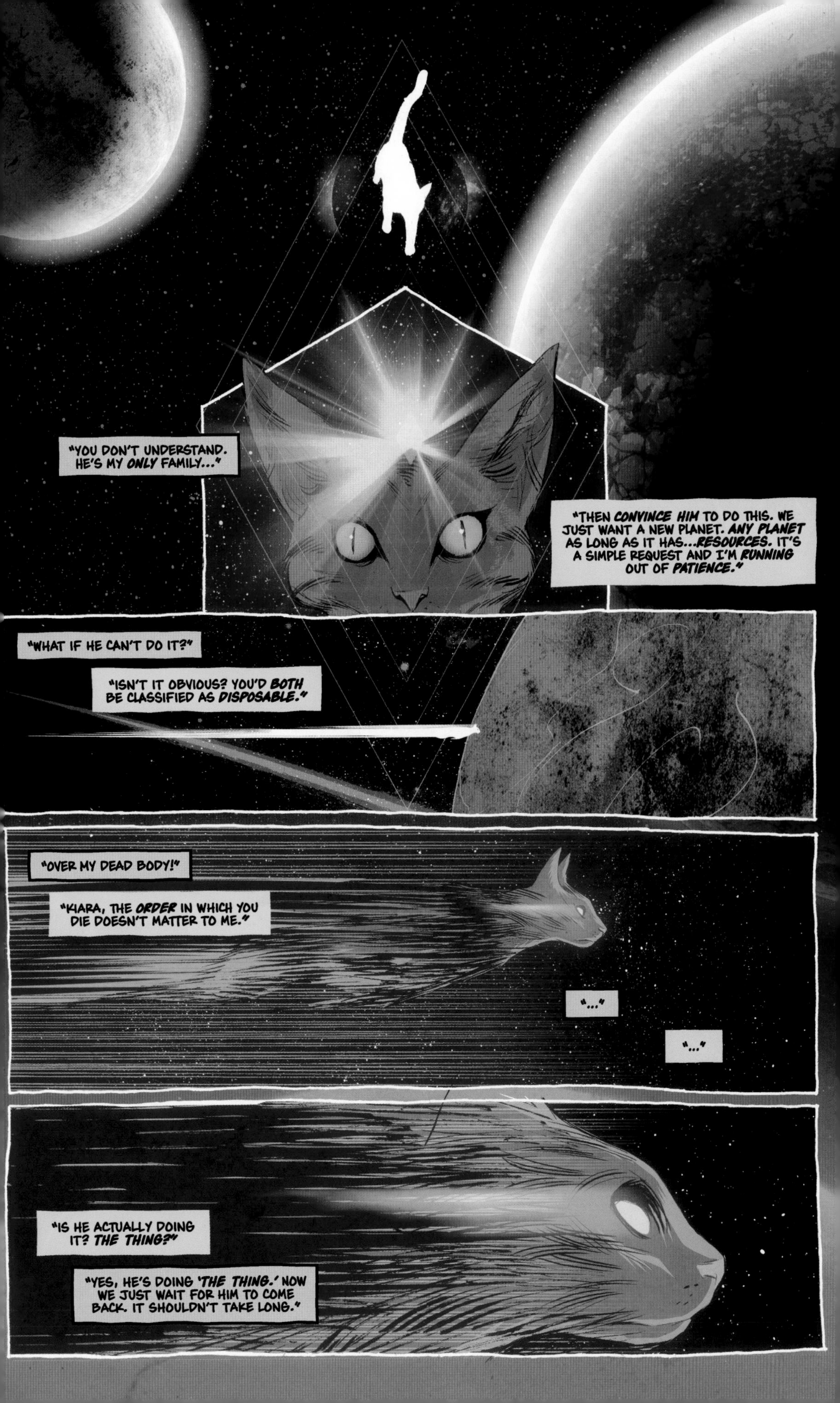
"YOU DON'T UNDERSTAND. HE'S MY ONLY FAMILY..."
"THEN CONVINCE HIM TO DO THIS. WE JUST WANT A NEW PLANET. ANY PLANET AS LONG AS IT HAS...RESOURCES. IT'S A SIMPLE REQUEST AND I'M RUNNING OUT OF PATIENCE."
"WHAT IF HE CAN'T DO IT?"
"ISN'T IT OBVIOUS? YOU'D BOTH BE CLASSIFIED AS DISPOSABLE."
"OVER MY DEAD BODY!"
"KIARA, THE ORDER IN WHICH YOU DIE DOESN'T MATTER TO ME."
"..."
"..."
"IS HE ACTUALLY DOING IT? THE THING?"
"YES, HE'S DOING 'THE THING.' NOW WE JUST WAIT FOR HIM TO COME BACK. IT SHOULDN'T TAKE LONG."

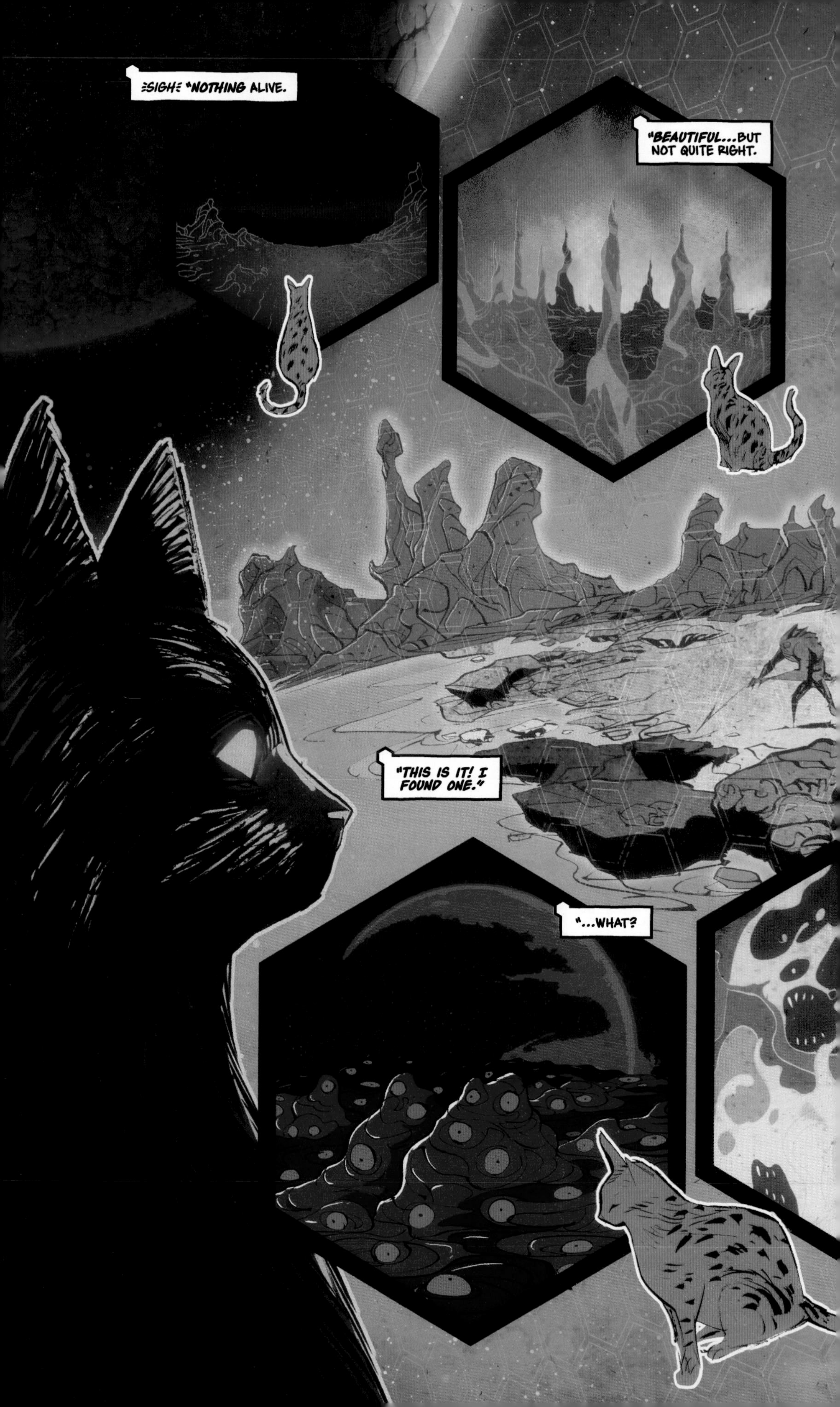

=SIGH= "NOTHING ALIVE.
"BEAUTIFUL...BUT NOT QUITE RIGHT.
"THIS IS IT! I FOUND ONE."
"...WHAT?

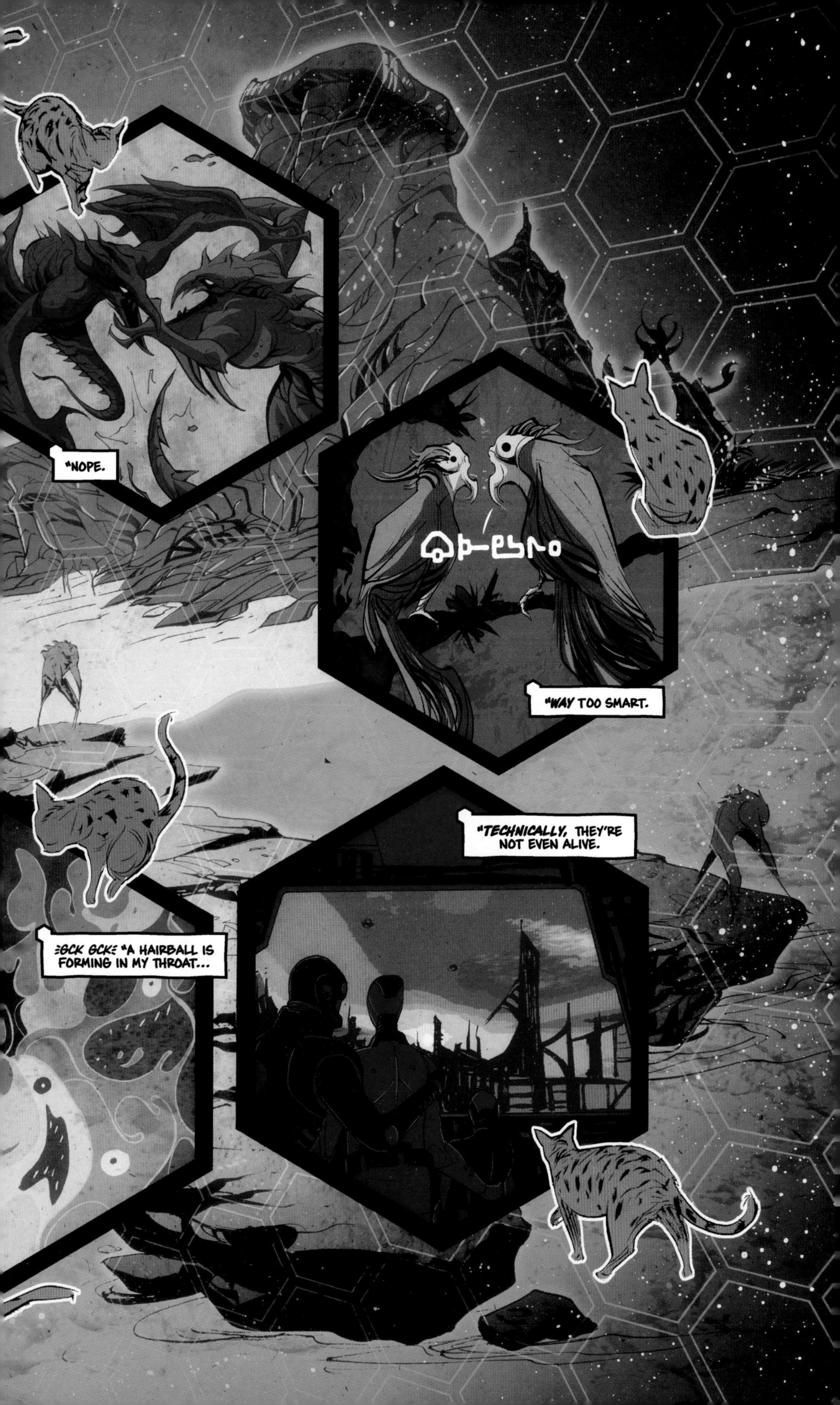
"NOPE.
"WAY TOO SMART.
"TECHNICALLY, THEY'RE NOT EVEN ALIVE.
GCK GCK "A HAIRBALL IS FORMING IN MY THROAT...

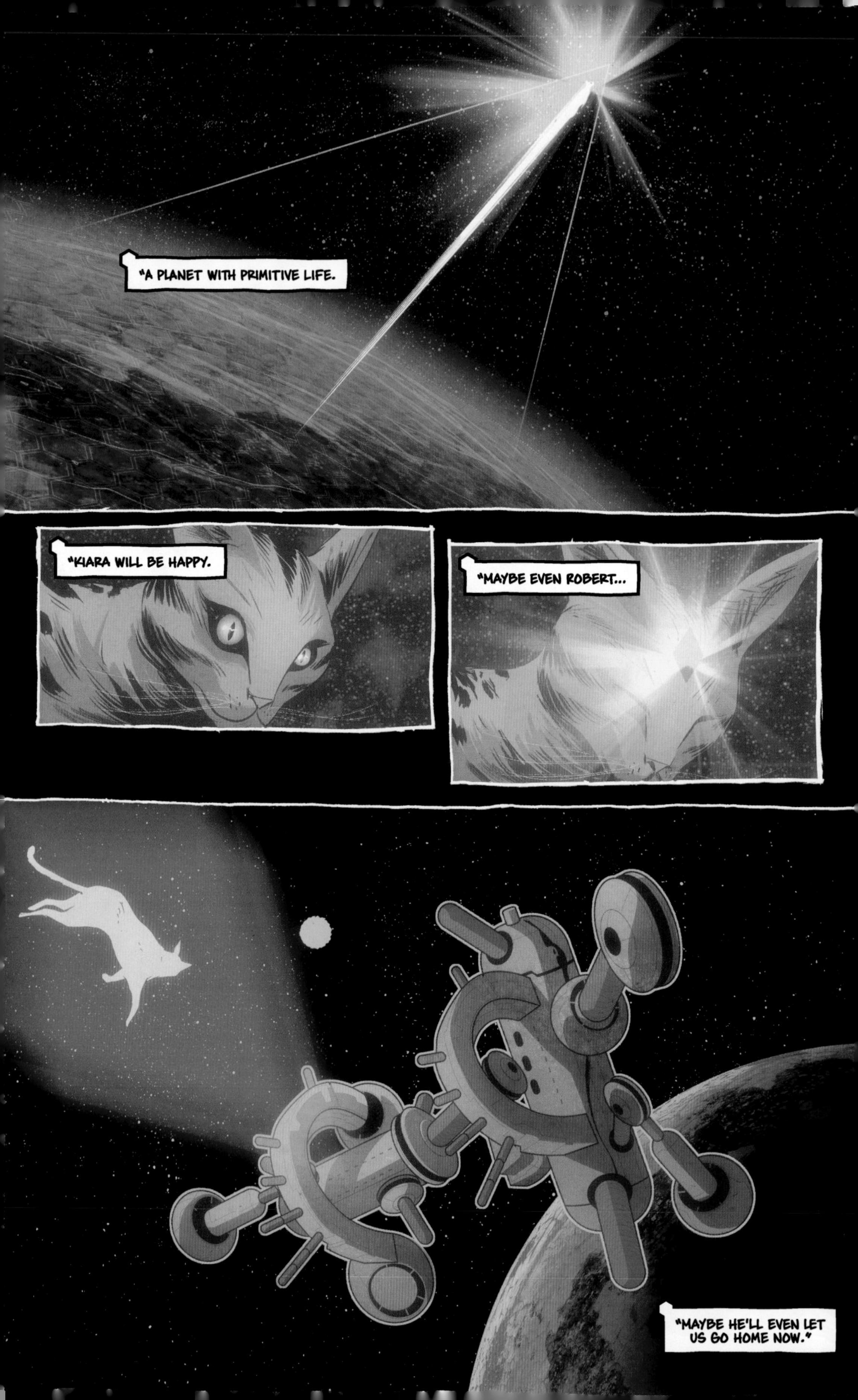
"A PLANET WITH PRIMITIVE LIFE.
"KIARA WILL BE HAPPY.
"MAYBE EVEN ROBERT...
"MAYBE HE'LL EVEN LET US GO HOME NOW."

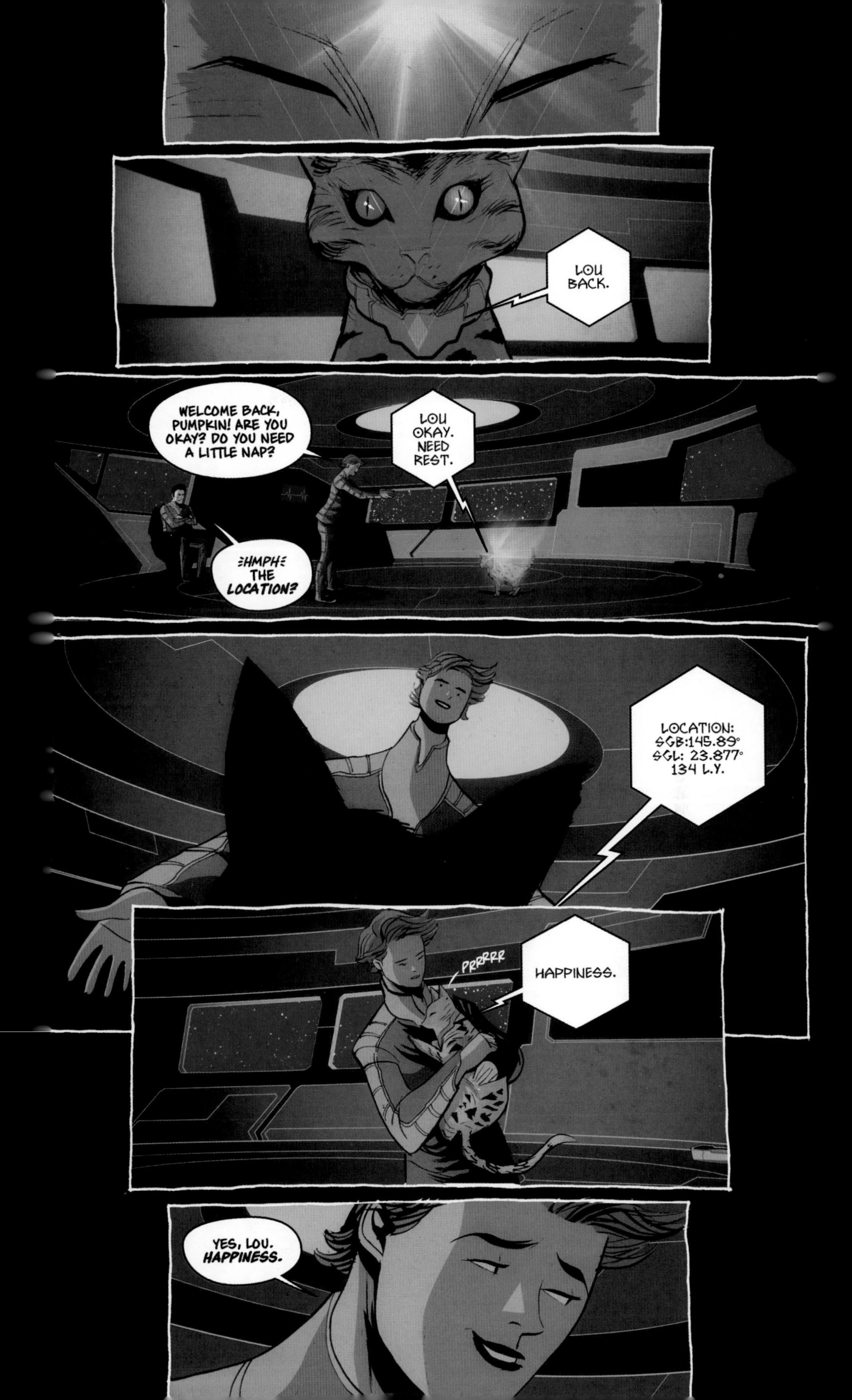
LOU BACK.
WELCOME BACK, PUMPKIN! ARE YOU OKAY? DO YOU NEED A LITTLE NAP?
LOU OKAY. NEED REST.
HMPH THE LOCATION?
LOCATION: SGB:145.89° SGL: 23.877° 134 L.Y.
PRRRRR
HAPPINESS.
YES, LOU. HAPPINESS.

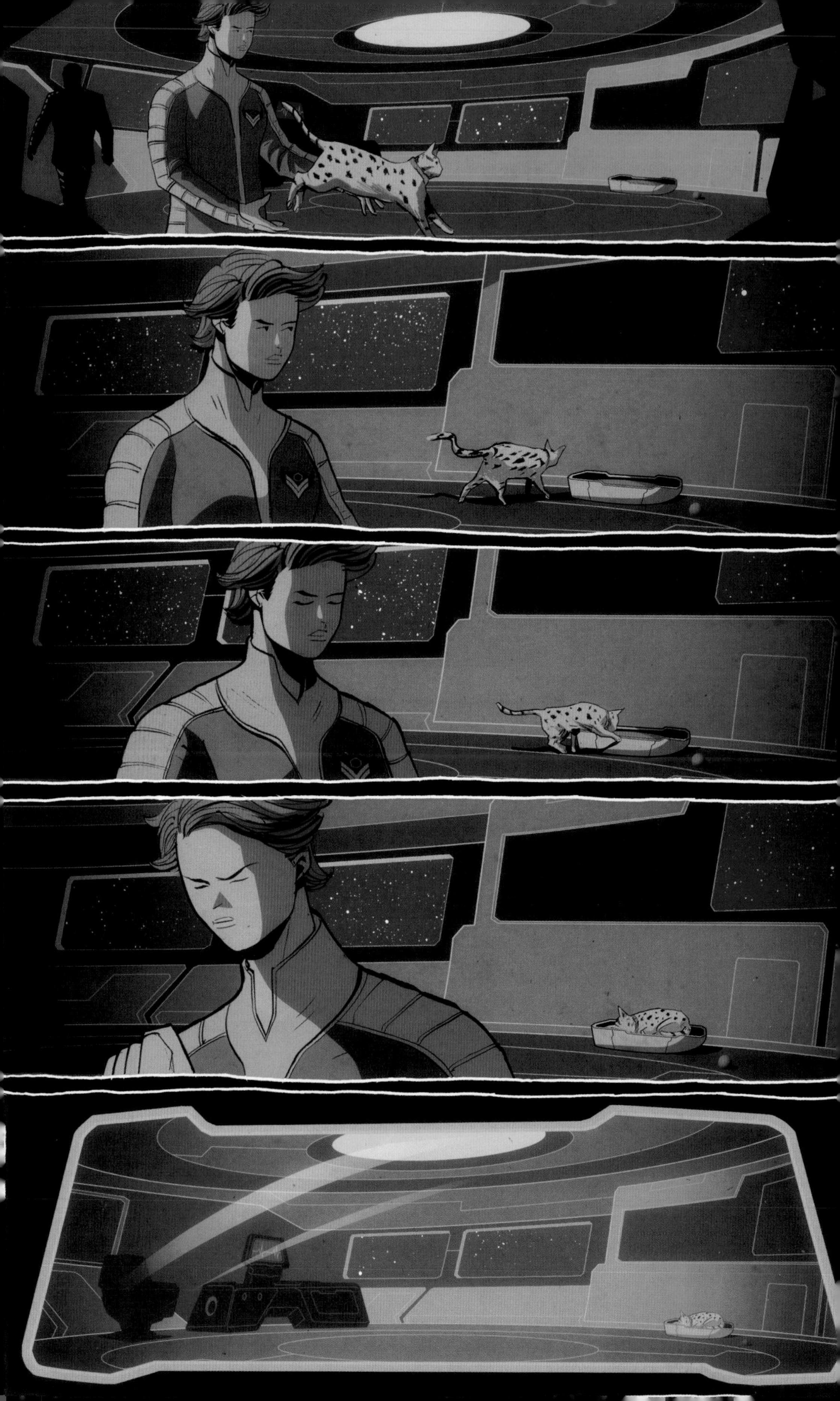

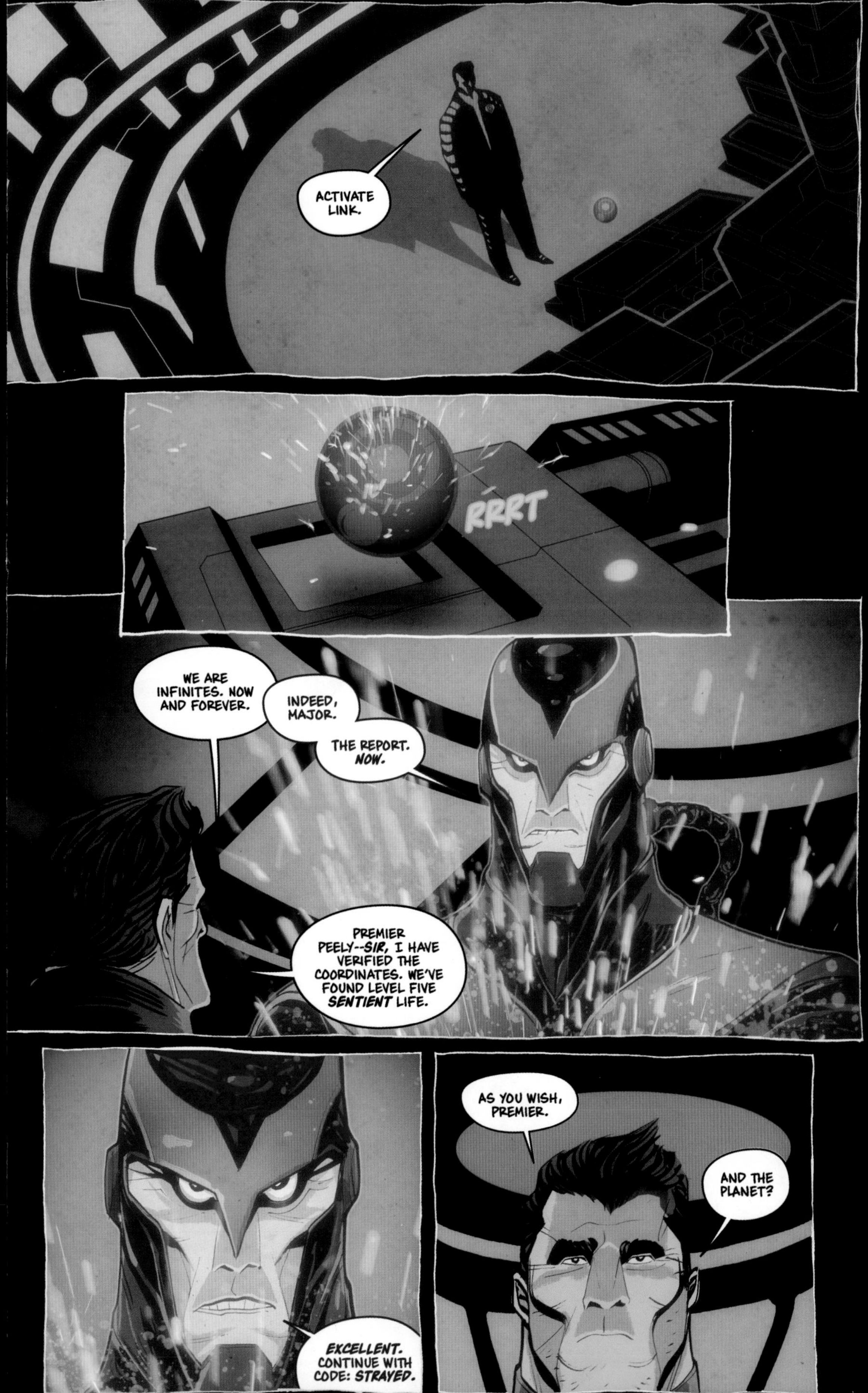
ACTIVATE LINK.
RRRT
WE ARE INFINITES. NOW AND FOREVER.
INDEED, MAJOR.
THE REPORT. *NOW.*
PREMIER PEELY--*SIR,* I HAVE VERIFIED THE COORDINATES. WE'VE FOUND LEVEL FIVE *SENTIENT* LIFE.
EXCELLENT. CONTINUE WITH CODE: *STRAYED.*
AS YOU WISH, PREMIER.
AND THE PLANET?

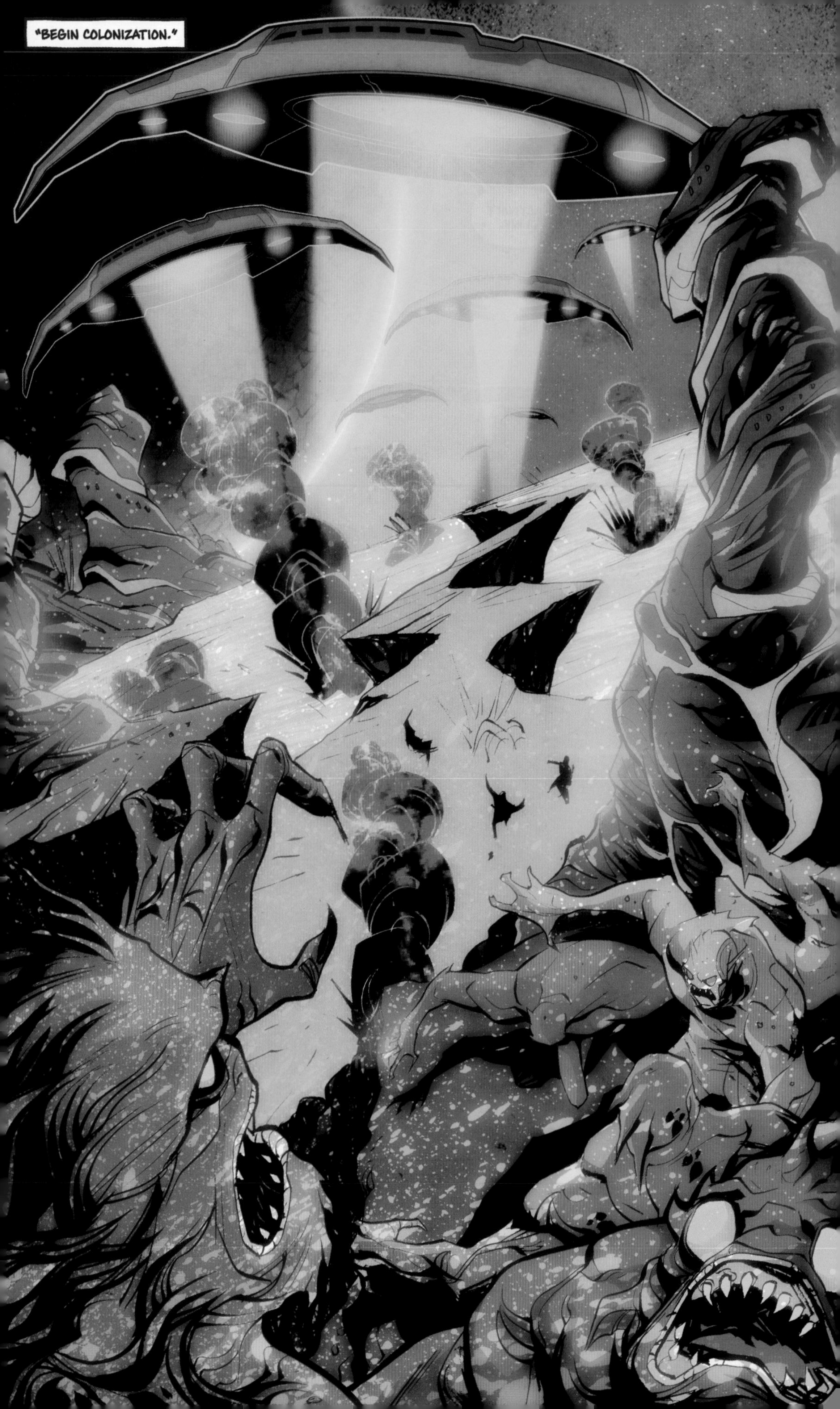
"BEGIN COLONIZATION."

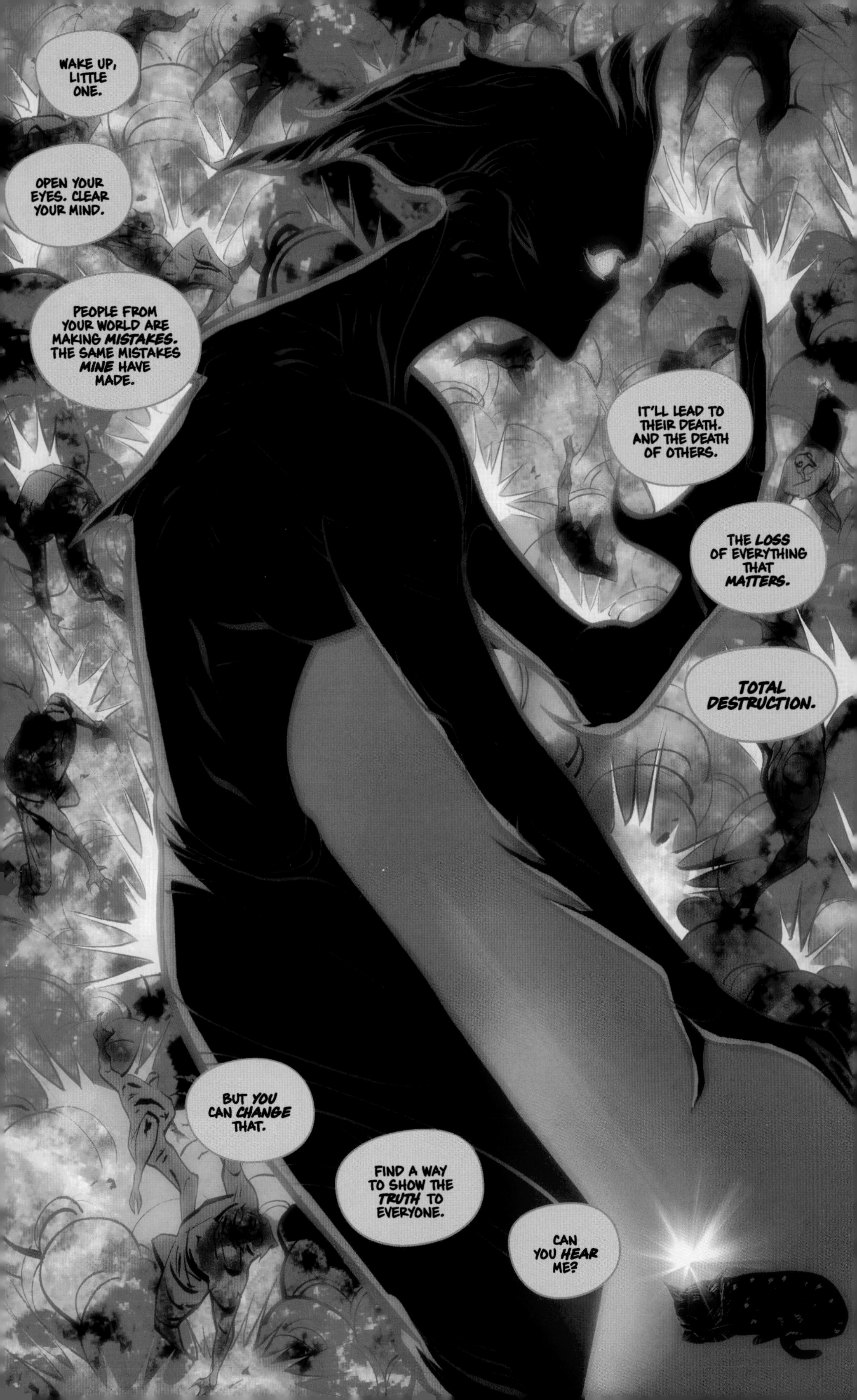
WAKE UP, LITTLE ONE.
OPEN YOUR EYES. CLEAR YOUR MIND.
PEOPLE FROM YOUR WORLD ARE MAKING *MISTAKES*. THE SAME MISTAKES *MINE* HAVE MADE.
IT'LL LEAD TO THEIR DEATH. AND THE DEATH OF OTHERS.
THE *LOSS* OF EVERYTHING THAT *MATTERS*.
TOTAL DESTRUCTION.
BUT *YOU* CAN *CHANGE* THAT.
FIND A WAY TO SHOW THE *TRUTH* TO EVERYONE.
CAN YOU *HEAR* ME?

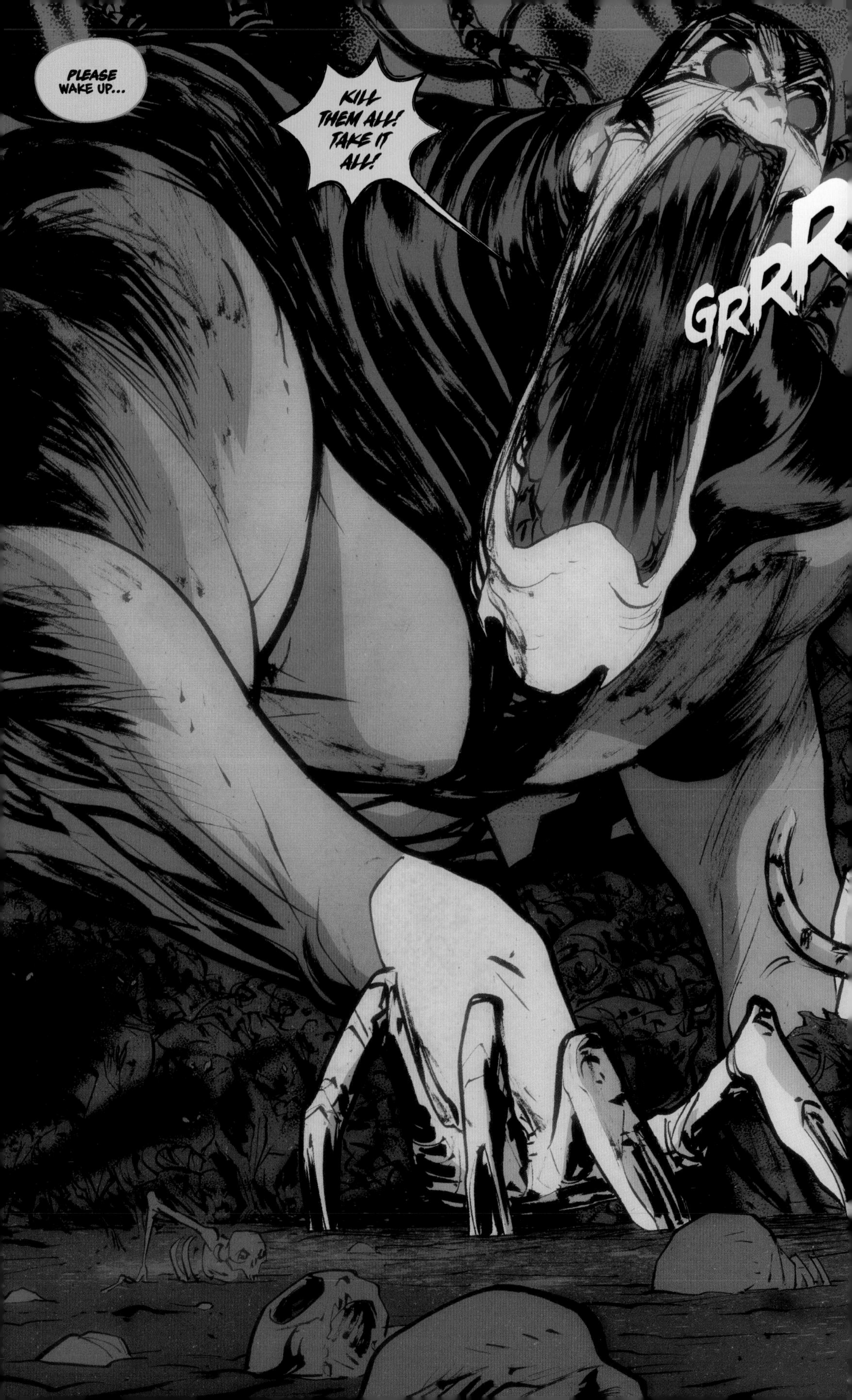
PLEASE WAKE UP...
KILL THEM ALL! TAKE IT ALL!
GRRR

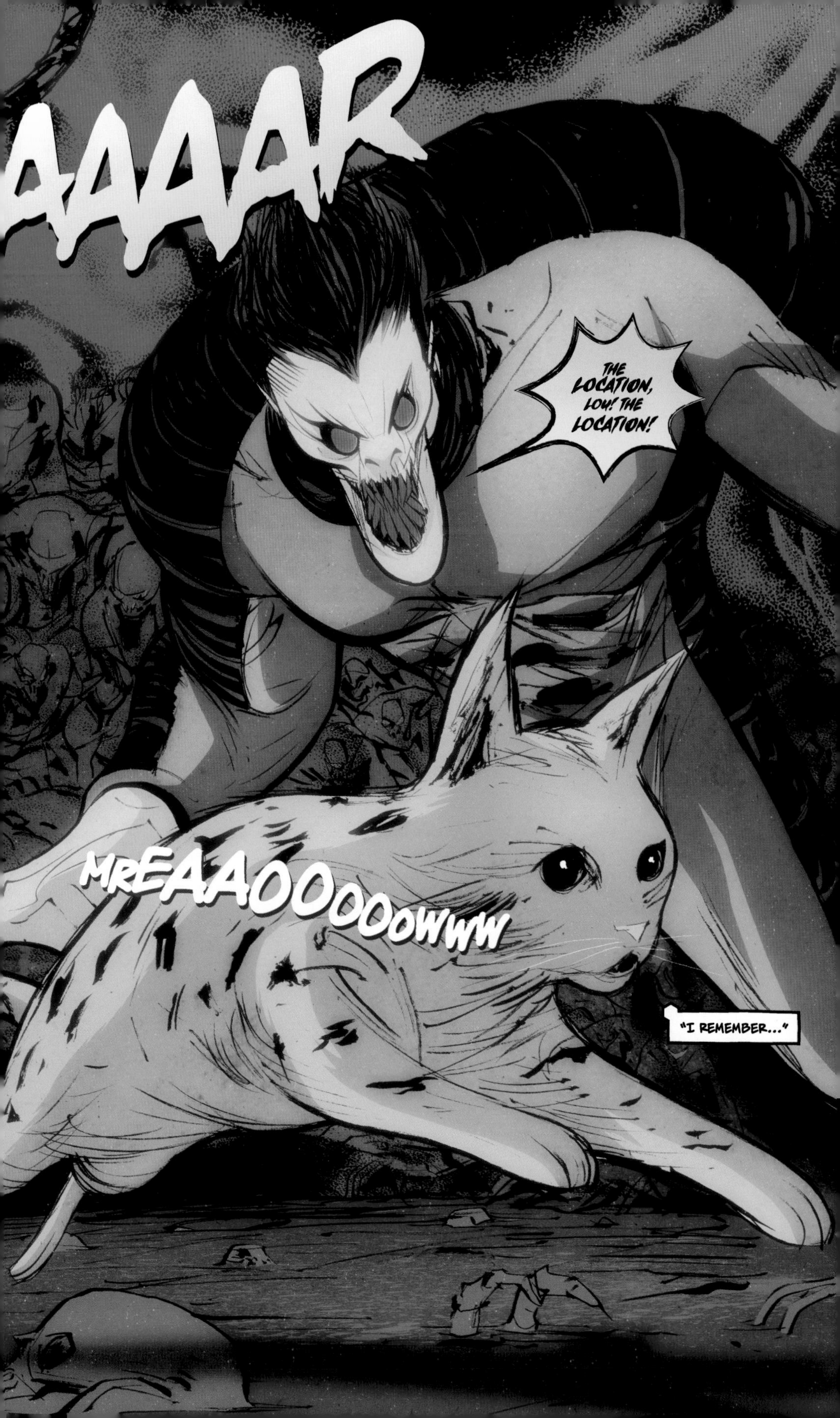
AAAAR
THE LOCATION, LOU! THE LOCATION!
MrEAAOOOOOOWWW
"I REMEMBER..."

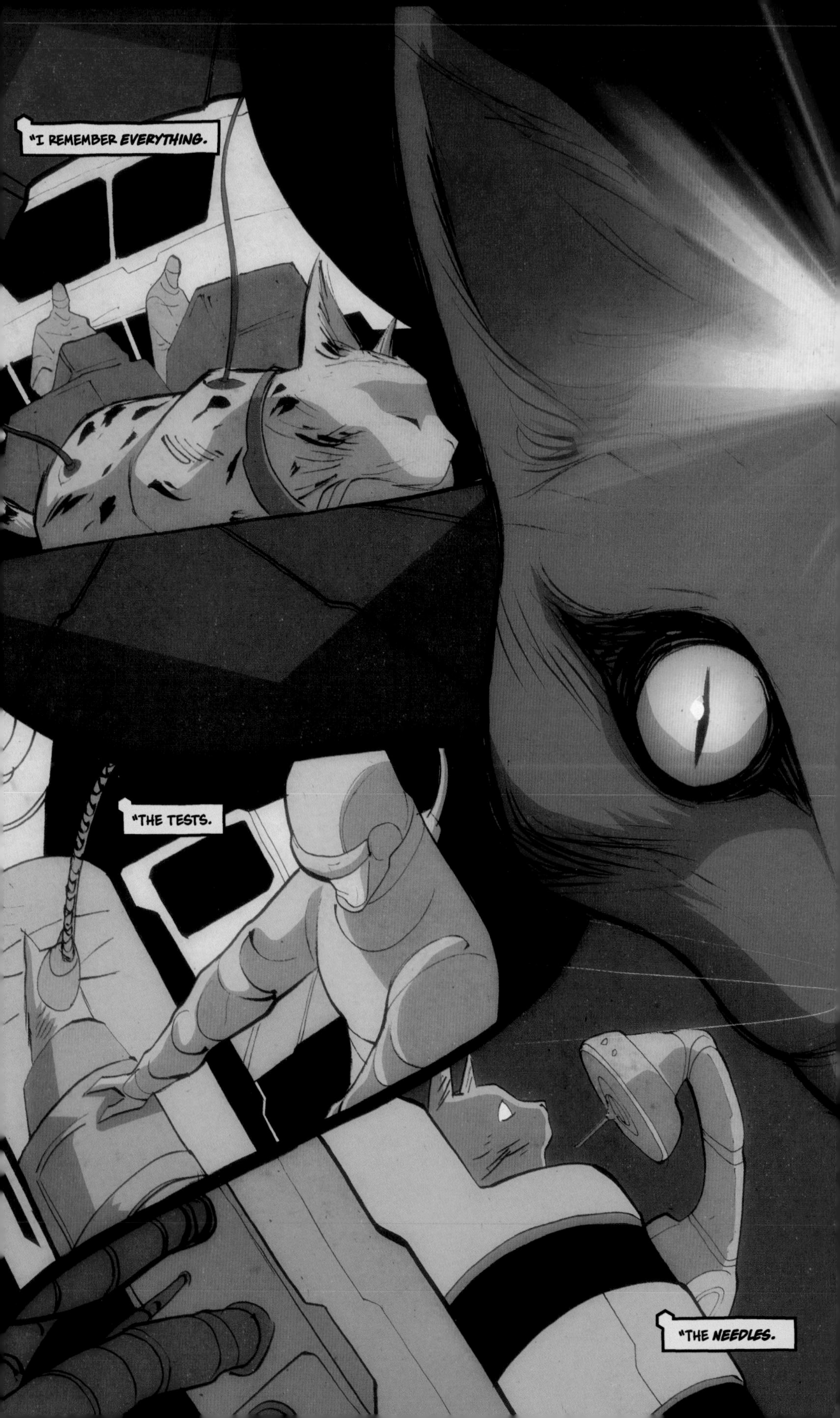
"I REMEMBER EVERYTHING.
"THE TESTS.
"THE NEEDLES.

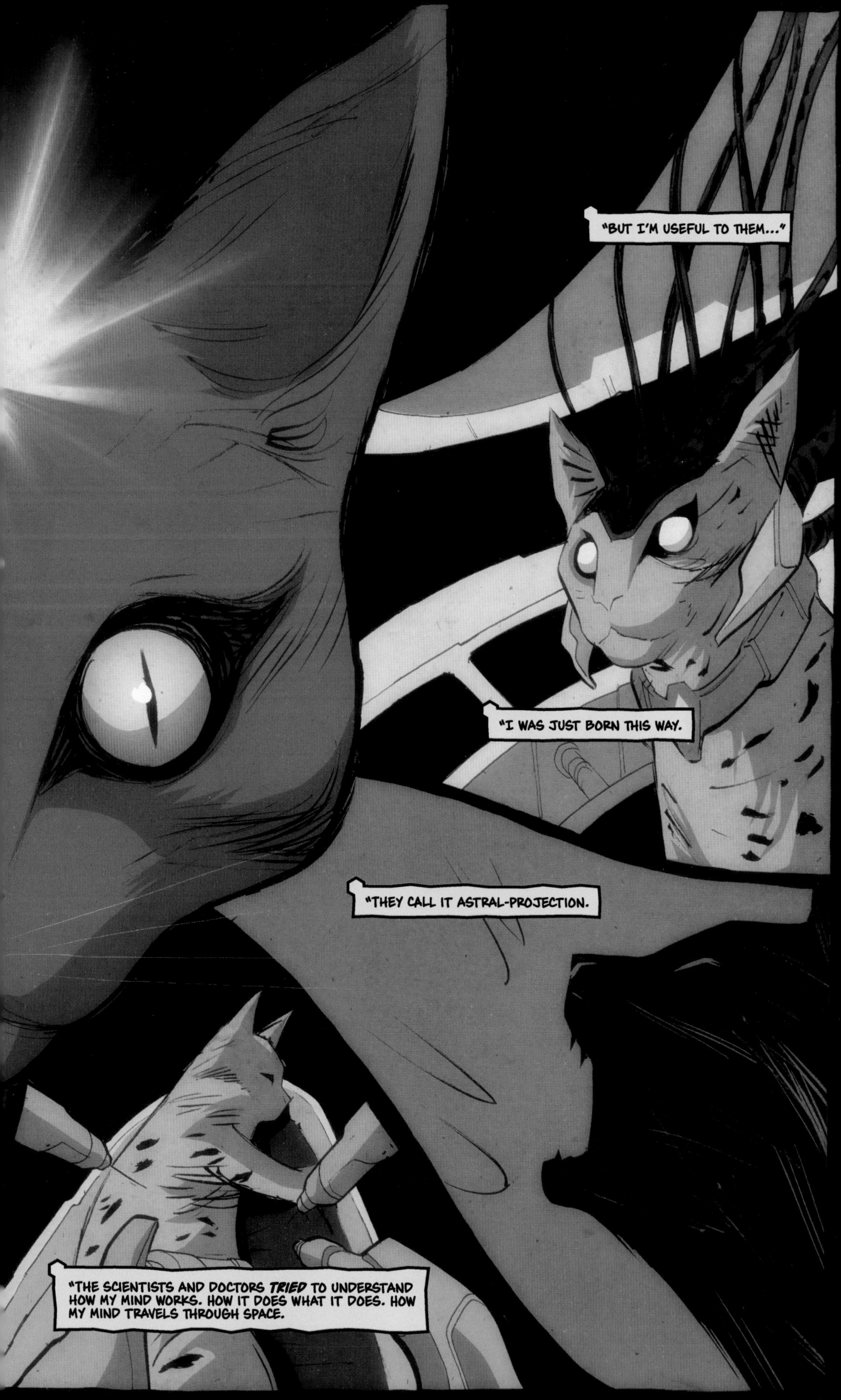
"BUT I'M USEFUL TO THEM..."
"I WAS JUST BORN THIS WAY.
"THEY CALL IT ASTRAL-PROJECTION.
"THE SCIENTISTS AND DOCTORS TRIED TO UNDERSTAND HOW MY MIND WORKS. HOW IT DOES WHAT IT DOES. HOW MY MIND TRAVELS THROUGH SPACE.

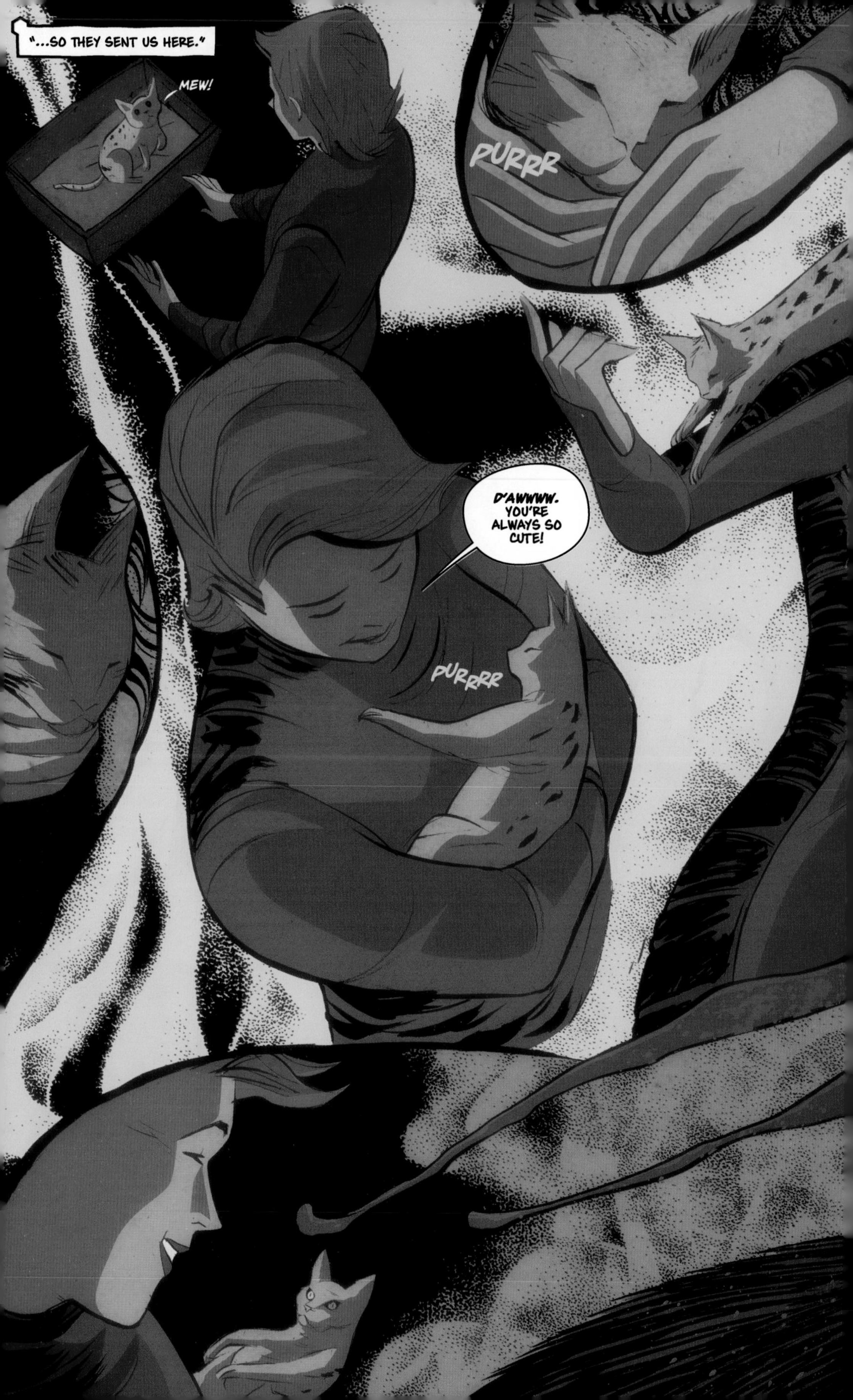
"...SO THEY SENT US HERE."
MEW!
PURRR
D'AWWWW. YOU'RE ALWAYS SO CUTE!
PURRRR

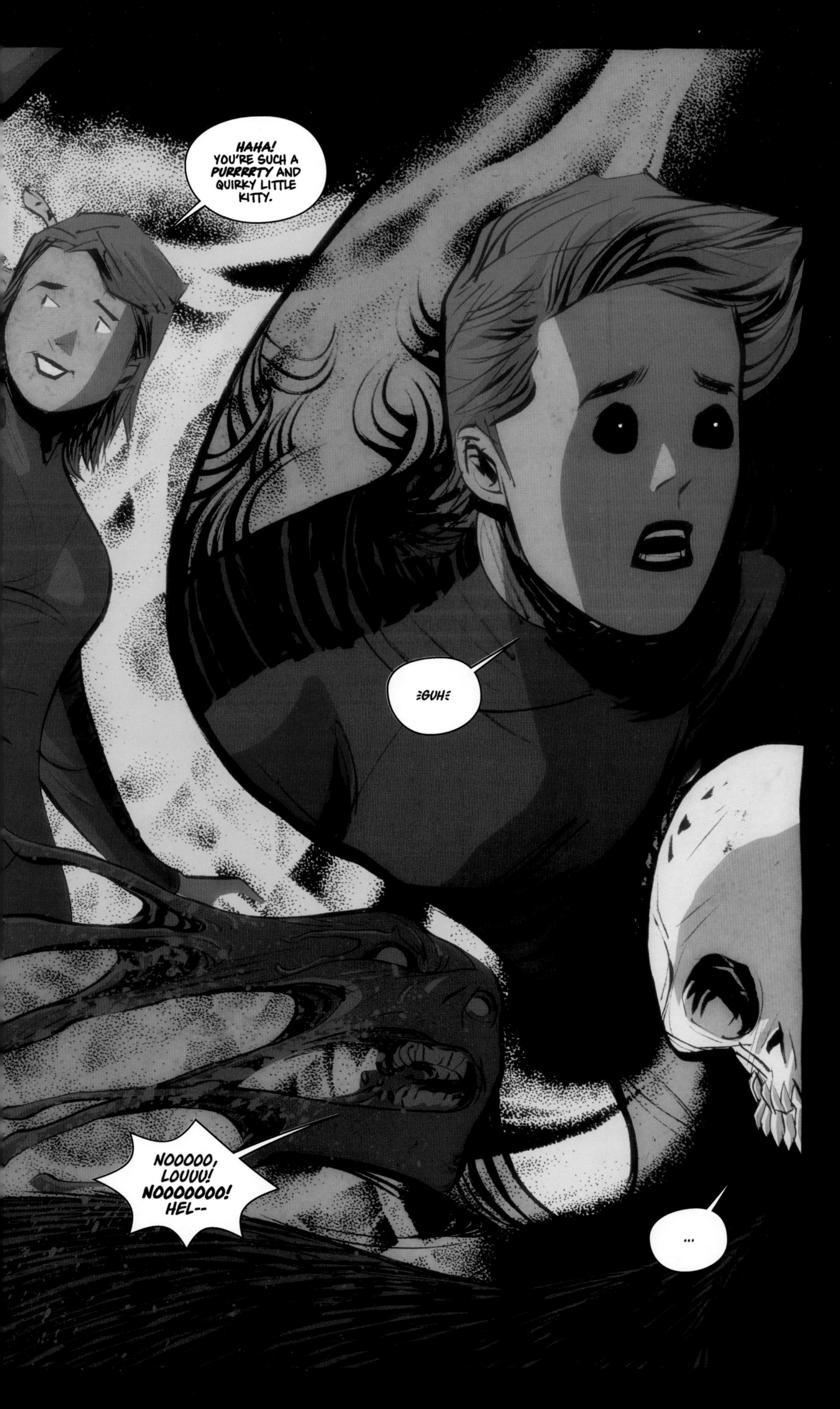
HAHA! YOU'RE SUCH A PURRRRTY AND QUIRKY LITTLE KITTY.
GUH
NOOOOO, LOUUU! NOOOOOOO! HEL--
...

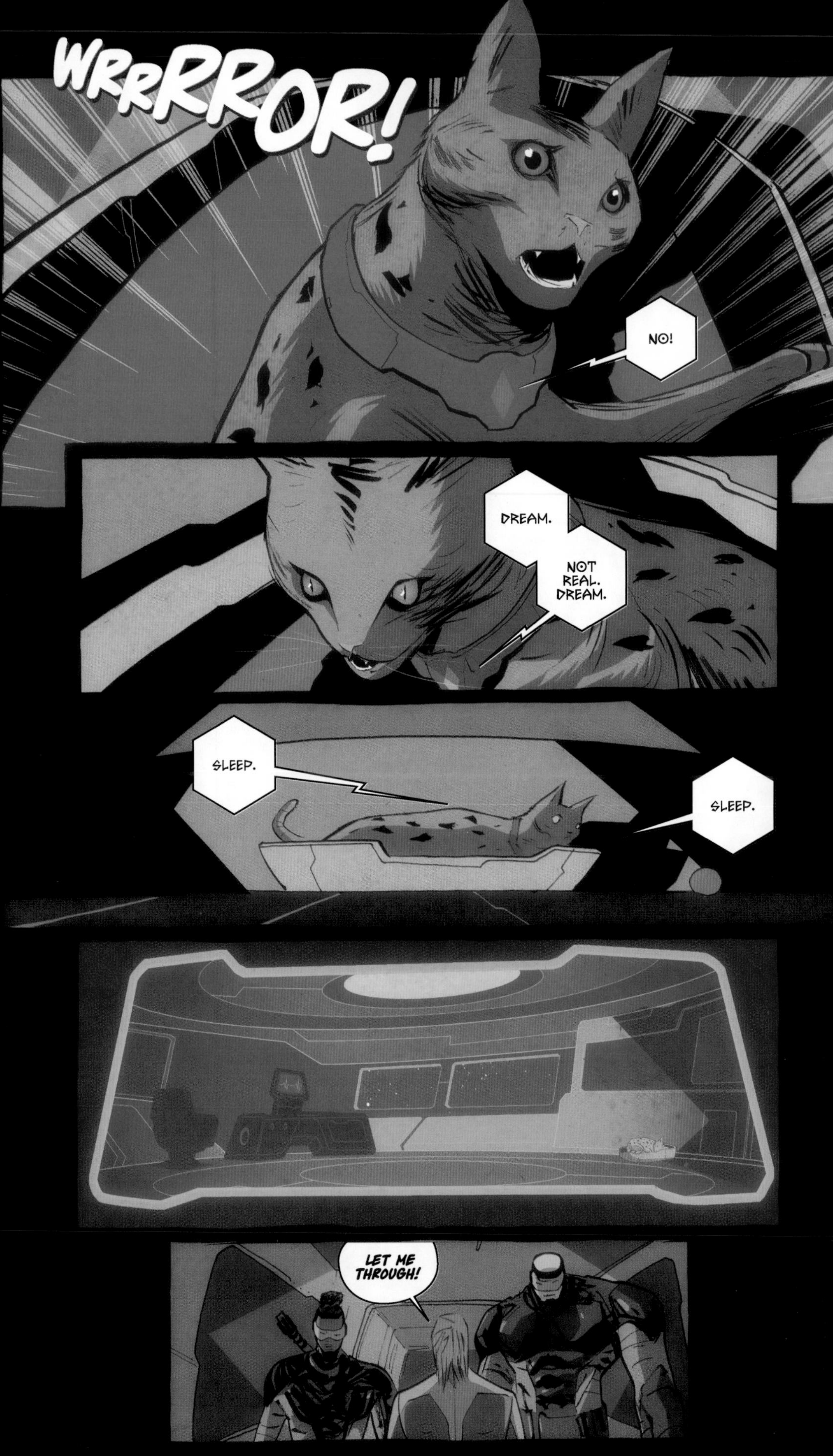
WRRRRROR!
NO!
DREAM.
NOT REAL. DREAM.
SLEEP.
SLEEP.
LET ME THROUGH!

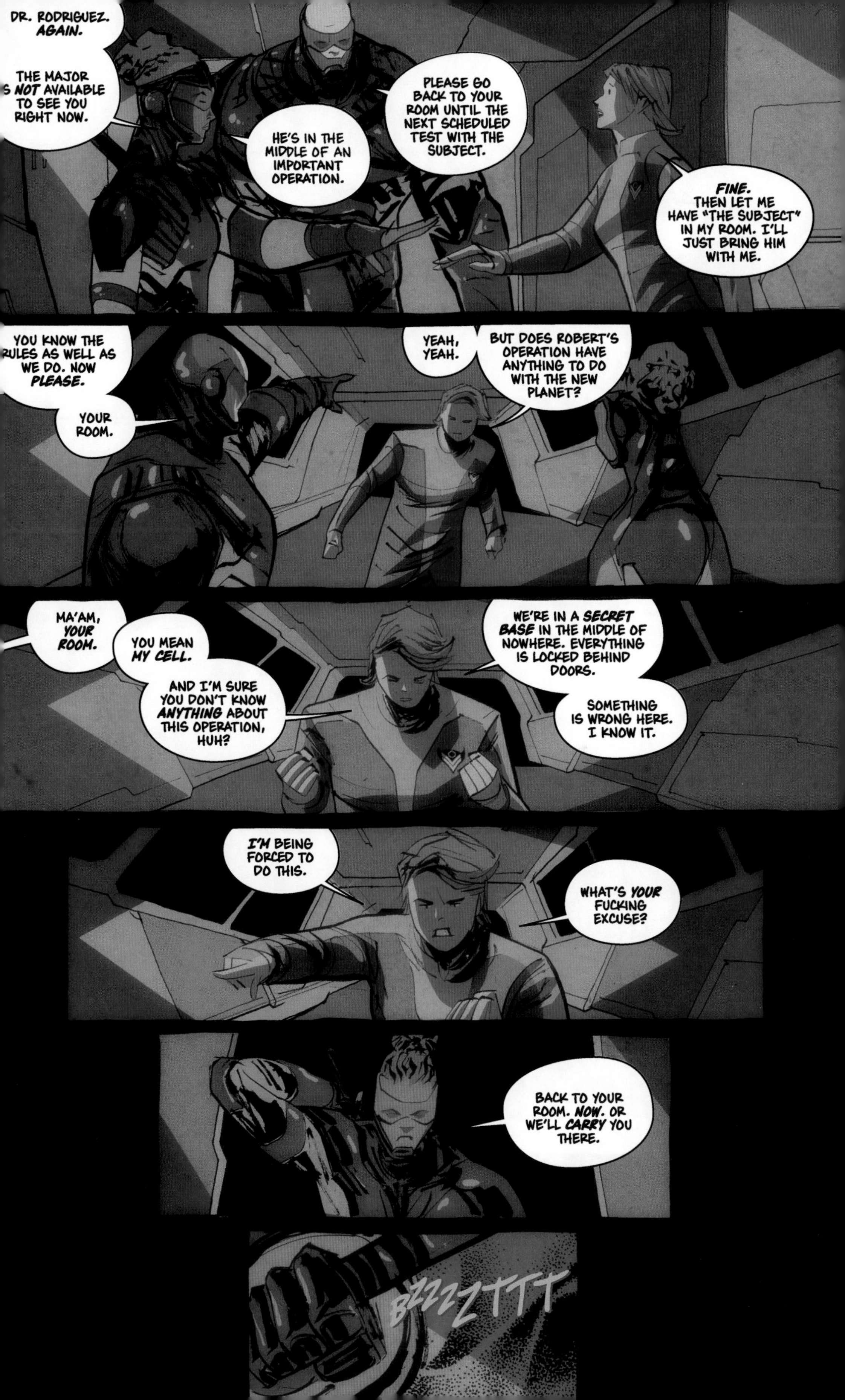
DR. RODRIGUEZ. AGAIN.
THE MAJOR IS NOT AVAILABLE TO SEE YOU RIGHT NOW.
HE'S IN THE MIDDLE OF AN IMPORTANT OPERATION.
PLEASE GO BACK TO YOUR ROOM UNTIL THE NEXT SCHEDULED TEST WITH THE SUBJECT.
FINE. THEN LET ME HAVE "THE SUBJECT" IN MY ROOM. I'LL JUST BRING HIM WITH ME.
YOU KNOW THE RULES AS WELL AS WE DO. NOW PLEASE.
YOUR ROOM.
YEAH, YEAH.
BUT DOES ROBERT'S OPERATION HAVE ANYTHING TO DO WITH THE NEW PLANET?
MA'AM, YOUR ROOM.
YOU MEAN MY CELL.
AND I'M SURE YOU DON'T KNOW ANYTHING ABOUT THIS OPERATION, HUH?
WE'RE IN A SECRET BASE IN THE MIDDLE OF NOWHERE. EVERYTHING IS LOCKED BEHIND DOORS.
SOMETHING IS WRONG HERE. I KNOW IT.
I'M BEING FORCED TO DO THIS.
WHAT'S YOUR FUCKING EXCUSE?
BACK TO YOUR ROOM. NOW. OR WE'LL CARRY YOU THERE.
BZZZZTTTT

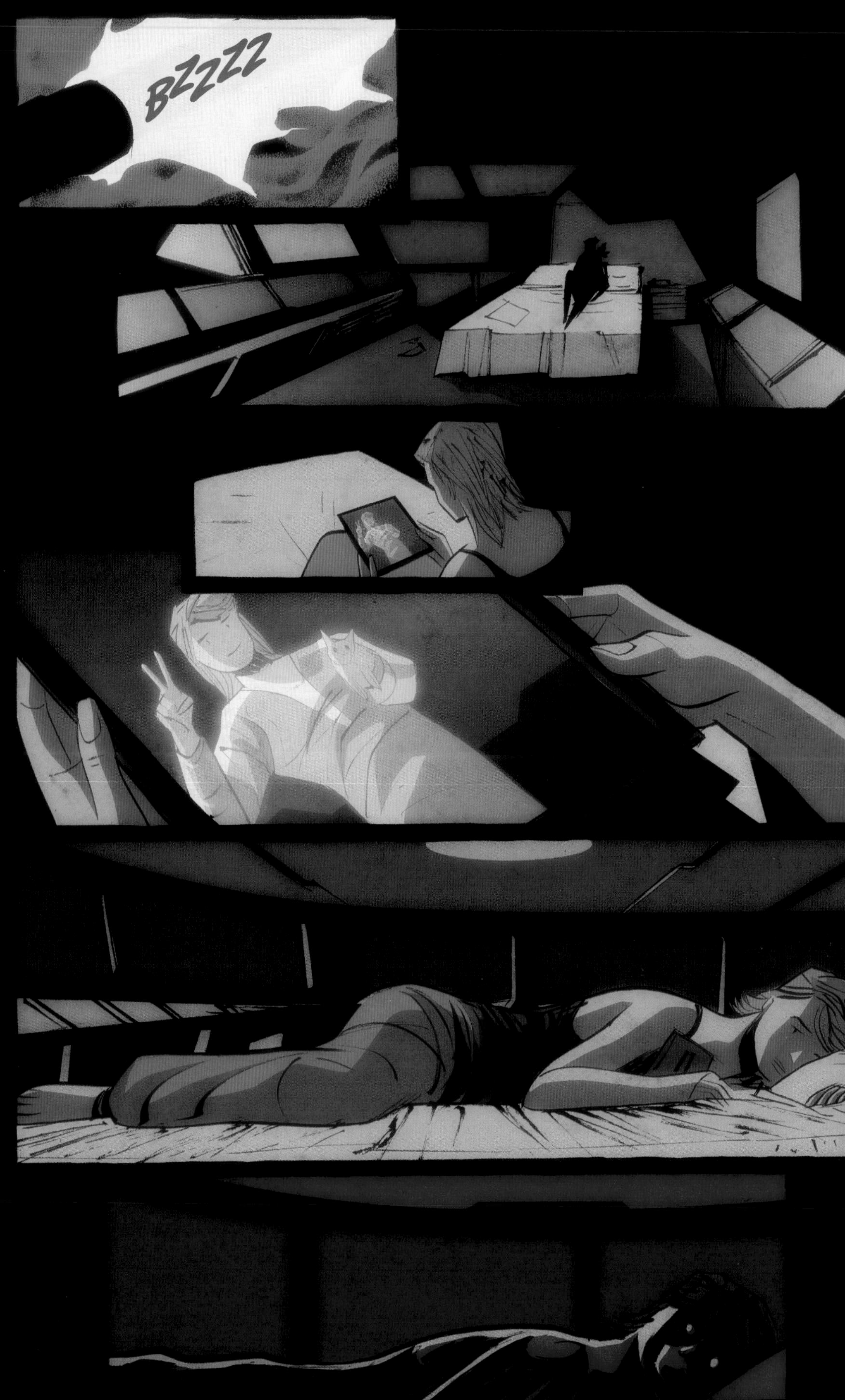
BZZZZ

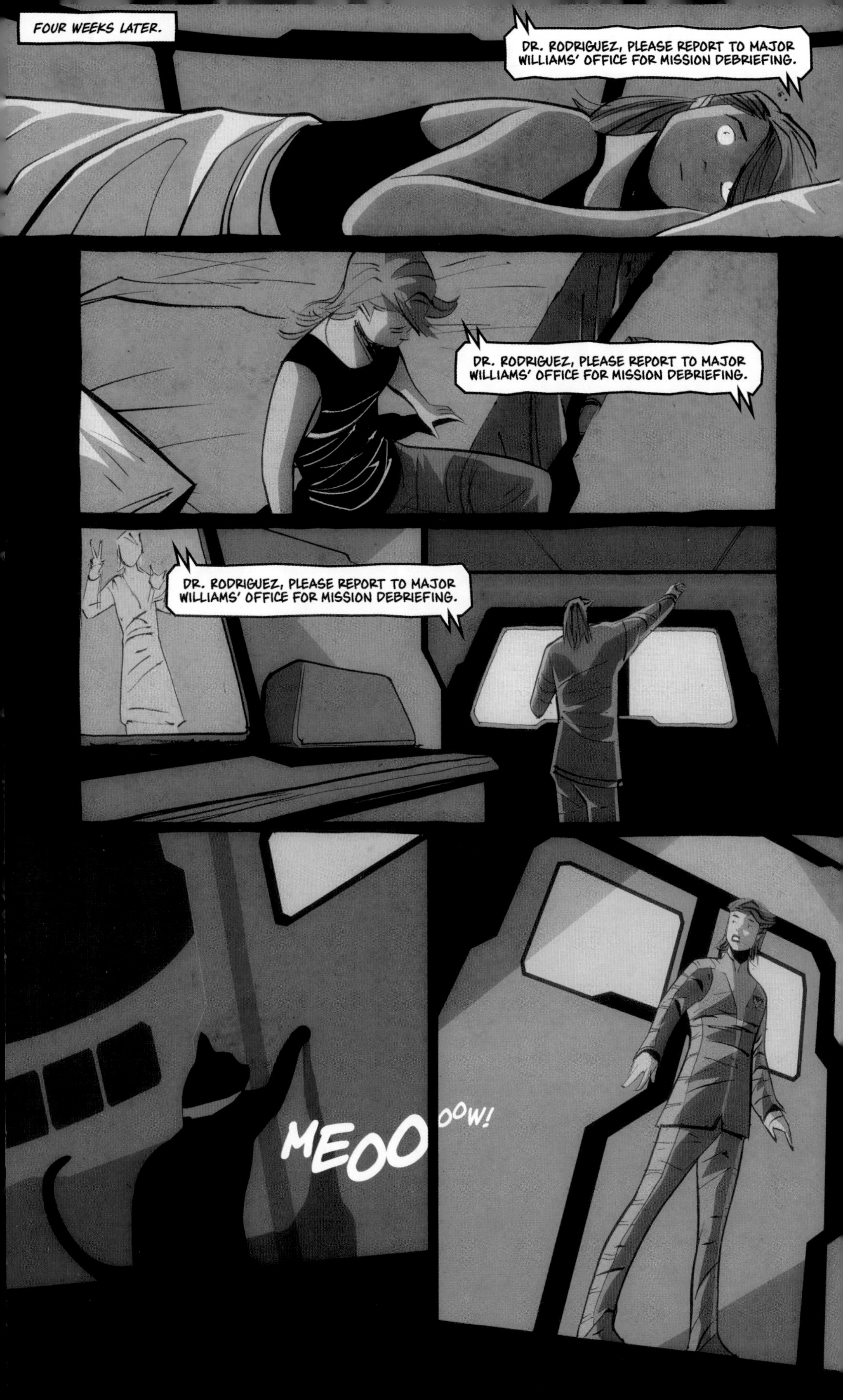
FOUR WEEKS LATER.
DR. RODRIGUEZ, PLEASE REPORT TO MAJOR WILLIAMS' OFFICE FOR MISSION DEBRIEFING.
DR. RODRIGUEZ, PLEASE REPORT TO MAJOR WILLIAMS' OFFICE FOR MISSION DEBRIEFING.
DR. RODRIGUEZ, PLEASE REPORT TO MAJOR WILLIAMS' OFFICE FOR MISSION DEBRIEFING.
MEOOOOW!

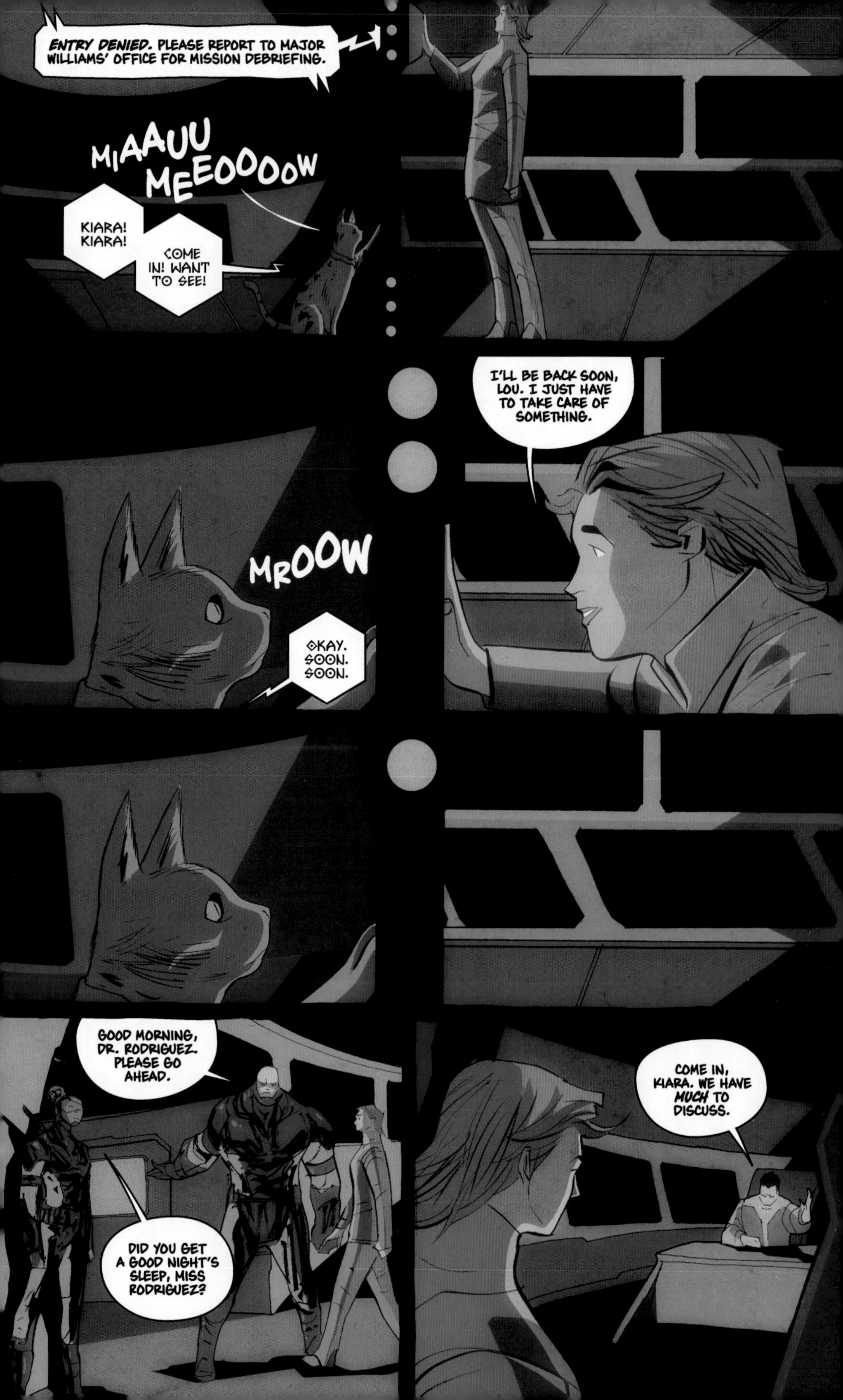
ENTRY DENIED. PLEASE REPORT TO MAJOR WILLIAMS' OFFICE FOR MISSION DEBRIEFING.
MIAAUU MEEOOOOW
KIARA! KIARA!
COME IN! WANT TO SEE!
I'LL BE BACK SOON, LOU. I JUST HAVE TO TAKE CARE OF SOMETHING.
MROOW
OKAY. SOON. SOON.
GOOD MORNING, DR. RODRIGUEZ. PLEASE GO AHEAD.
DID YOU GET A GOOD NIGHT'S SLEEP, MISS RODRIGUEZ?
COME IN, KIARA. WE HAVE MUCH TO DISCUSS.

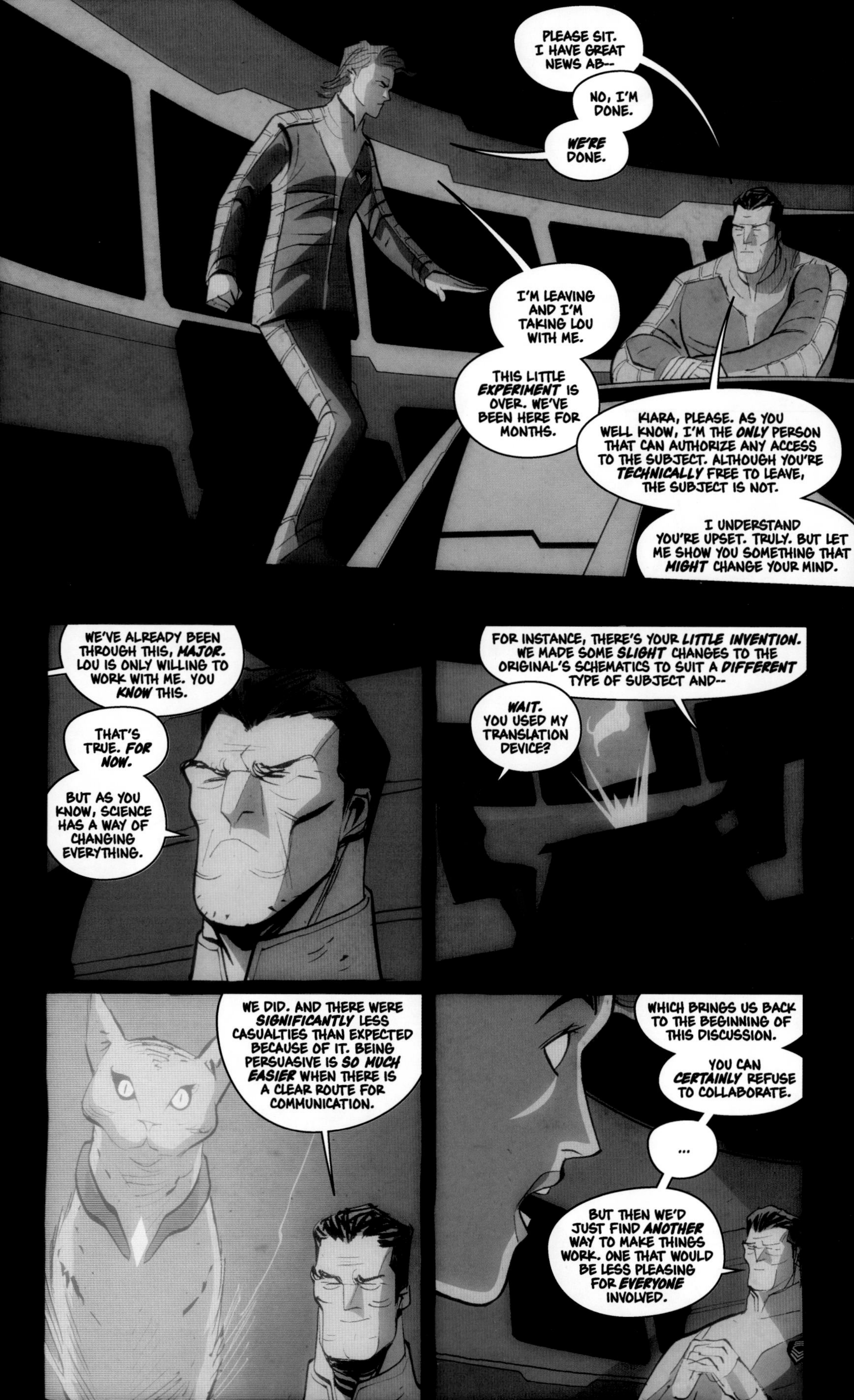
PLEASE SIT. I HAVE GREAT NEWS AB--
NO, I'M DONE.
WE'RE DONE.
I'M LEAVING AND I'M TAKING LOU WITH ME.
THIS LITTLE EXPERIMENT IS OVER. WE'VE BEEN HERE FOR MONTHS.
KIARA, PLEASE. AS YOU WELL KNOW, I'M THE ONLY PERSON THAT CAN AUTHORIZE ANY ACCESS TO THE SUBJECT. ALTHOUGH YOU'RE TECHNICALLY FREE TO LEAVE, THE SUBJECT IS NOT.
I UNDERSTAND YOU'RE UPSET. TRULY. BUT LET ME SHOW YOU SOMETHING THAT MIGHT CHANGE YOUR MIND.
WE'VE ALREADY BEEN THROUGH THIS, MAJOR. LOU IS ONLY WILLING TO WORK WITH ME. YOU KNOW THIS.
THAT'S TRUE. FOR NOW.
BUT AS YOU KNOW, SCIENCE HAS A WAY OF CHANGING EVERYTHING.
FOR INSTANCE, THERE'S YOUR LITTLE INVENTION. WE MADE SOME SLIGHT CHANGES TO THE ORIGINAL'S SCHEMATICS TO SUIT A DIFFERENT TYPE OF SUBJECT AND--
WAIT. YOU USED MY TRANSLATION DEVICE?
WE DID. AND THERE WERE SIGNIFICANTLY LESS CASUALTIES THAN EXPECTED BECAUSE OF IT. BEING PERSUASIVE IS SO MUCH EASIER WHEN THERE IS A CLEAR ROUTE FOR COMMUNICATION.
WHICH BRINGS US BACK TO THE BEGINNING OF THIS DISCUSSION.
YOU CAN CERTAINLY REFUSE TO COLLABORATE.
...
BUT THEN WE'D JUST FIND ANOTHER WAY TO MAKE THINGS WORK. ONE THAT WOULD BE LESS PLEASING FOR EVERYONE INVOLVED.

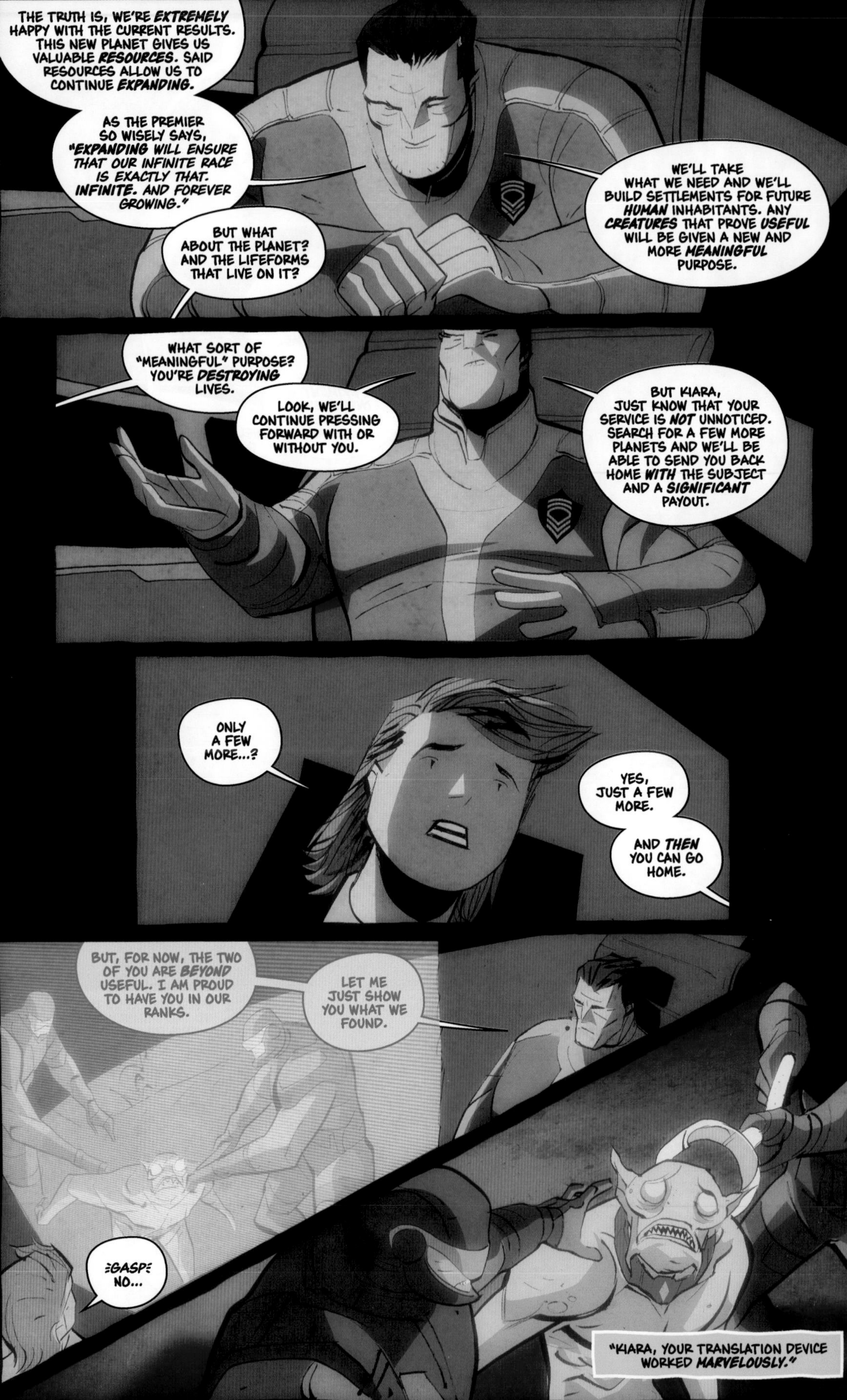
THE TRUTH IS, WE'RE EXTREMELY HAPPY WITH THE CURRENT RESULTS. THIS NEW PLANET GIVES US VALUABLE RESOURCES. SAID RESOURCES ALLOW US TO CONTINUE EXPANDING.
AS THE PREMIER SO WISELY SAYS, "EXPANDING WILL ENSURE THAT OUR INFINITE RACE IS EXACTLY THAT. INFINITE. AND FOREVER GROWING."
WE'LL TAKE WHAT WE NEED AND WE'LL BUILD SETTLEMENTS FOR FUTURE HUMAN INHABITANTS. ANY CREATURES THAT PROVE USEFUL WILL BE GIVEN A NEW AND MORE MEANINGFUL PURPOSE.
BUT WHAT ABOUT THE PLANET? AND THE LIFEFORMS THAT LIVE ON IT?
WHAT SORT OF "MEANINGFUL" PURPOSE? YOU'RE DESTROYING LIVES.
LOOK, WE'LL CONTINUE PRESSING FORWARD WITH OR WITHOUT YOU.
BUT KIARA, JUST KNOW THAT YOUR SERVICE IS NOT UNNOTICED. SEARCH FOR A FEW MORE PLANETS AND WE'LL BE ABLE TO SEND YOU BACK HOME WITH THE SUBJECT AND A SIGNIFICANT PAYOUT.
ONLY A FEW MORE...?
YES, JUST A FEW MORE.
AND THEN YOU CAN GO HOME.
BUT, FOR NOW, THE TWO OF YOU ARE BEYOND USEFUL. I AM PROUD TO HAVE YOU IN OUR RANKS.
LET ME JUST SHOW YOU WHAT WE FOUND.
GASP NO...
"KIARA, YOUR TRANSLATION DEVICE WORKED MARVELOUSLY."

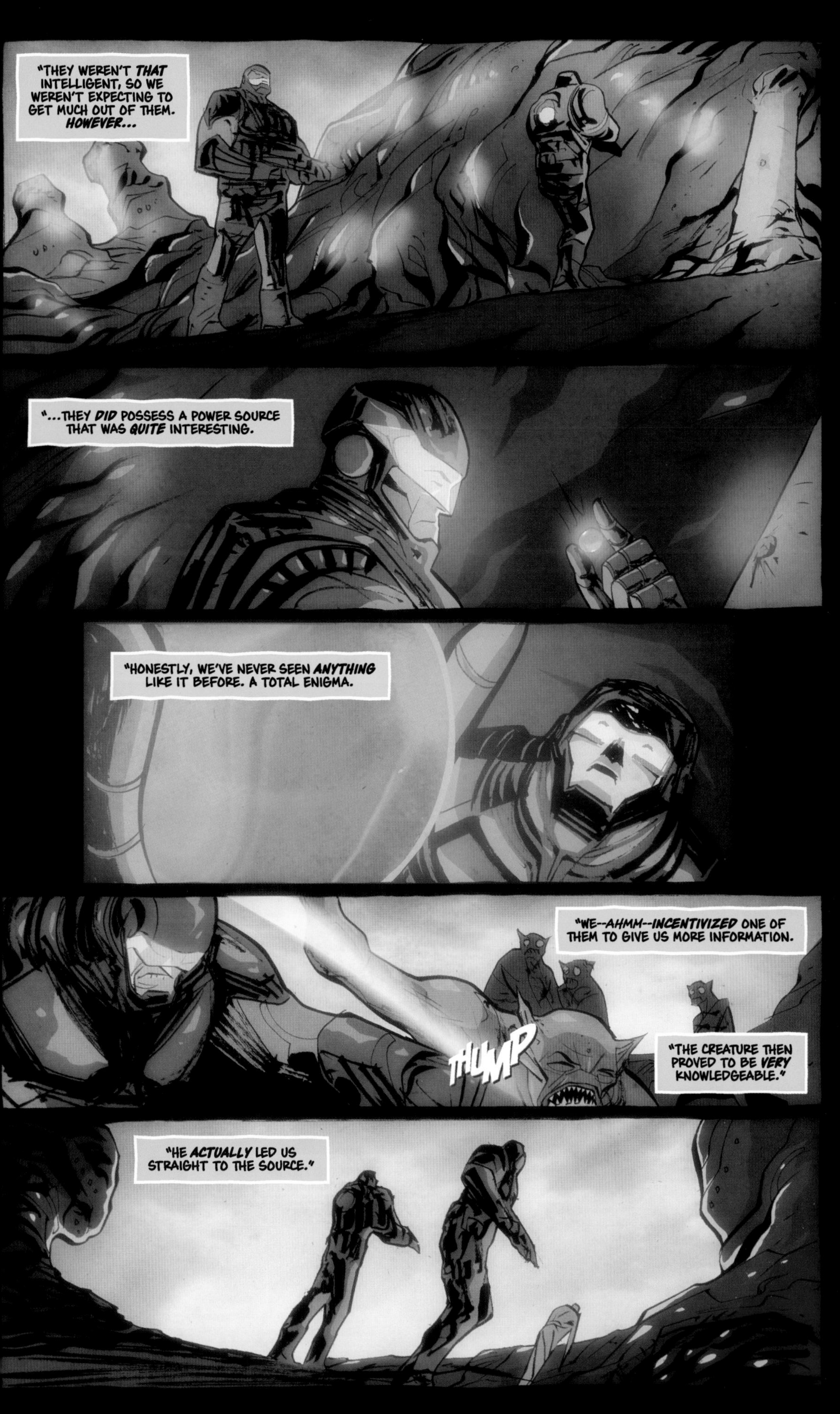
"THEY WEREN'T THAT INTELLIGENT, SO WE WEREN'T EXPECTING TO GET MUCH OUT OF THEM. HOWEVER...
"...THEY DID POSSESS A POWER SOURCE THAT WAS QUITE INTERESTING.
"HONESTLY, WE'VE NEVER SEEN ANYTHING LIKE IT BEFORE. A TOTAL ENIGMA.
"WE--AHMM--INCENTIVIZED ONE OF THEM TO GIVE US MORE INFORMATION.
THUMP
"THE CREATURE THEN PROVED TO BE VERY KNOWLEDGEABLE."
"HE ACTUALLY LED US STRAIGHT TO THE SOURCE."

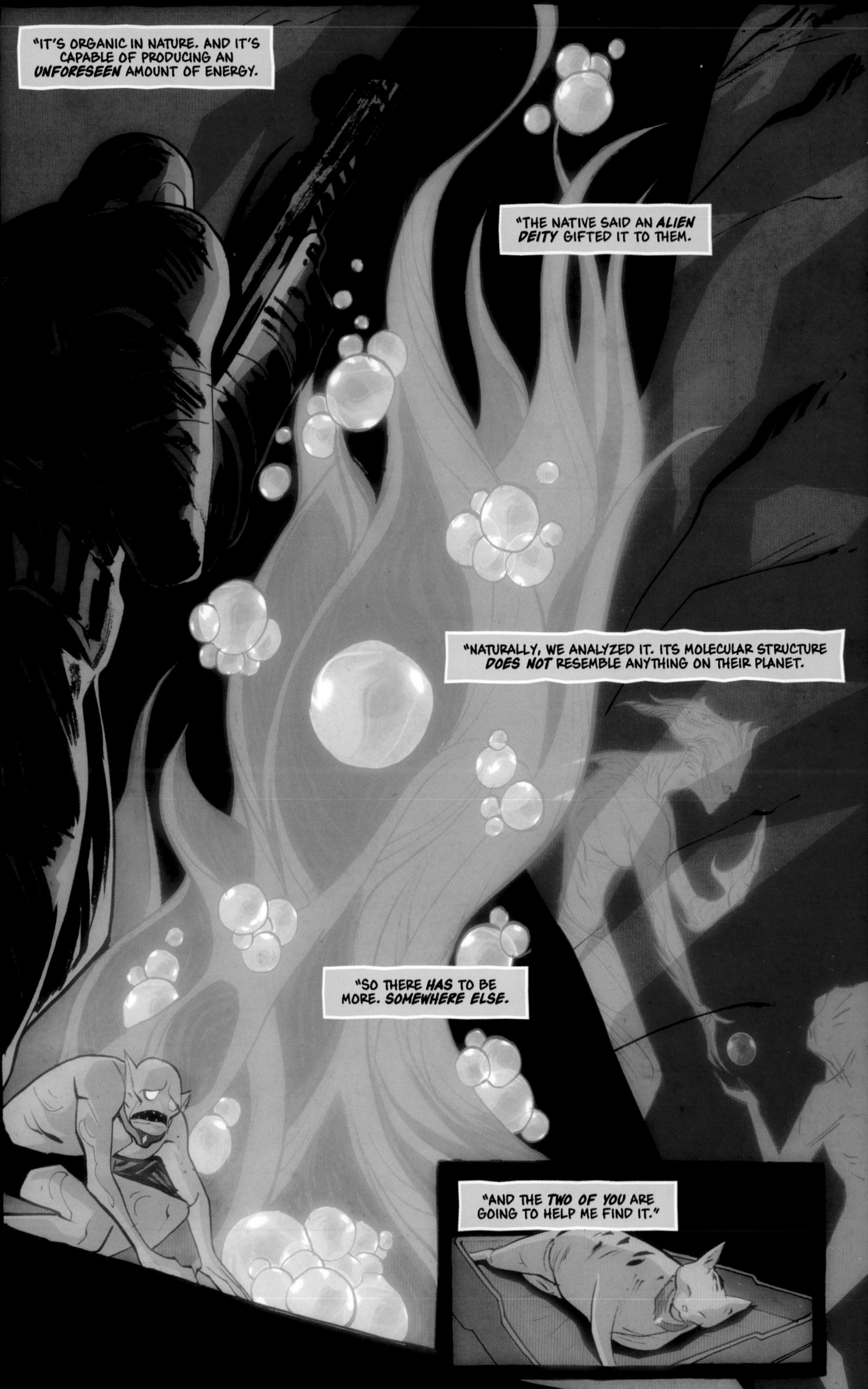
"IT'S ORGANIC IN NATURE. AND IT'S CAPABLE OF PRODUCING AN *UNFORESEEN* AMOUNT OF ENERGY.
"THE NATIVE SAID AN *ALIEN DEITY* GIFTED IT TO THEM.
"NATURALLY, WE ANALYZED IT. ITS MOLECULAR STRUCTURE *DOES NOT* RESEMBLE ANYTHING ON THEIR PLANET.
"SO THERE *HAS* TO BE MORE. *SOMEWHERE ELSE*.
"AND THE *TWO OF YOU* ARE GOING TO HELP ME FIND IT."

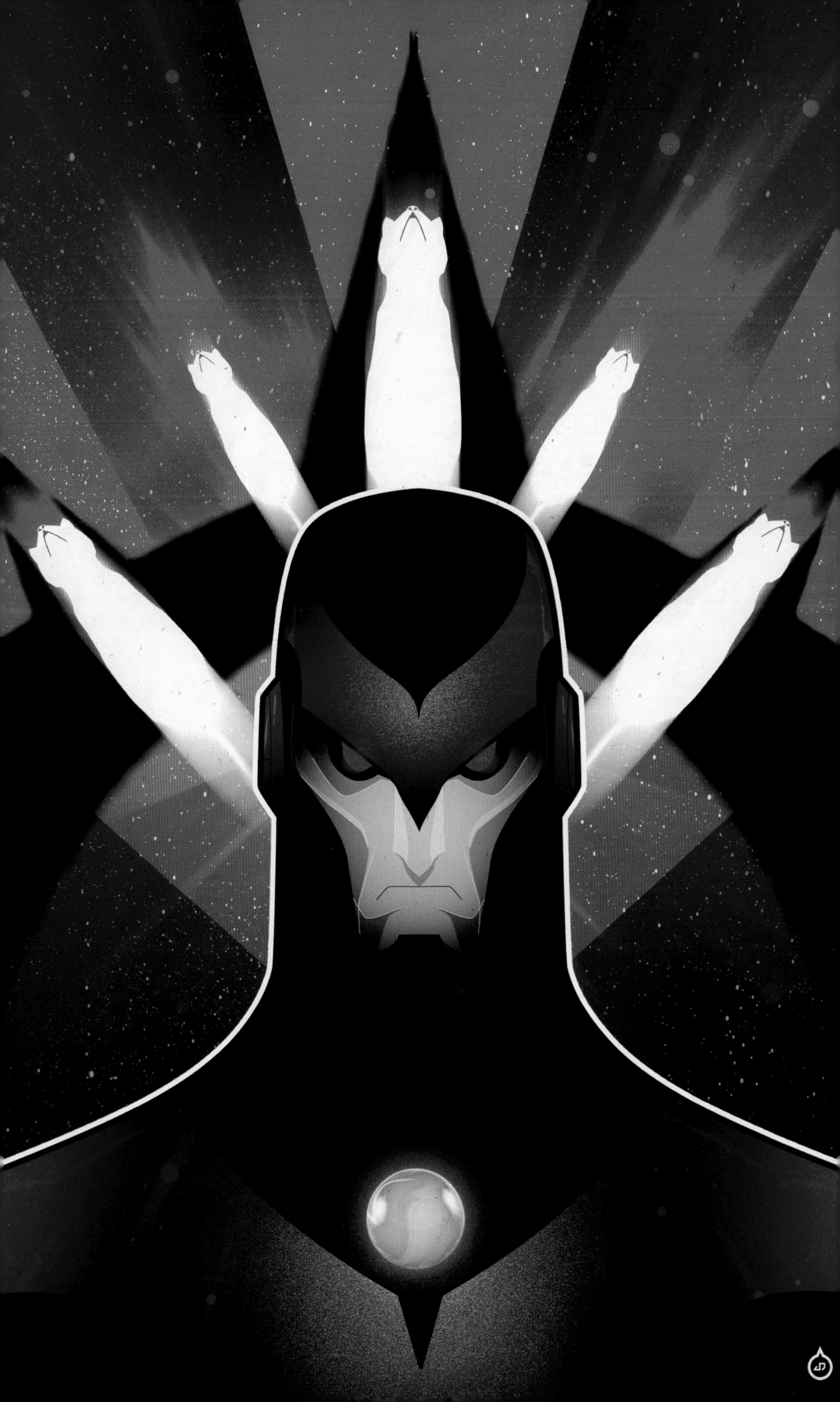

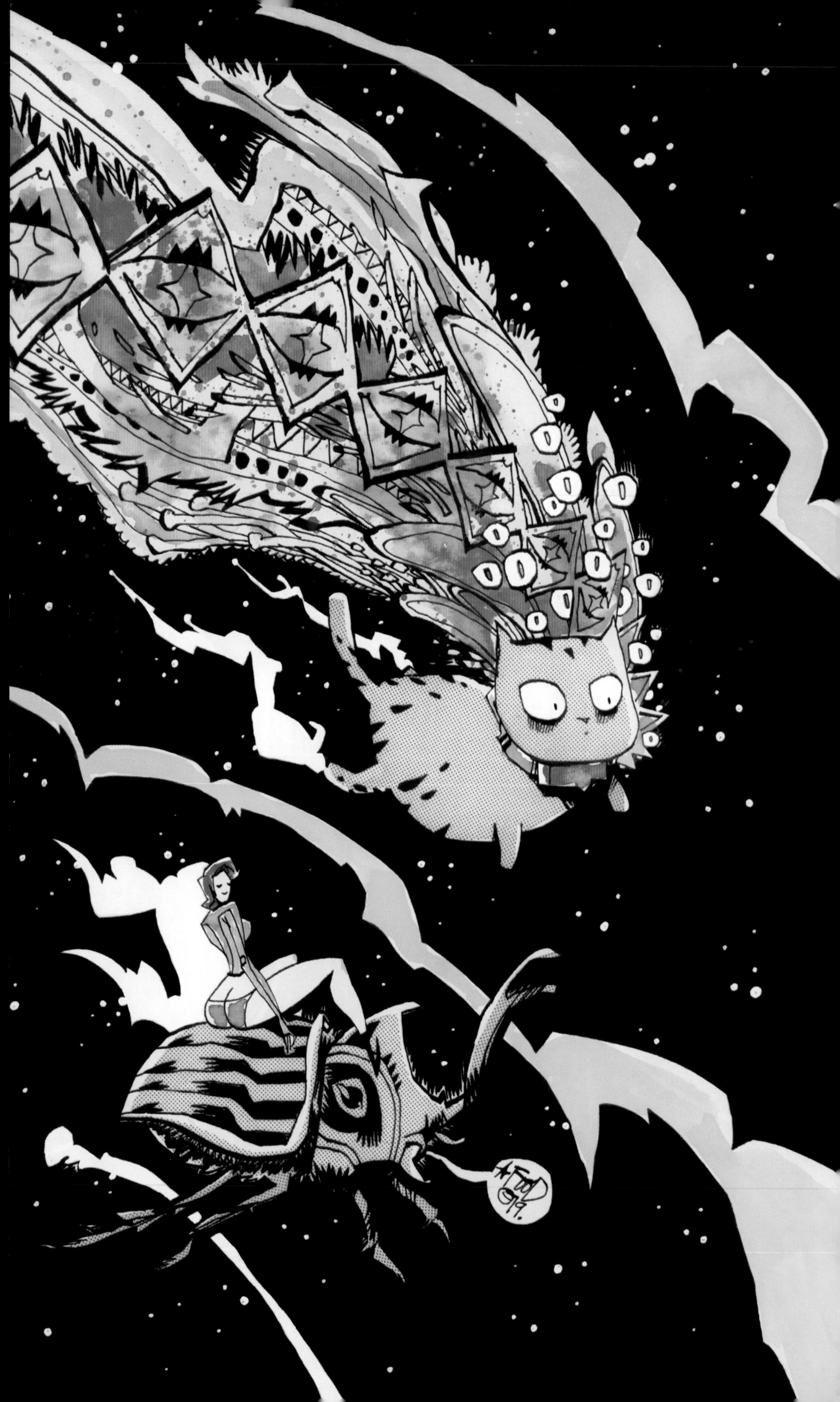

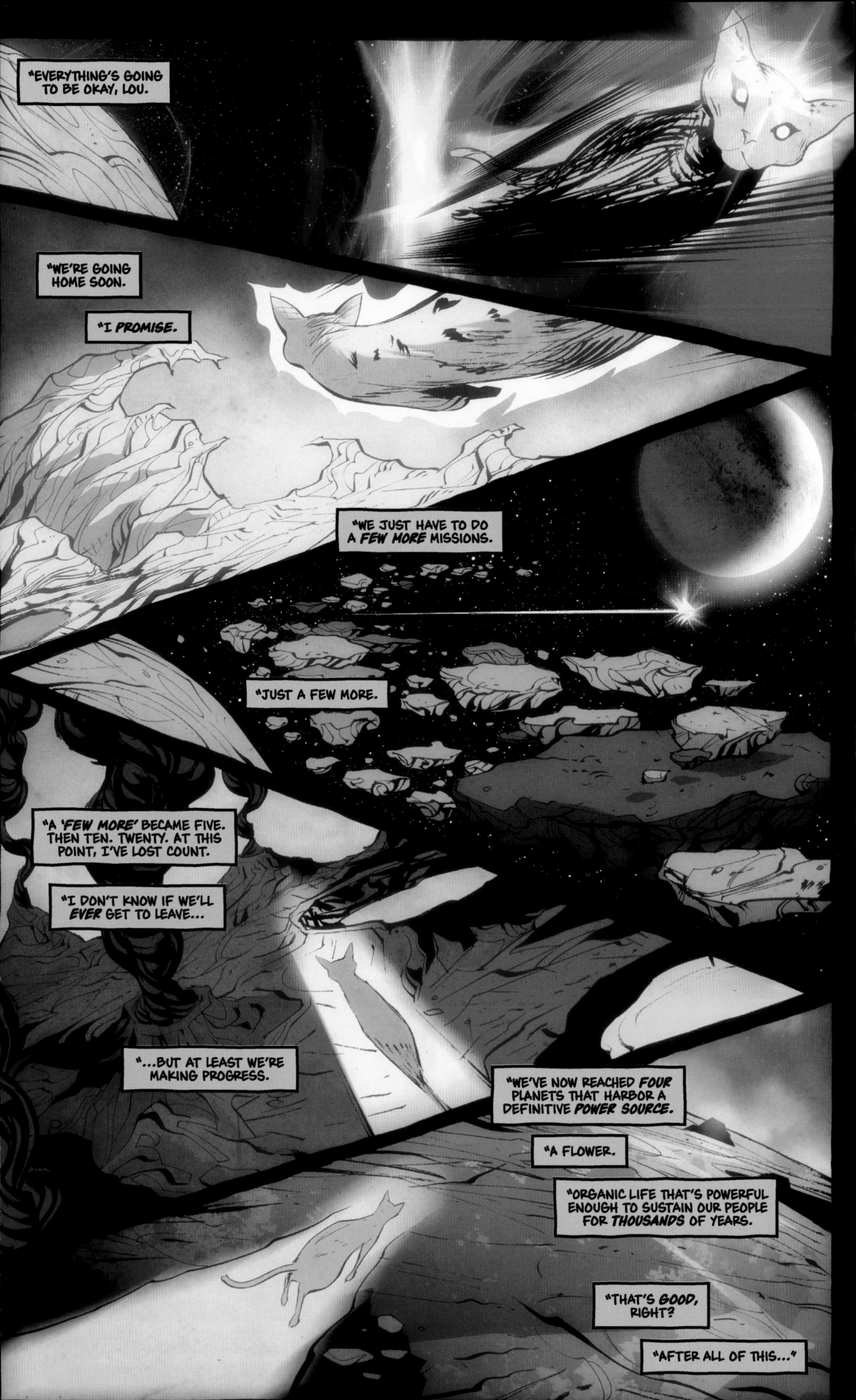
"EVERYTHING'S GOING TO BE OKAY, LOU.
"WE'RE GOING HOME SOON.
"I PROMISE.
"WE JUST HAVE TO DO A FEW MORE MISSIONS.
"JUST A FEW MORE.
"A 'FEW MORE' BECAME FIVE. THEN TEN. TWENTY. AT THIS POINT, I'VE LOST COUNT.
"I DON'T KNOW IF WE'LL EVER GET TO LEAVE...
"...BUT AT LEAST WE'RE MAKING PROGRESS.
"WE'VE NOW REACHED FOUR PLANETS THAT HARBOR A DEFINITIVE POWER SOURCE.
"A FLOWER.
"ORGANIC LIFE THAT'S POWERFUL ENOUGH TO SUSTAIN OUR PEOPLE FOR THOUSANDS OF YEARS.
"THAT'S GOOD, RIGHT?
"AFTER ALL OF THIS..."

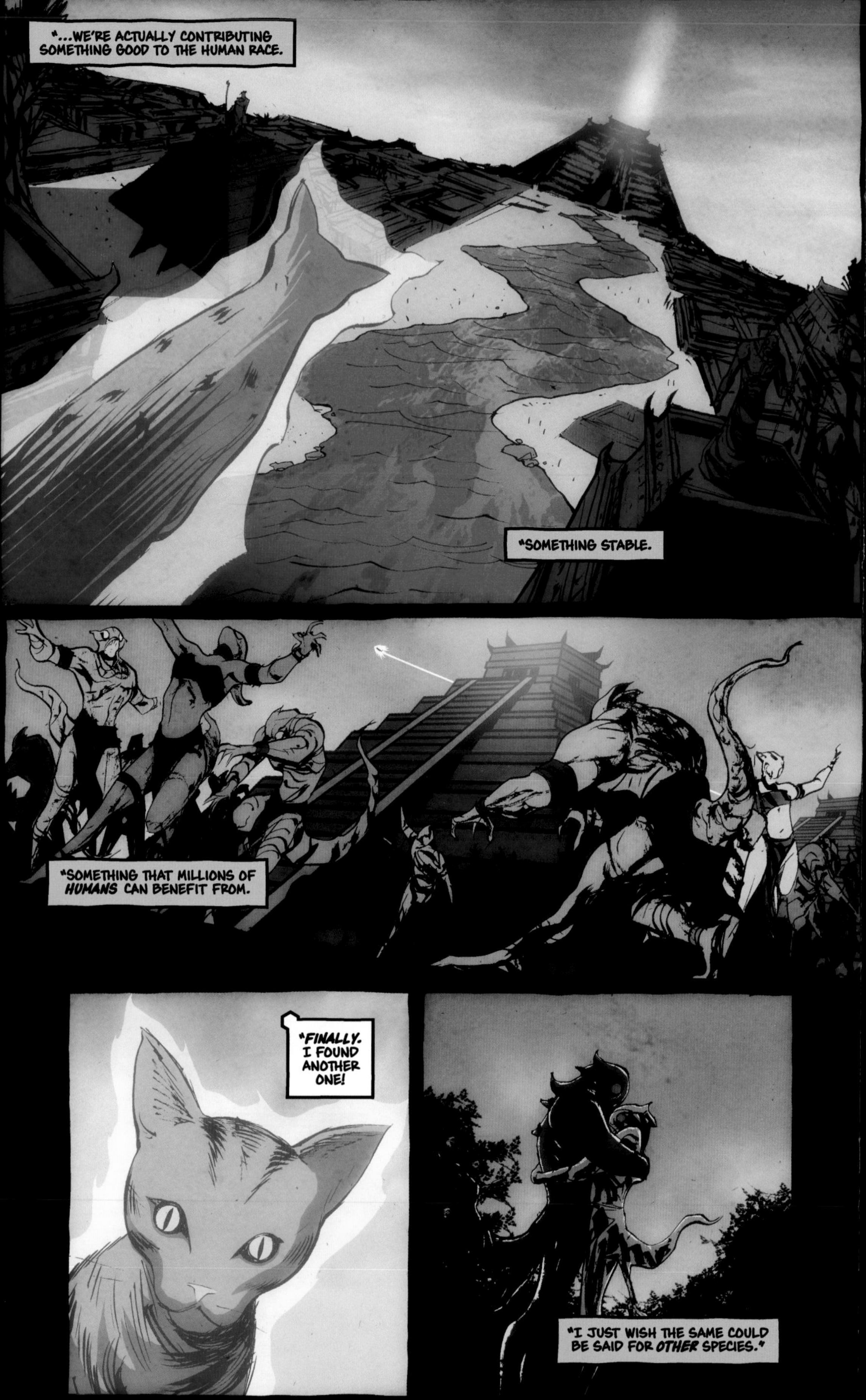
"...WE'RE ACTUALLY CONTRIBUTING SOMETHING GOOD TO THE HUMAN RACE.
"SOMETHING STABLE.
"SOMETHING THAT MILLIONS OF *HUMANS* CAN BENEFIT FROM.
"*FINALLY.* I FOUND ANOTHER ONE!
"I JUST WISH THE SAME COULD BE SAID FOR *OTHER* SPECIES."

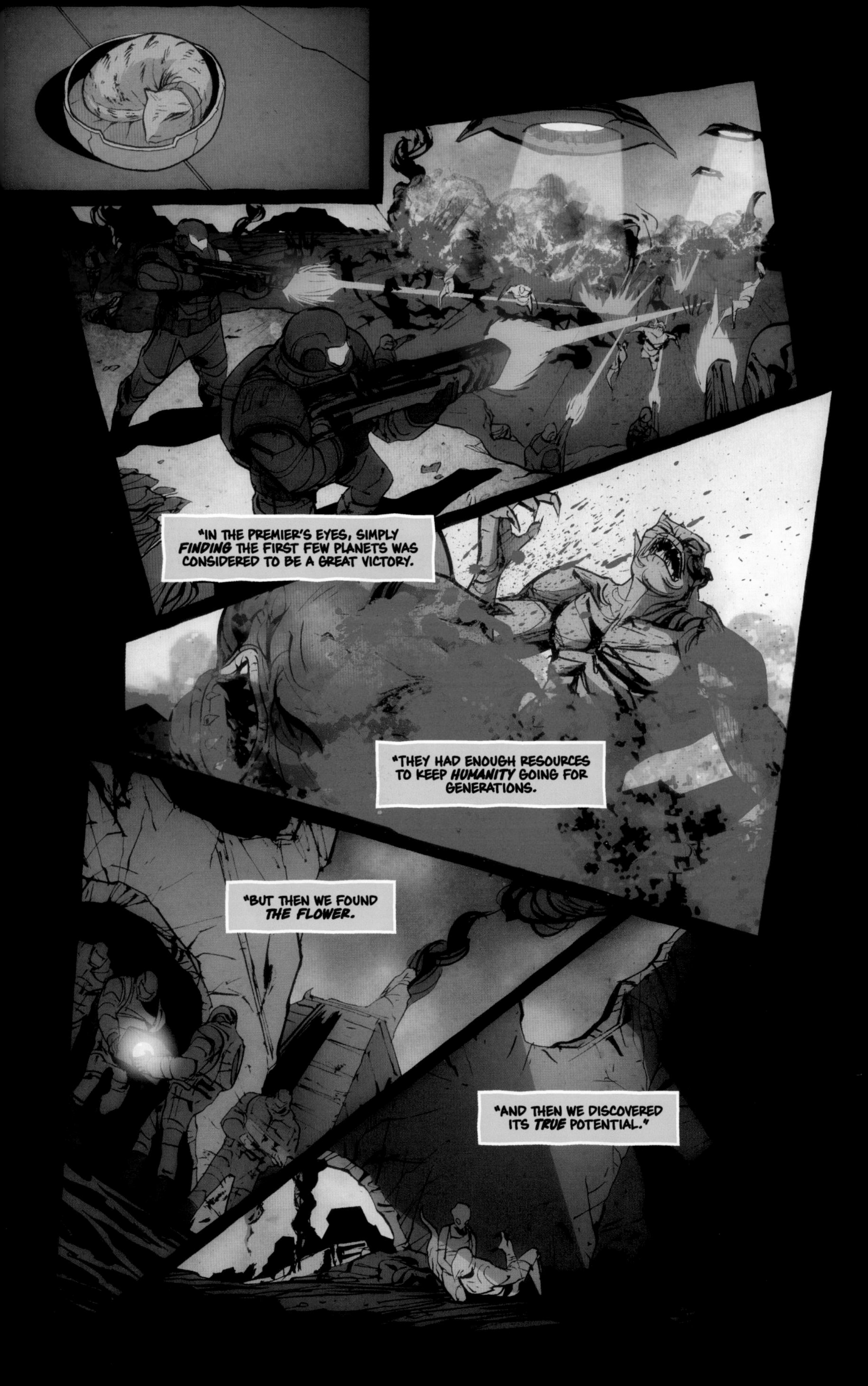
"IN THE PREMIER'S EYES, SIMPLY FINDING THE FIRST FEW PLANETS WAS CONSIDERED TO BE A GREAT VICTORY.
"THEY HAD ENOUGH RESOURCES TO KEEP HUMANITY GOING FOR GENERATIONS.
"BUT THEN WE FOUND THE FLOWER.
"AND THEN WE DISCOVERED ITS TRUE POTENTIAL."

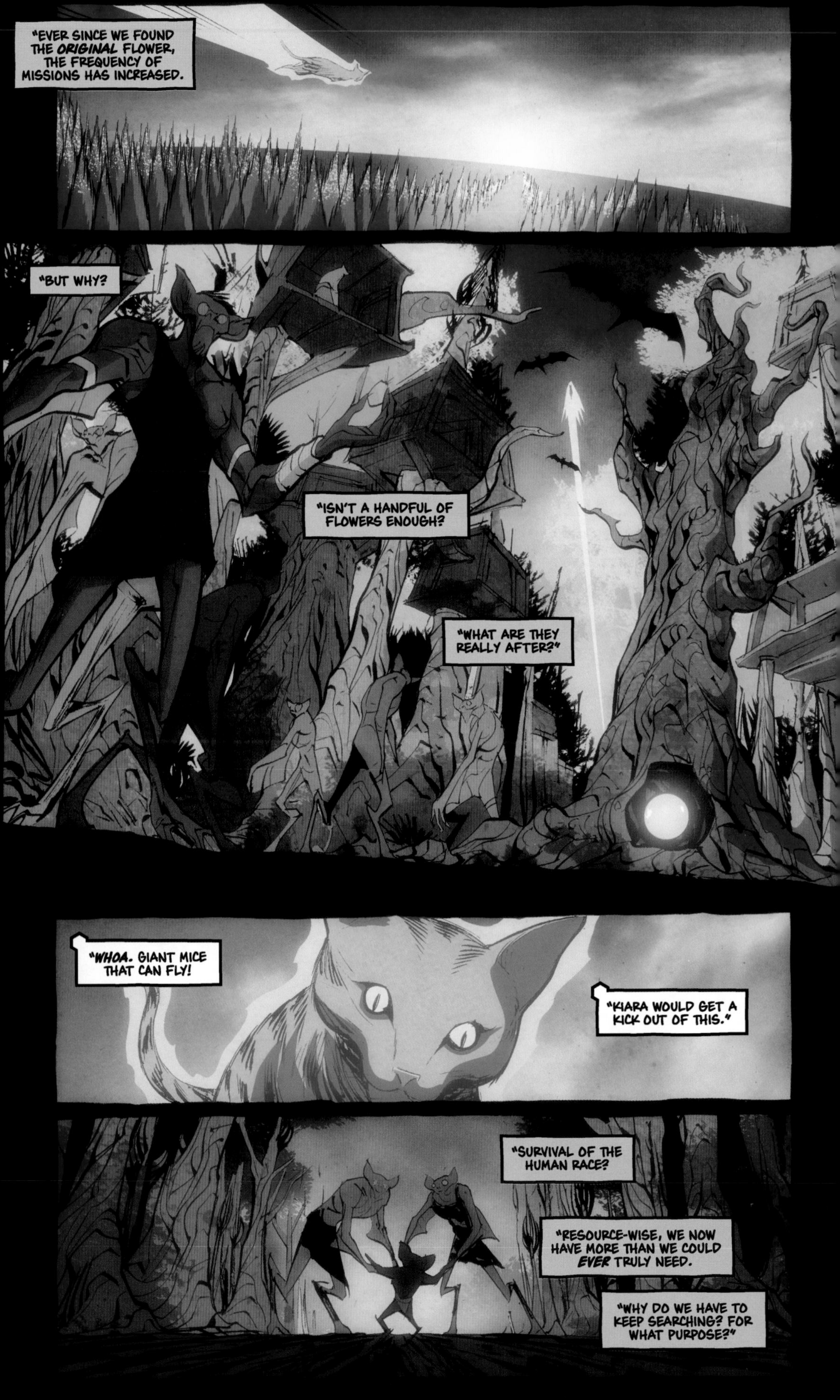
"EVER SINCE WE FOUND THE *ORIGINAL* FLOWER, THE FREQUENCY OF MISSIONS HAS INCREASED.
"BUT WHY?
"ISN'T A HANDFUL OF FLOWERS ENOUGH?
"WHAT ARE THEY REALLY AFTER?"
"*WHOA*. GIANT MICE THAT CAN FLY!
"KIARA WOULD GET A KICK OUT OF THIS."
"SURVIVAL OF THE HUMAN RACE?
"RESOURCE-WISE, WE NOW HAVE MORE THAN WE COULD *EVER* TRULY NEED.
"WHY DO WE HAVE TO KEEP SEARCHING? FOR WHAT PURPOSE?"

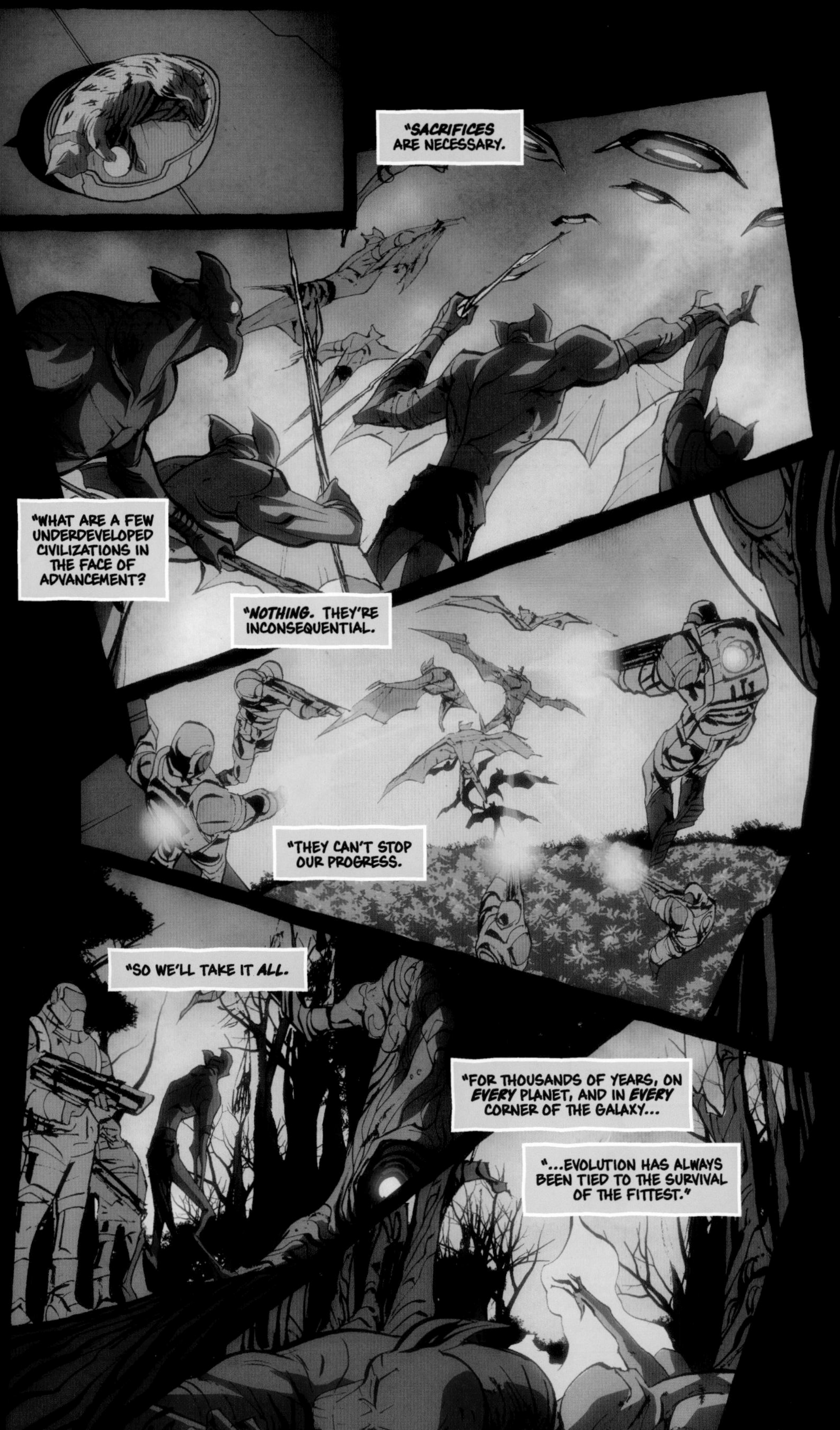
"SACRIFICES ARE NECESSARY.
"WHAT ARE A FEW UNDERDEVELOPED CIVILIZATIONS IN THE FACE OF ADVANCEMENT?
"NOTHING. THEY'RE INCONSEQUENTIAL.
"THEY CAN'T STOP OUR PROGRESS.
"SO WE'LL TAKE IT ALL.
"FOR THOUSANDS OF YEARS, ON EVERY PLANET, AND IN EVERY CORNER OF THE GALAXY...
"...EVOLUTION HAS ALWAYS BEEN TIED TO THE SURVIVAL OF THE FITTEST."

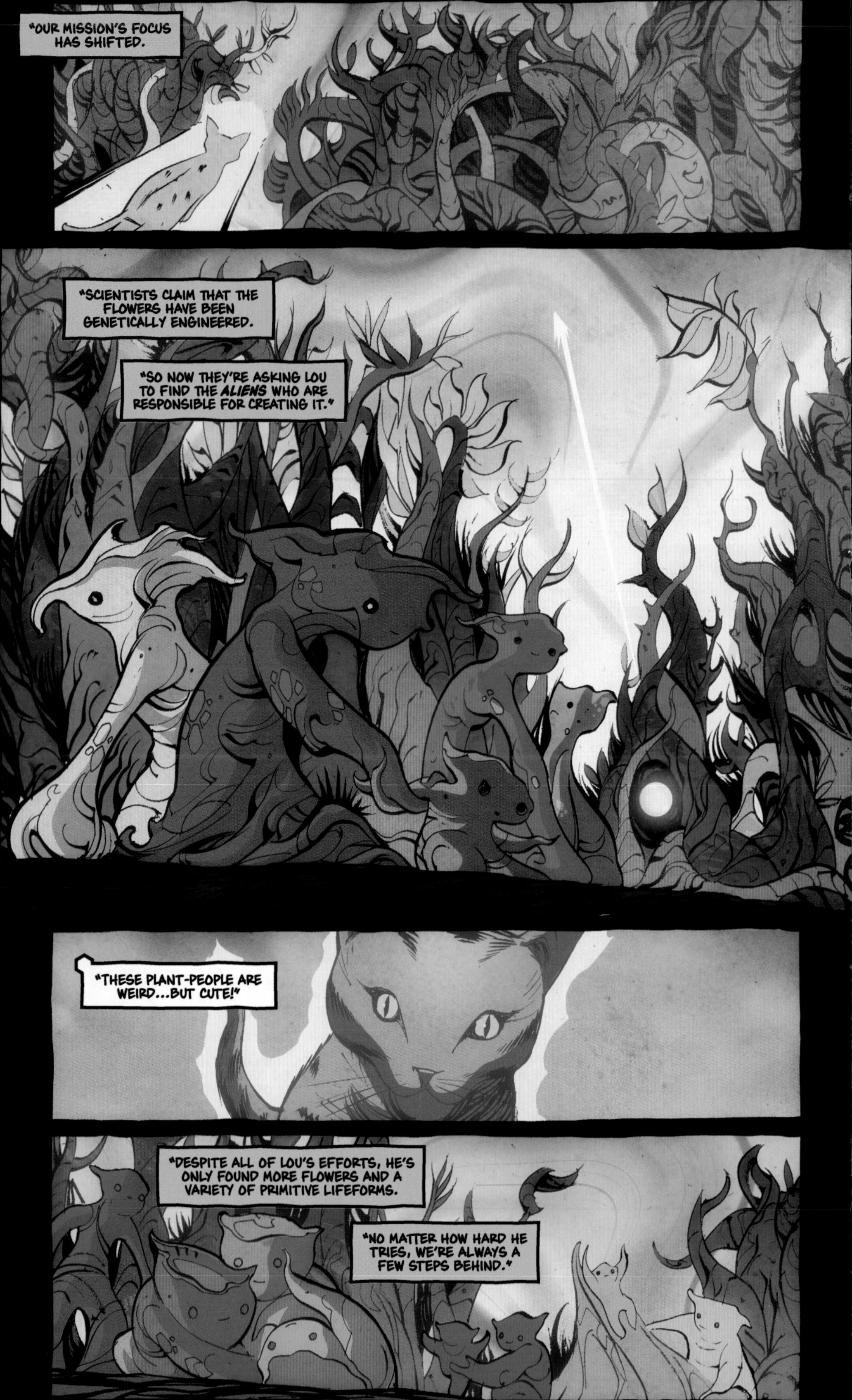
"OUR MISSION'S FOCUS HAS SHIFTED.
"SCIENTISTS CLAIM THAT THE FLOWERS HAVE BEEN GENETICALLY ENGINEERED.
"SO NOW THEY'RE ASKING LOU TO FIND THE *ALIENS* WHO ARE RESPONSIBLE FOR CREATING IT."
"THESE PLANT-PEOPLE ARE WEIRD...BUT CUTE!"
"DESPITE ALL OF LOU'S EFFORTS, HE'S ONLY FOUND MORE FLOWERS AND A VARIETY OF PRIMITIVE LIFEFORMS.
"NO MATTER HOW HARD HE TRIES, WE'RE ALWAYS A FEW STEPS BEHIND."

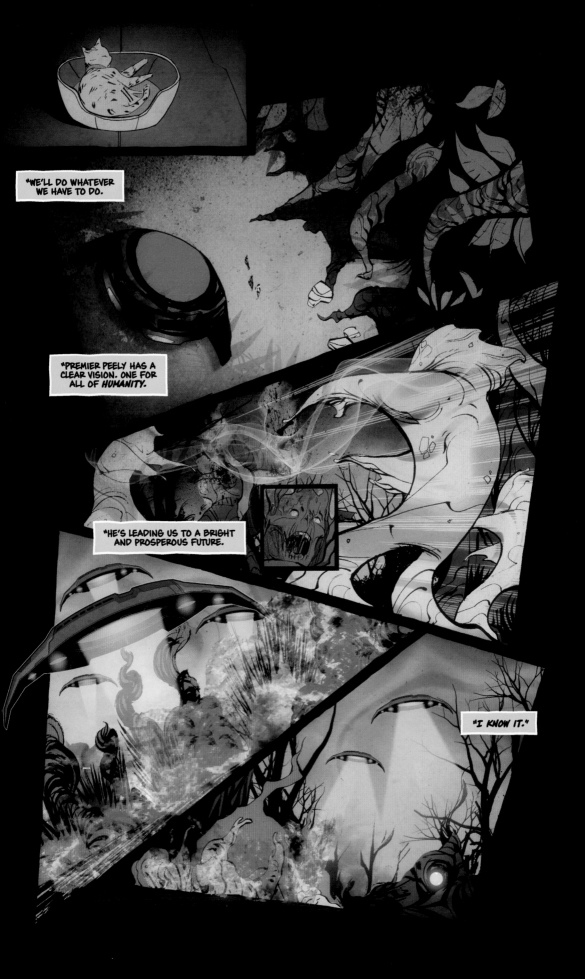

*WE'LL DO WHATEVER WE HAVE TO DO.

*PREMIER PEELY HAS A CLEAR VISION. ONE FOR ALL OF *HUMANITY*.

*HE'S LEADING US TO A BRIGHT AND PROSPEROUS FUTURE.

"I KNOW IT."

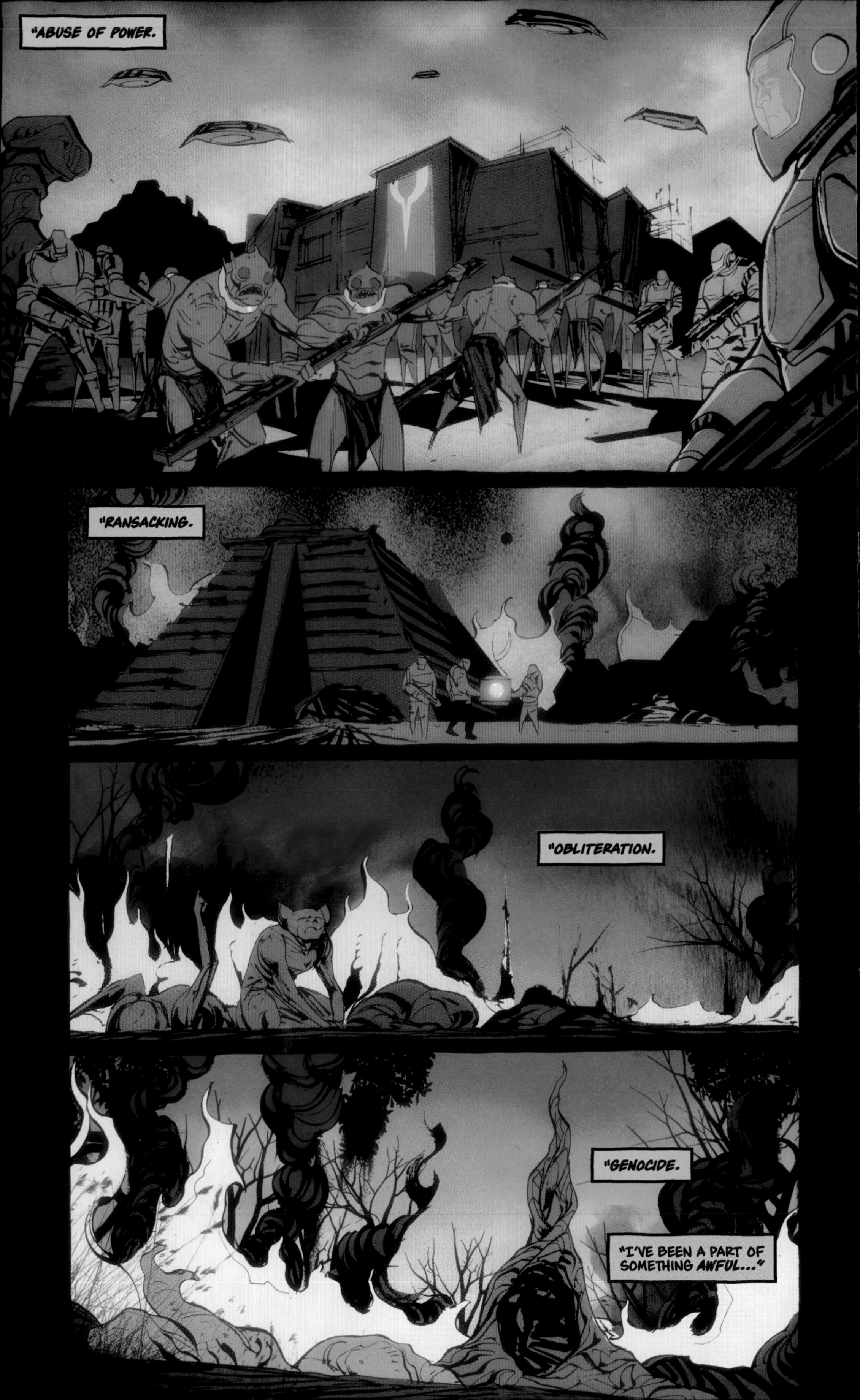
"ABUSE OF POWER.
"RANSACKING.
"OBLITERATION.
"GENOCIDE.
"I'VE BEEN A PART OF SOMETHING AWFUL..."

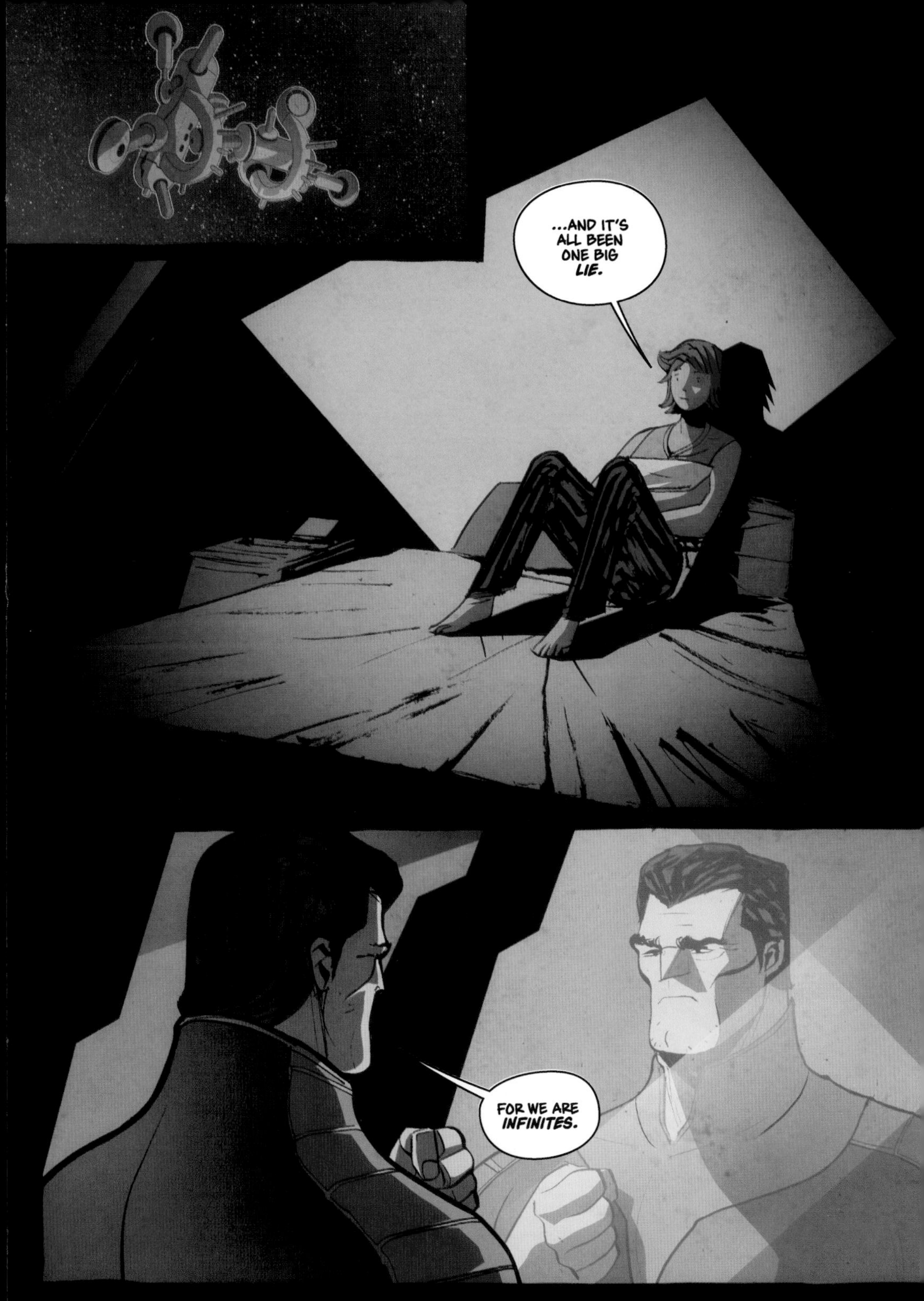
...AND IT'S ALL BEEN ONE BIG *LIE.*
FOR WE ARE *INFINITES.*

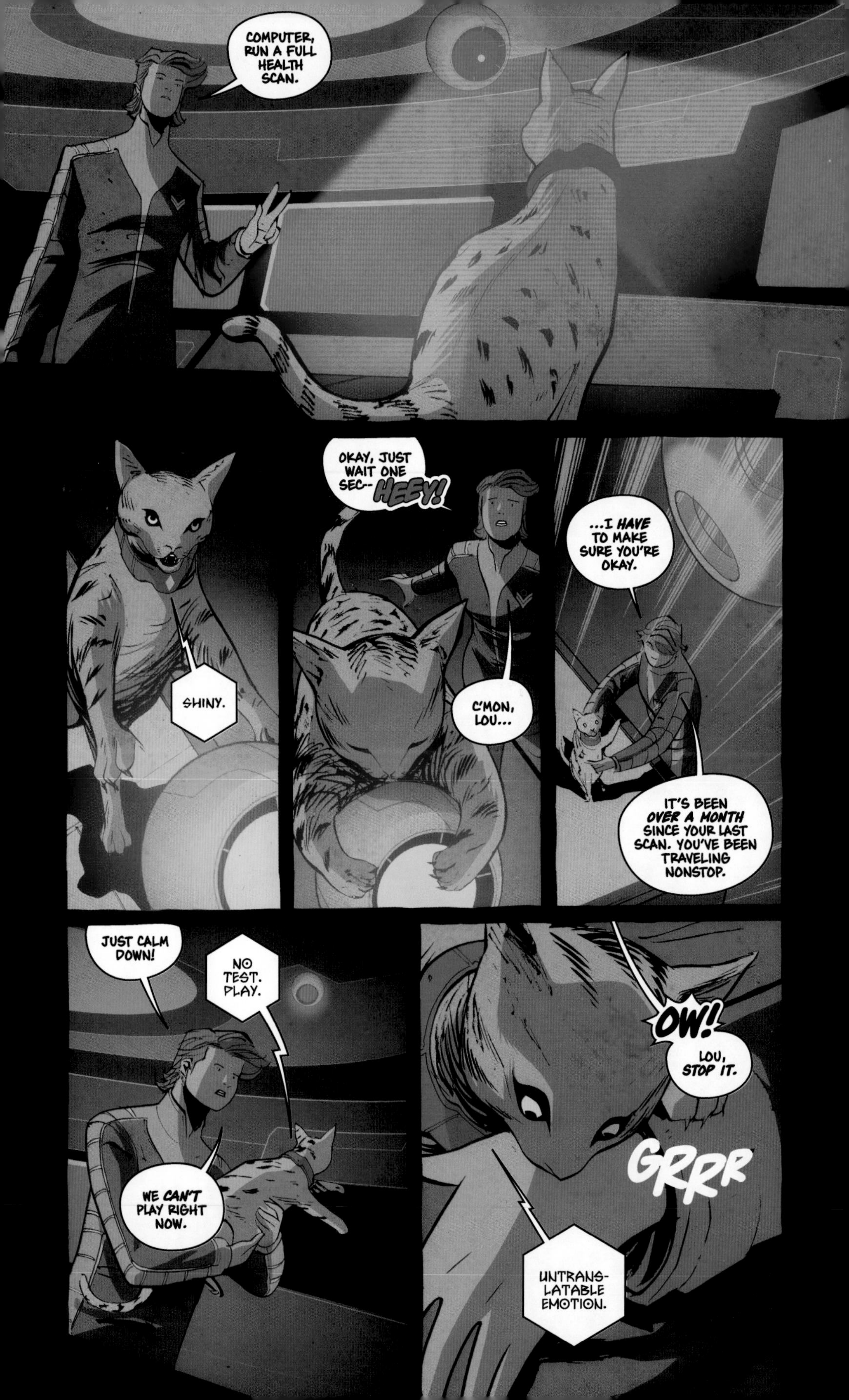
COMPUTER, RUN A FULL HEALTH SCAN.
SHINY.
OKAY, JUST WAIT ONE SEC-- HEEY!
C'MON, LOU...
...I HAVE TO MAKE SURE YOU'RE OKAY.
IT'S BEEN OVER A MONTH SINCE YOUR LAST SCAN. YOU'VE BEEN TRAVELING NONSTOP.
JUST CALM DOWN!
NO TEST. PLAY.
WE CAN'T PLAY RIGHT NOW.
OW!
LOU, STOP IT.
GRRR
UNTRANS-LATABLE EMOTION.

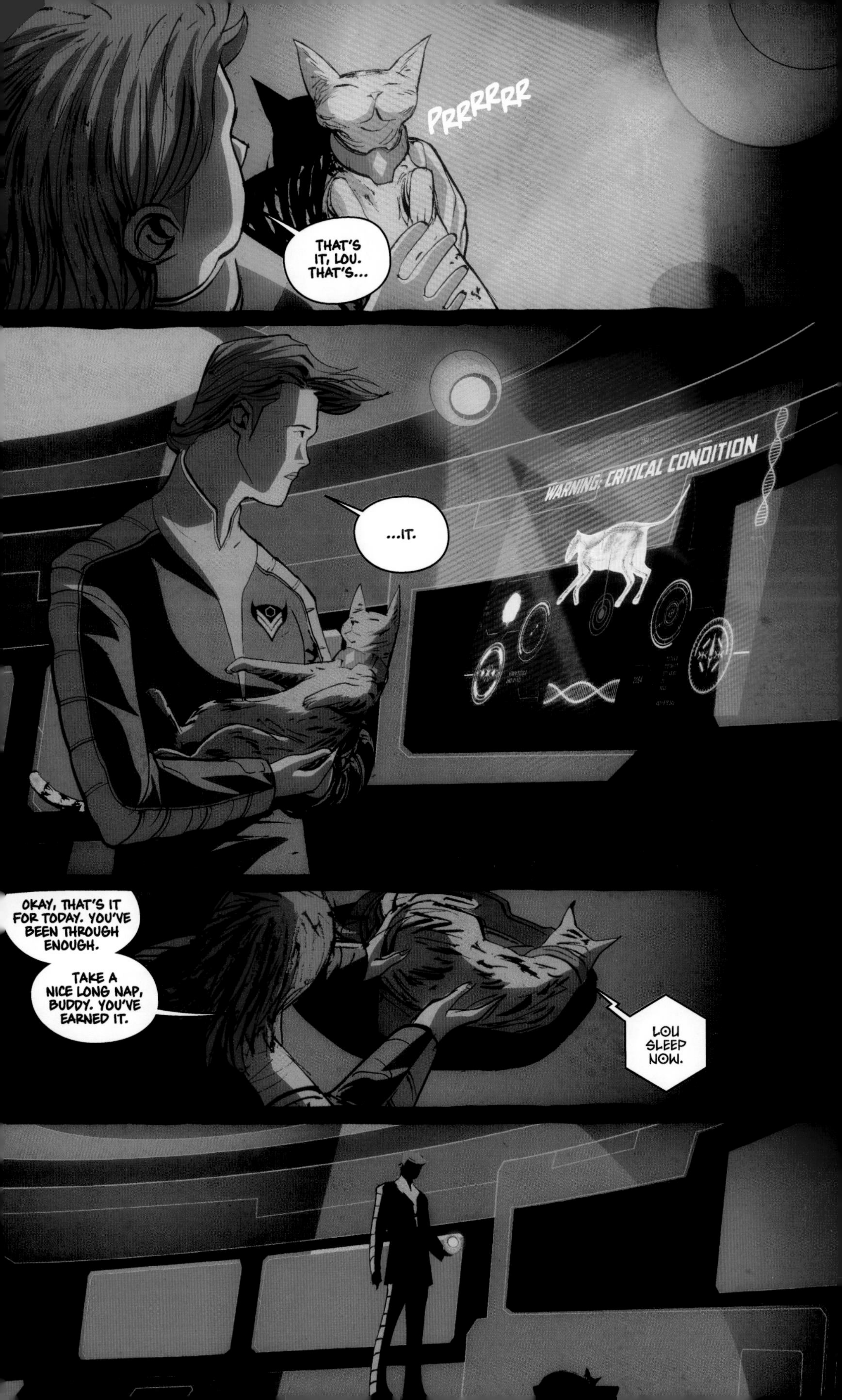
PRRRRRR
THAT'S IT, LOU. THAT'S...
WARNING: CRITICAL CONDITION
...IT.
OKAY, THAT'S IT FOR TODAY. YOU'VE BEEN THROUGH ENOUGH.
TAKE A NICE LONG NAP, BUDDY. YOU'VE EARNED IT.
LOU SLEEP NOW.

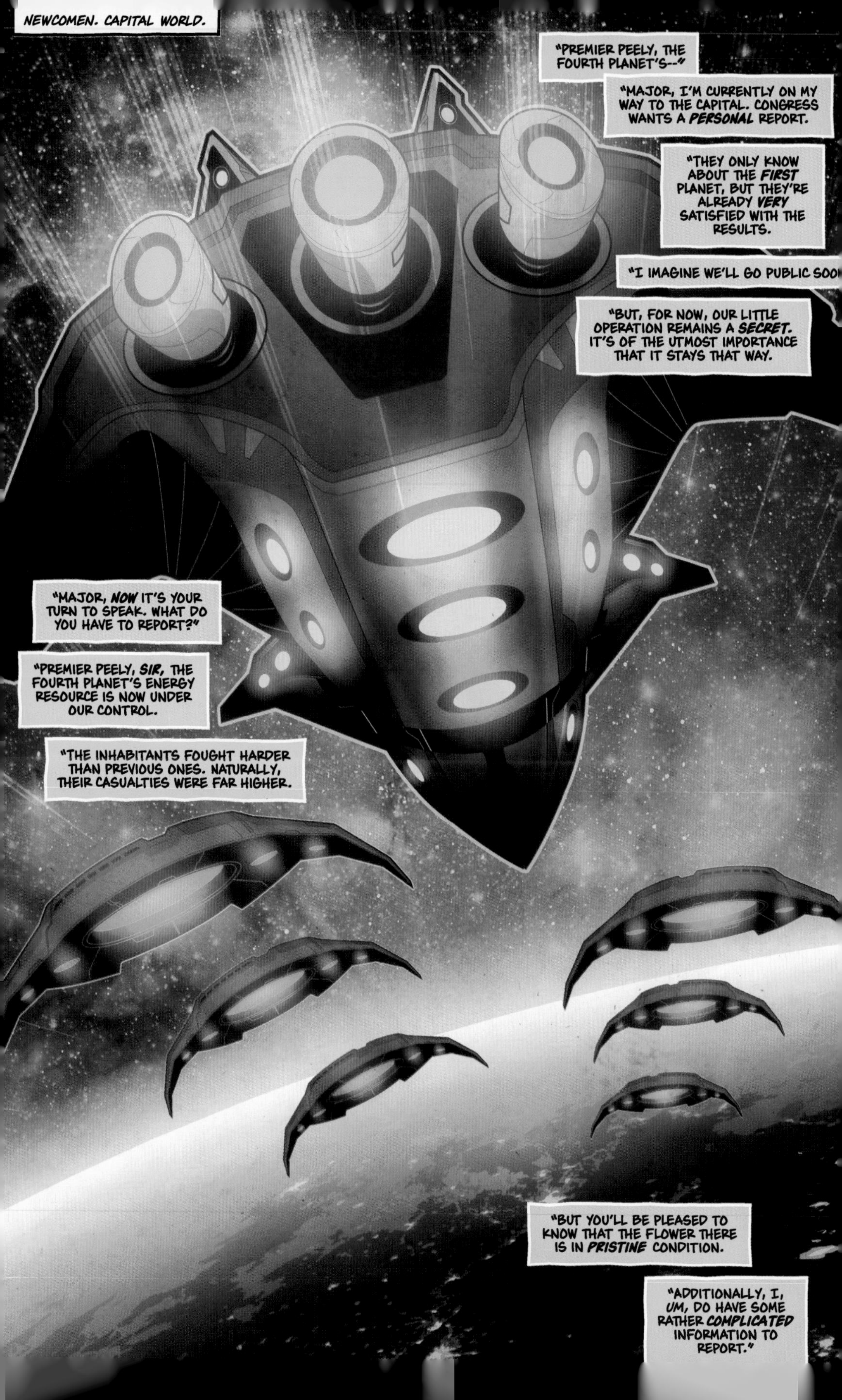
NEWCOMEN. CAPITAL WORLD.
"PREMIER PEELY, THE FOURTH PLANET'S--"
"MAJOR, I'M CURRENTLY ON MY WAY TO THE CAPITAL. CONGRESS WANTS A PERSONAL REPORT.
"THEY ONLY KNOW ABOUT THE FIRST PLANET, BUT THEY'RE ALREADY VERY SATISFIED WITH THE RESULTS.
"I IMAGINE WE'LL GO PUBLIC SOO
"BUT, FOR NOW, OUR LITTLE OPERATION REMAINS A SECRET. IT'S OF THE UTMOST IMPORTANCE THAT IT STAYS THAT WAY.
"MAJOR, NOW IT'S YOUR TURN TO SPEAK. WHAT DO YOU HAVE TO REPORT?"
"PREMIER PEELY, SIR, THE FOURTH PLANET'S ENERGY RESOURCE IS NOW UNDER OUR CONTROL.
"THE INHABITANTS FOUGHT HARDER THAN PREVIOUS ONES. NATURALLY, THEIR CASUALTIES WERE FAR HIGHER.
"BUT YOU'LL BE PLEASED TO KNOW THAT THE FLOWER THERE IS IN PRISTINE CONDITION.
"ADDITIONALLY, I, UM, DO HAVE SOME RATHER COMPLICATED INFORMATION TO REPORT."

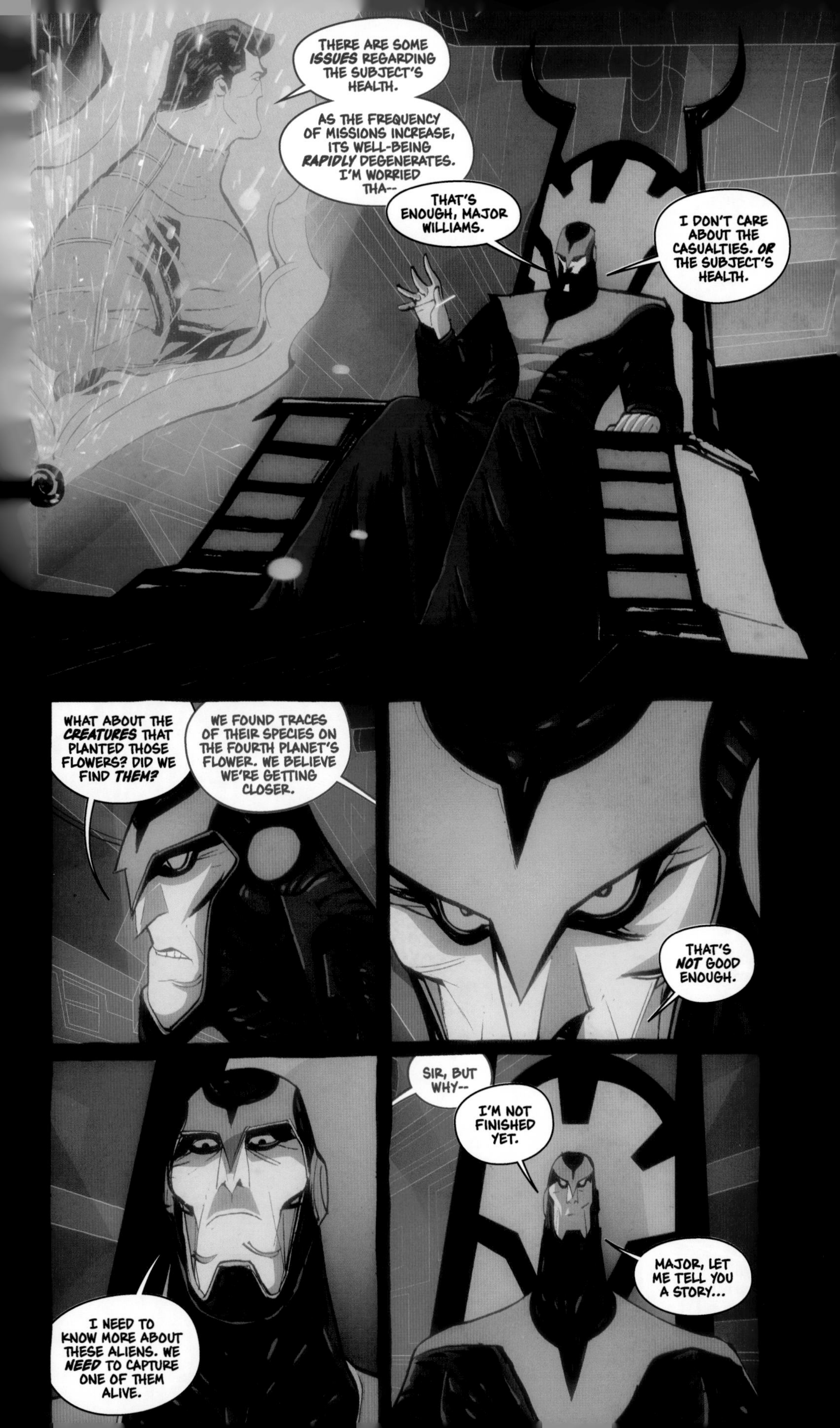
THERE ARE SOME ISSUES REGARDING THE SUBJECT'S HEALTH.
AS THE FREQUENCY OF MISSIONS INCREASE, ITS WELL-BEING RAPIDLY DEGENERATES. I'M WORRIED THA--
THAT'S ENOUGH, MAJOR WILLIAMS.
I DON'T CARE ABOUT THE CASUALTIES. OR THE SUBJECT'S HEALTH.
WHAT ABOUT THE CREATURES THAT PLANTED THOSE FLOWERS? DID WE FIND THEM?
WE FOUND TRACES OF THEIR SPECIES ON THE FOURTH PLANET'S FLOWER. WE BELIEVE WE'RE GETTING CLOSER.
THAT'S NOT GOOD ENOUGH.
I NEED TO KNOW MORE ABOUT THESE ALIENS. WE NEED TO CAPTURE ONE OF THEM ALIVE.
SIR, BUT WHY--
I'M NOT FINISHED YET.
MAJOR, LET ME TELL YOU A STORY...

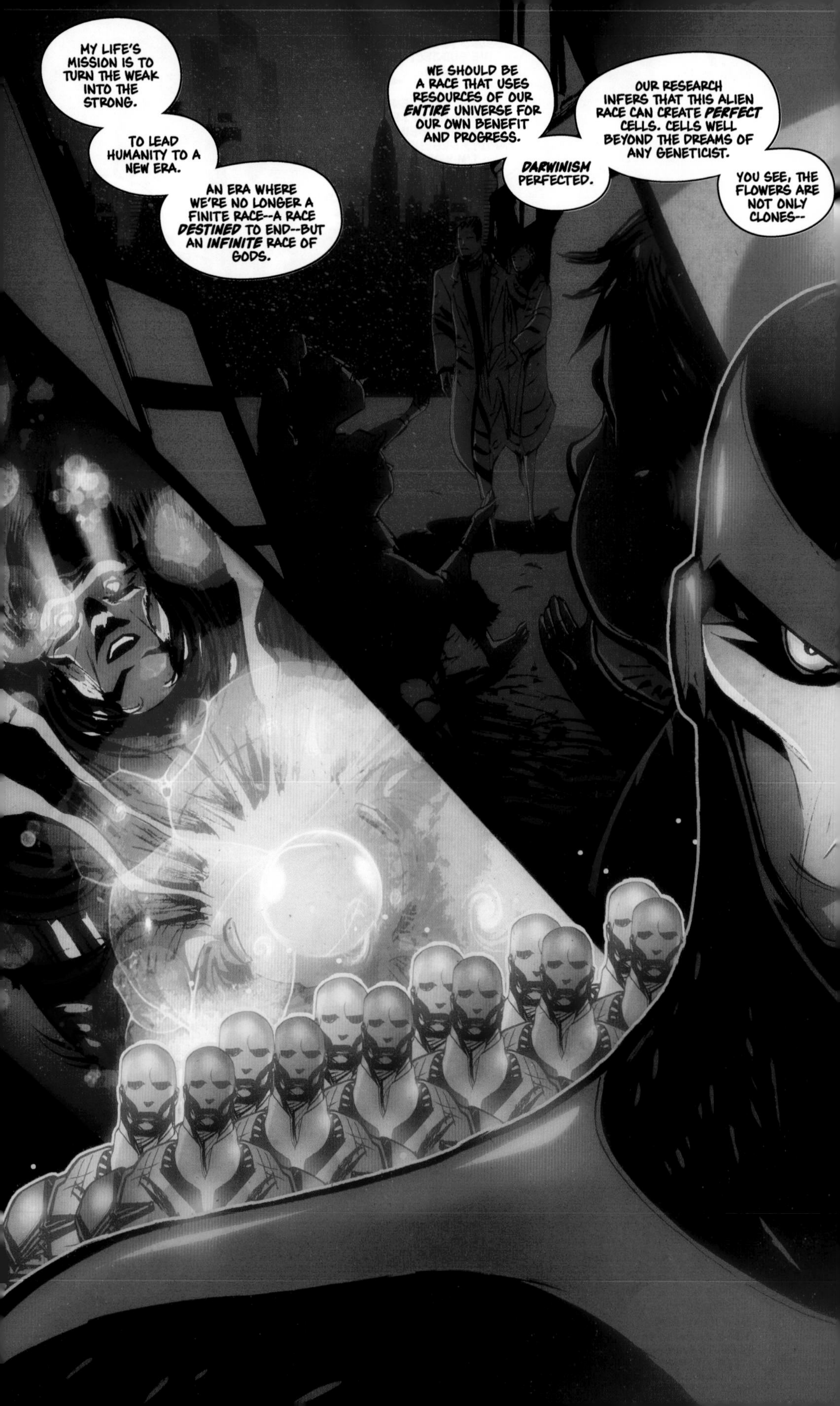
MY LIFE'S MISSION IS TO TURN THE WEAK INTO THE STRONG.
TO LEAD HUMANITY TO A NEW ERA.
AN ERA WHERE WE'RE NO LONGER A FINITE RACE--A RACE *DESTINED* TO END--BUT AN *INFINITE* RACE OF GODS.
WE SHOULD BE A RACE THAT USES RESOURCES OF OUR *ENTIRE* UNIVERSE FOR OUR OWN BENEFIT AND PROGRESS.
DARWINISM PERFECTED.
OUR RESEARCH INFERS THAT THIS ALIEN RACE CAN CREATE *PERFECT* CELLS. CELLS WELL BEYOND THE DREAMS OF ANY GENETICIST.
YOU SEE, THE FLOWERS ARE NOT ONLY CLONES--

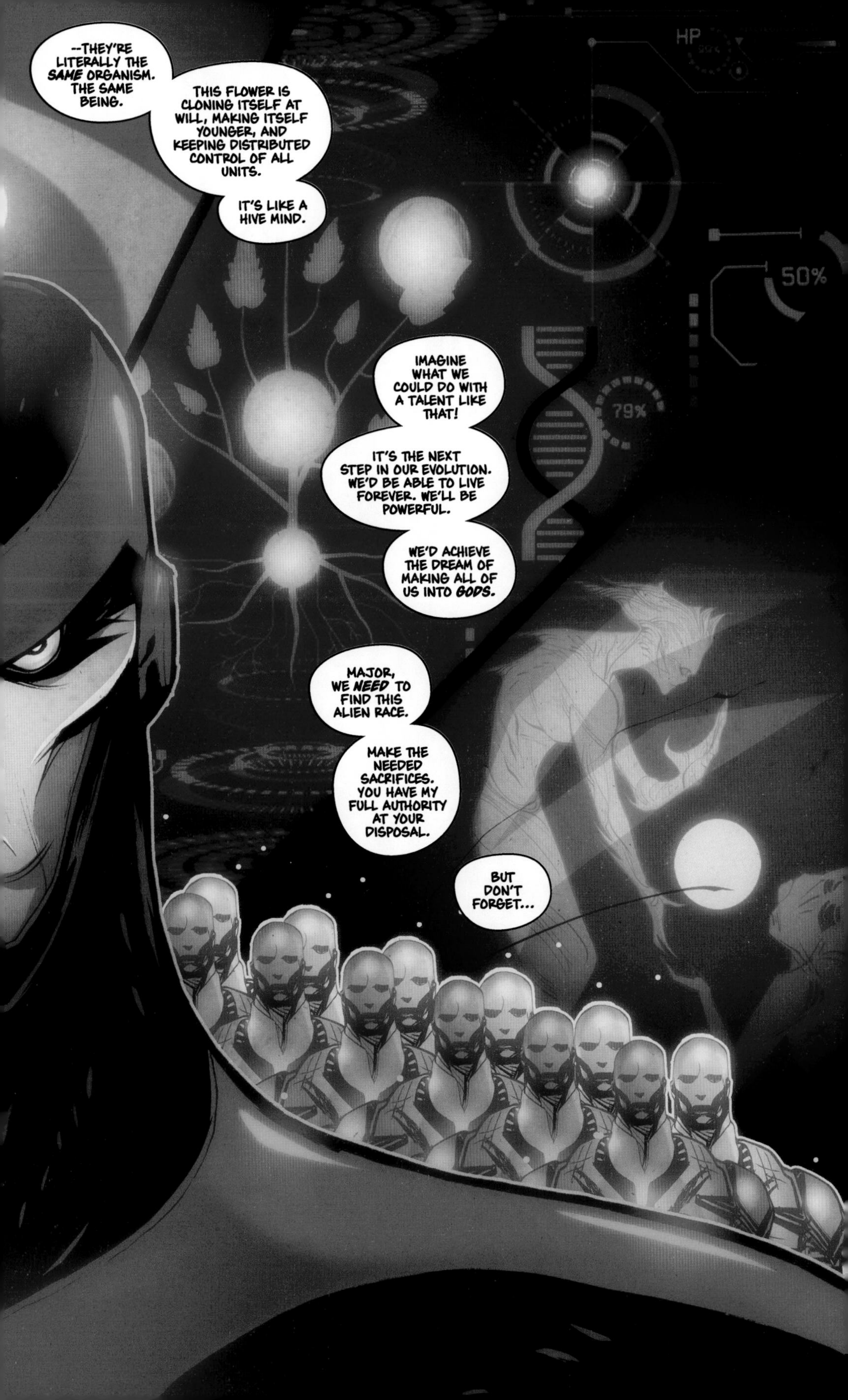
--THEY'RE LITERALLY THE SAME ORGANISM. THE SAME BEING.
THIS FLOWER IS CLONING ITSELF AT WILL, MAKING ITSELF YOUNGER, AND KEEPING DISTRIBUTED CONTROL OF ALL UNITS.
IT'S LIKE A HIVE MIND.
HP
50%
79%
IMAGINE WHAT WE COULD DO WITH A TALENT LIKE THAT!
IT'S THE NEXT STEP IN OUR EVOLUTION. WE'D BE ABLE TO LIVE FOREVER. WE'LL BE POWERFUL.
WE'D ACHIEVE THE DREAM OF MAKING ALL OF US INTO GODS.
MAJOR, WE NEED TO FIND THIS ALIEN RACE.
MAKE THE NEEDED SACRIFICES. YOU HAVE MY FULL AUTHORITY AT YOUR DISPOSAL.
BUT DON'T FORGET...

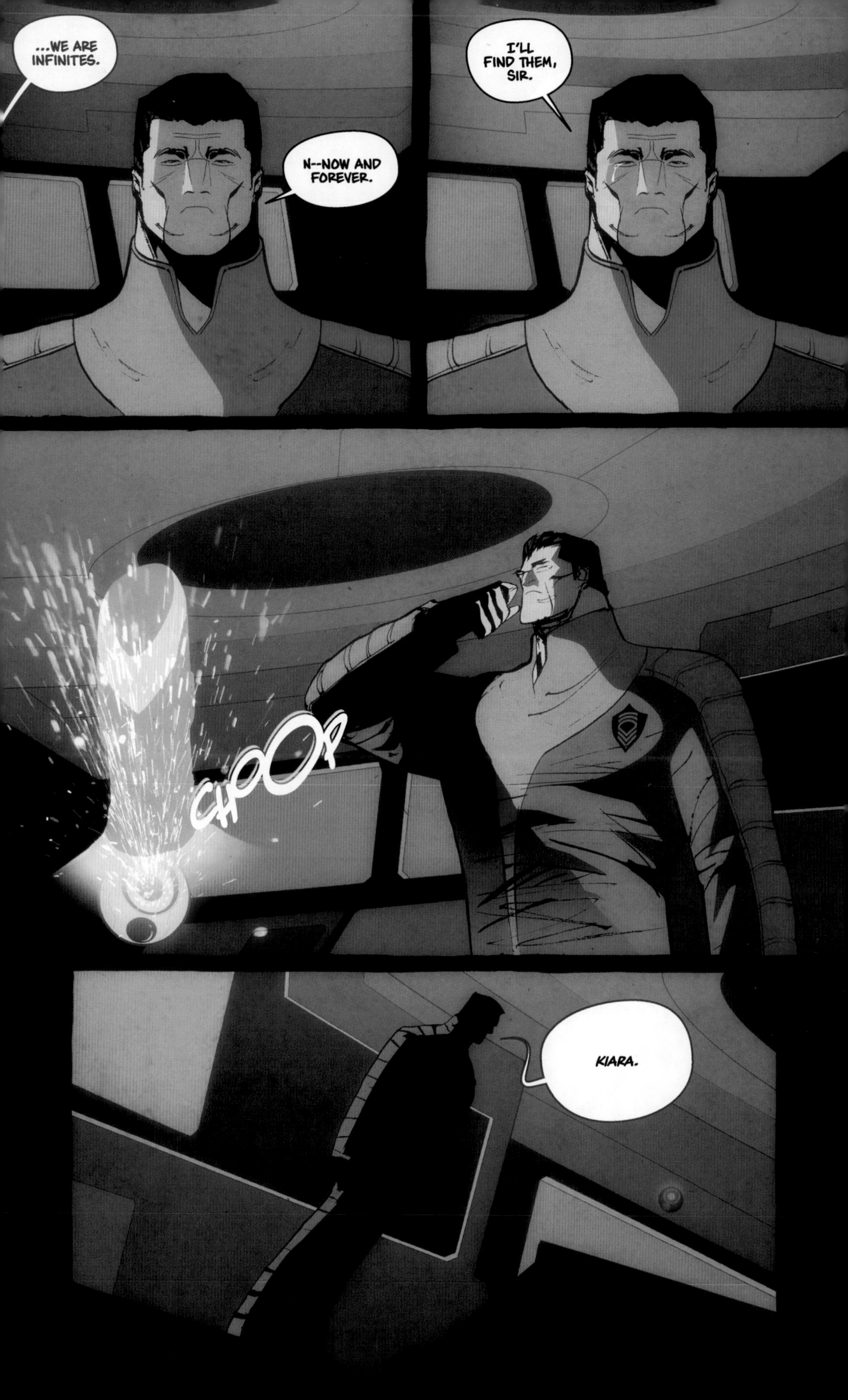
...WE ARE INFINITES.
N--NOW AND FOREVER.
I'LL FIND THEM, SIR.
CHOOP
KIARA.

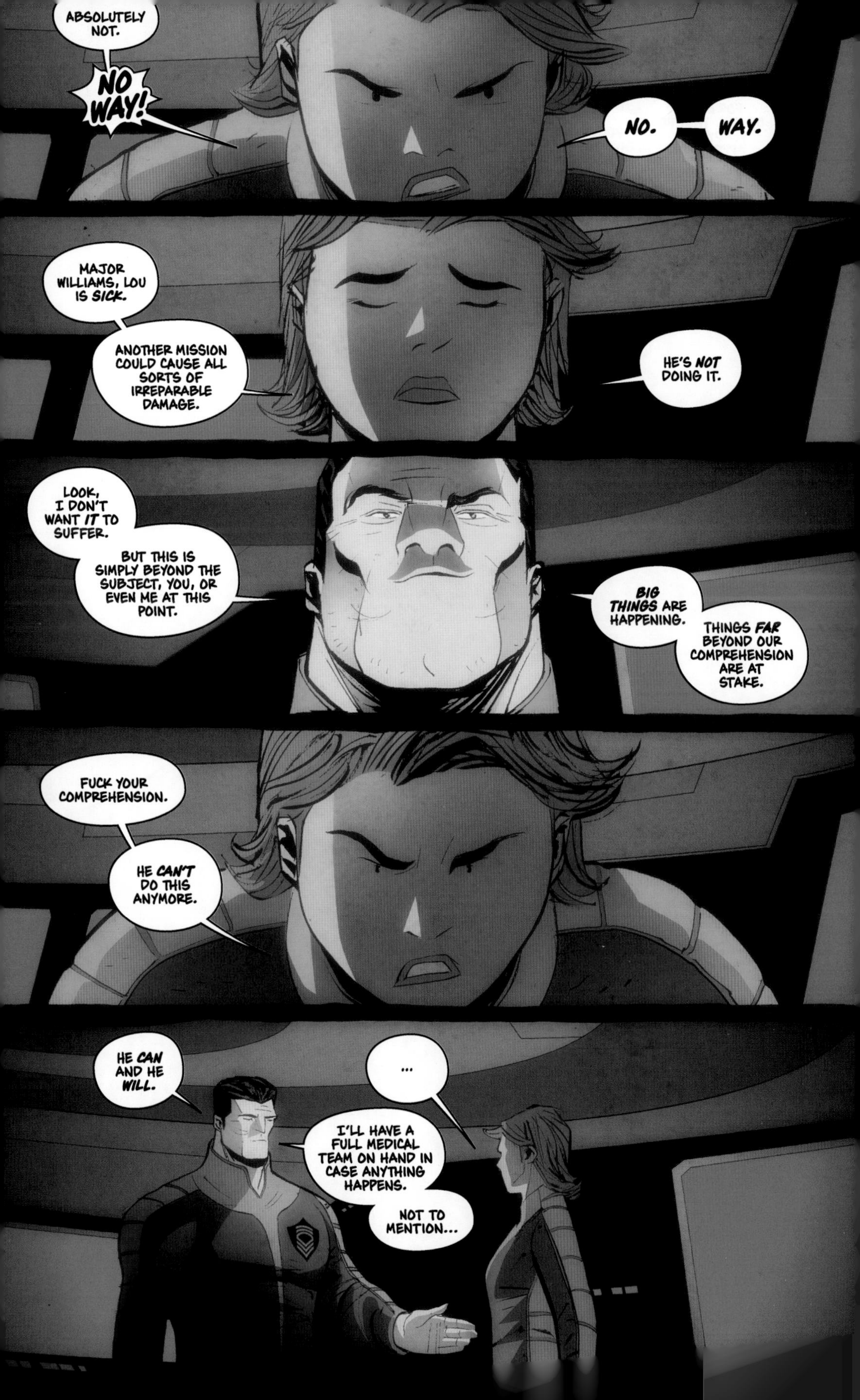
ABSOLUTELY NOT.
NO WAY!
NO.
WAY.
MAJOR WILLIAMS, LOU IS SICK.
ANOTHER MISSION COULD CAUSE ALL SORTS OF IRREPARABLE DAMAGE.
HE'S NOT DOING IT.
LOOK, I DON'T WANT IT TO SUFFER.
BUT THIS IS SIMPLY BEYOND THE SUBJECT, YOU, OR EVEN ME AT THIS POINT.
BIG THINGS ARE HAPPENING.
THINGS FAR BEYOND OUR COMPREHENSION ARE AT STAKE.
FUCK YOUR COMPREHENSION.
HE CAN'T DO THIS ANYMORE.
HE CAN AND HE WILL.
...
I'LL HAVE A FULL MEDICAL TEAM ON HAND IN CASE ANYTHING HAPPENS.
NOT TO MENTION...

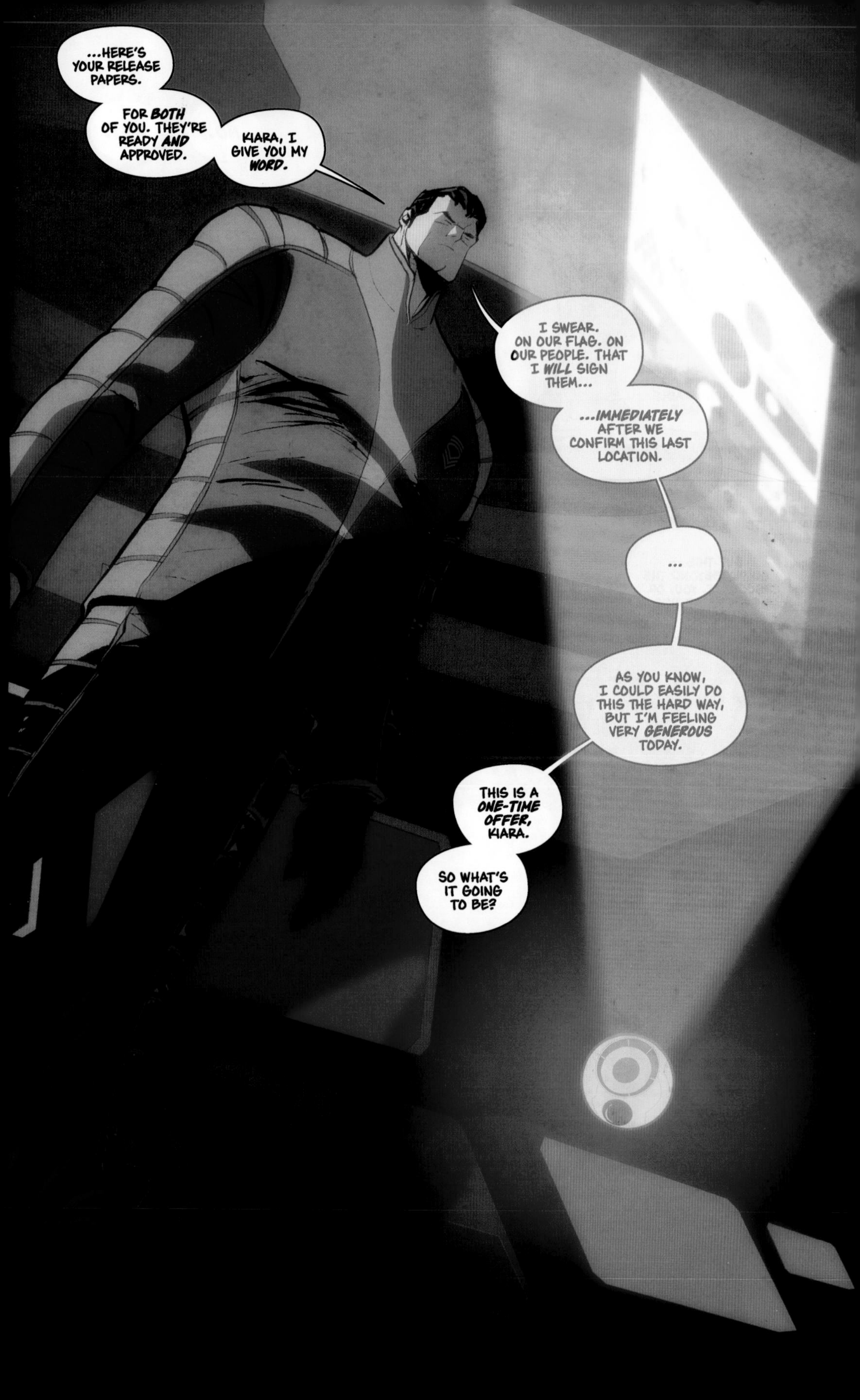
...HERE'S YOUR RELEASE PAPERS.
FOR BOTH OF YOU. THEY'RE READY AND APPROVED.
KIARA, I GIVE YOU MY WORD.
I SWEAR. ON OUR FLAG. ON OUR PEOPLE. THAT I WILL SIGN THEM...
...IMMEDIATELY AFTER WE CONFIRM THIS LAST LOCATION.
...
AS YOU KNOW, I COULD EASILY DO THIS THE HARD WAY, BUT I'M FEELING VERY GENEROUS TODAY.
THIS IS A ONE-TIME OFFER, KIARA.
SO WHAT'S IT GOING TO BE?

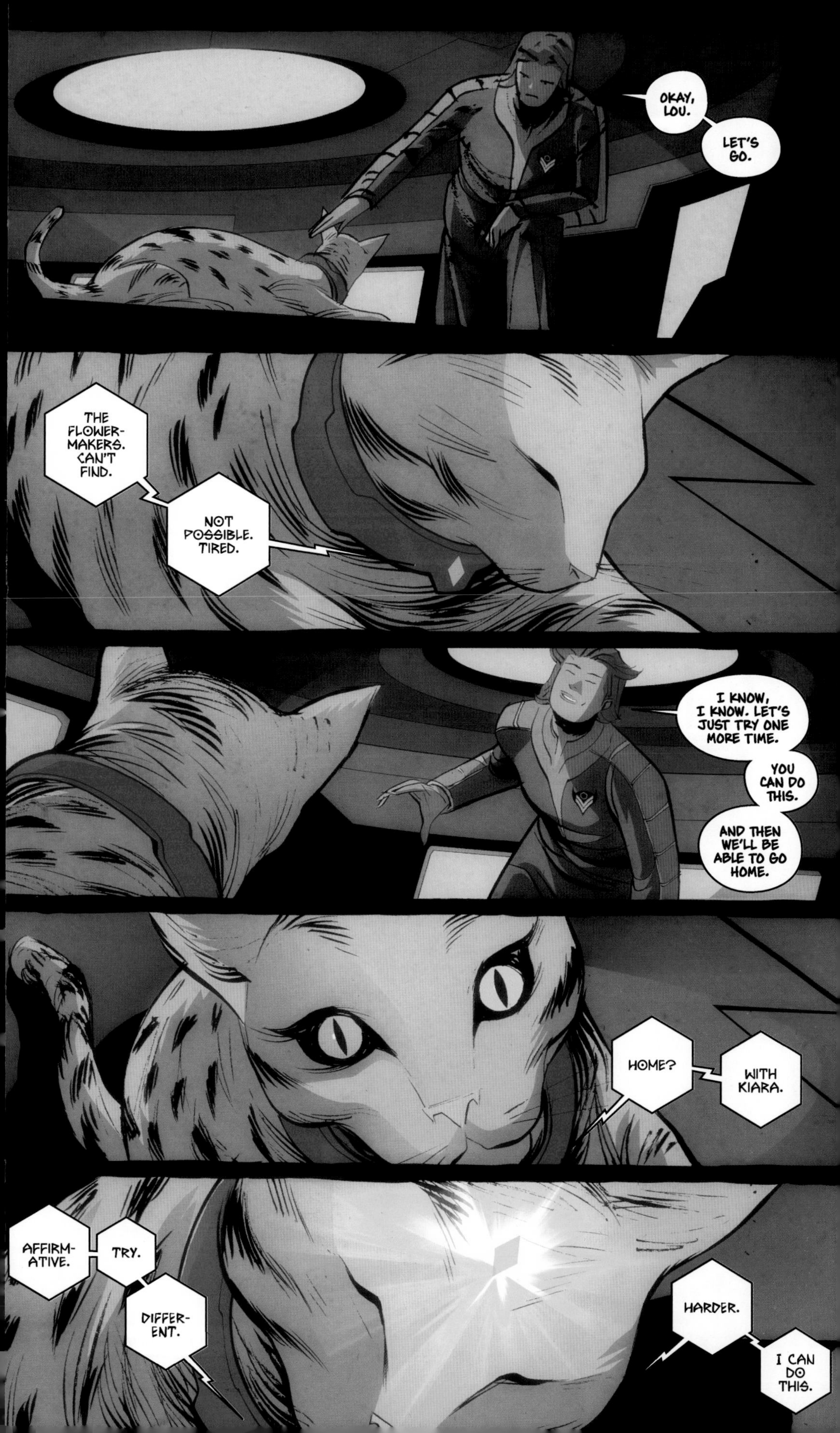
OKAY, LOU.
LET'S GO.
THE FLOWER-MAKERS. CAN'T FIND.
NOT POSSIBLE. TIRED.
I KNOW, I KNOW. LET'S JUST TRY ONE MORE TIME.
YOU CAN DO THIS.
AND THEN WE'LL BE ABLE TO GO HOME.
HOME?
WITH KIARA.
AFFIRM-ATIVE.
TRY.
DIFFER-ENT.
HARDER.
I CAN DO THIS.

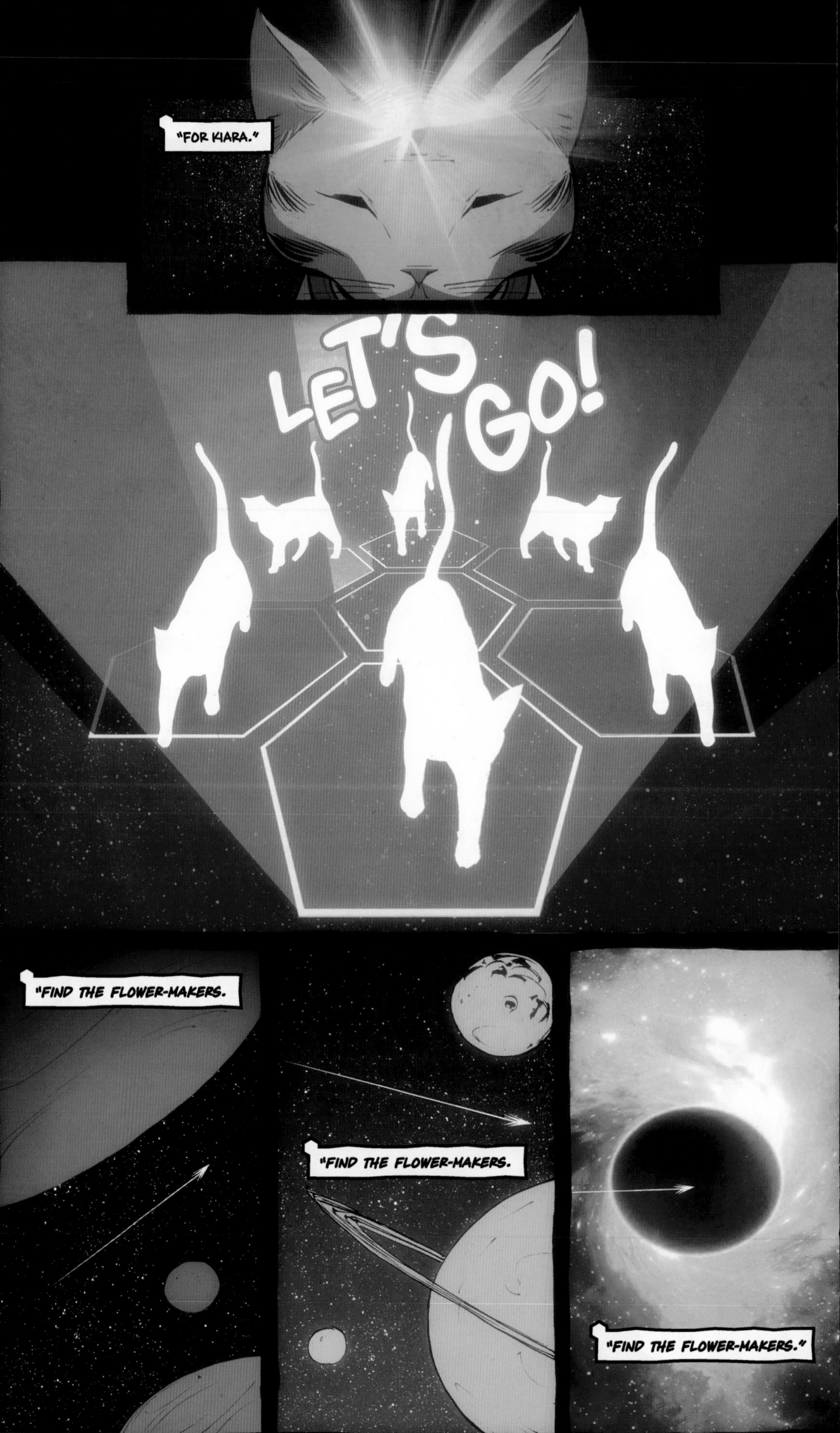
"FOR KIARA."
LET'S GO!
"FIND THE FLOWER-MAKERS.
"FIND THE FLOWER-MAKERS.
"FIND THE FLOWER-MAKERS."

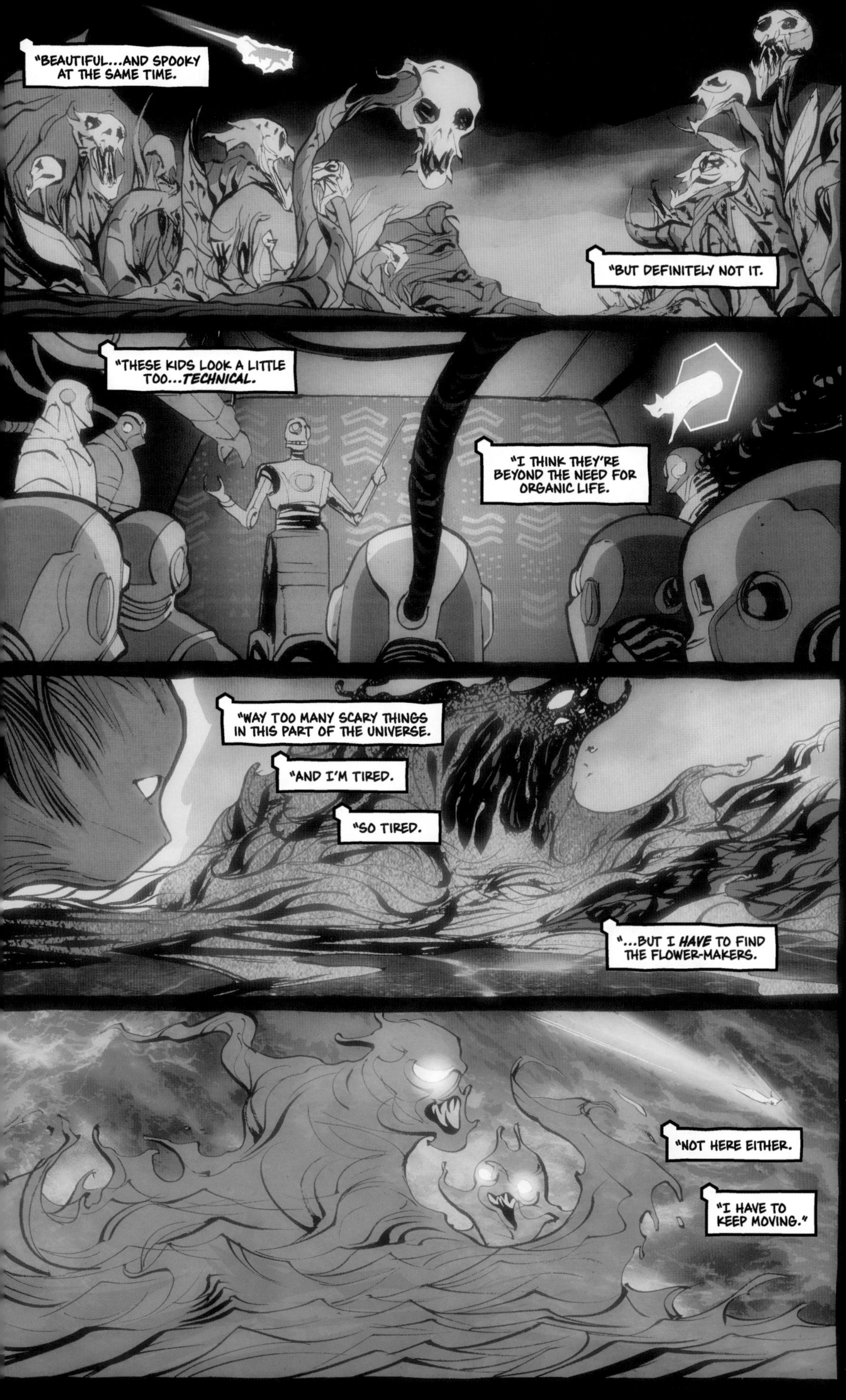
"BEAUTIFUL...AND SPOOKY AT THE SAME TIME.
"BUT DEFINITELY NOT IT.
"THESE KIDS LOOK A LITTLE TOO...*TECHNICAL*.
"I THINK THEY'RE BEYOND THE NEED FOR ORGANIC LIFE.
"WAY TOO MANY SCARY THINGS IN THIS PART OF THE UNIVERSE.
"AND I'M TIRED.
"SO TIRED.
"...BUT I *HAVE* TO FIND THE FLOWER-MAKERS.
"NOT HERE EITHER.
"I HAVE TO KEEP MOVING."

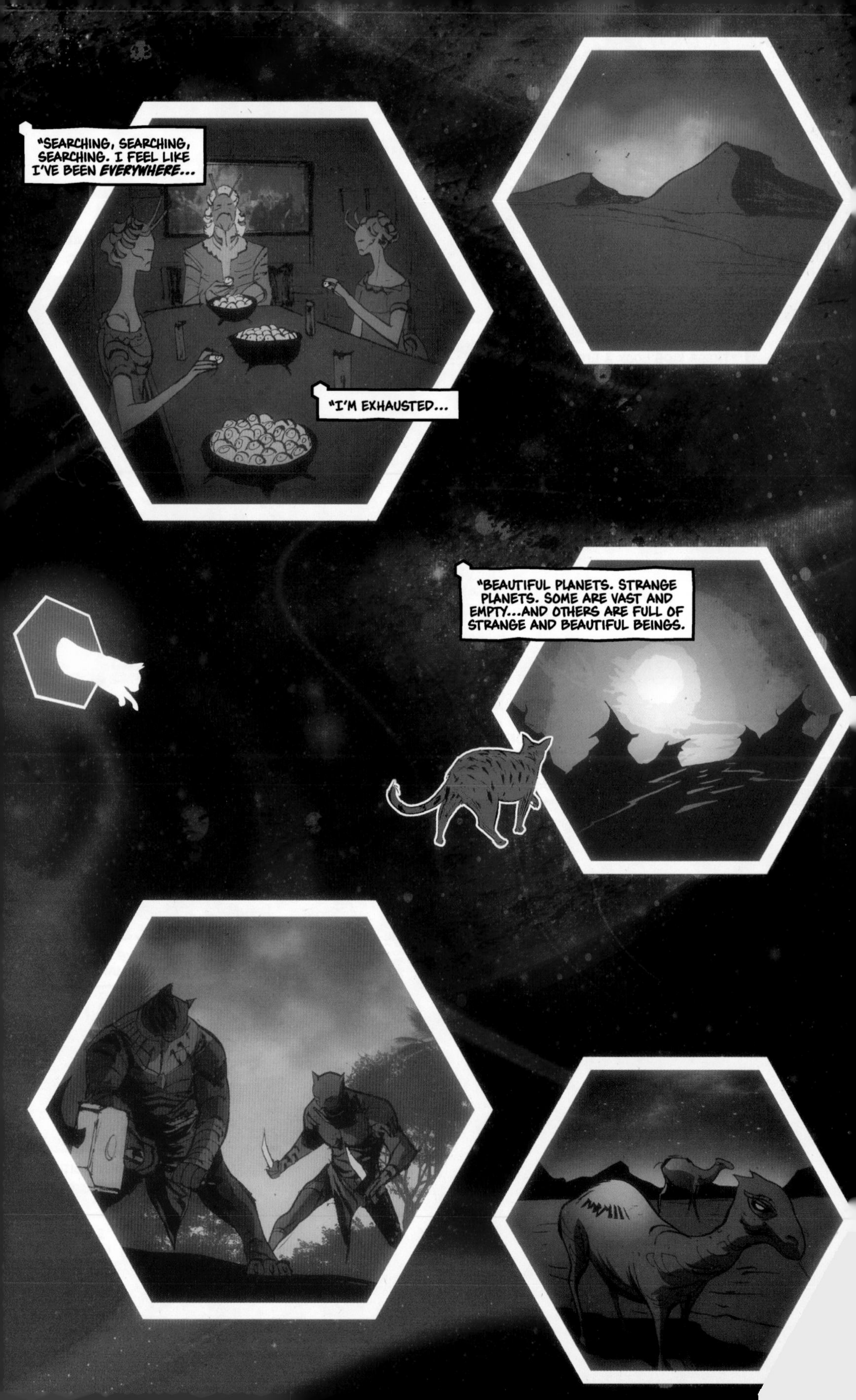
"SEARCHING, SEARCHING, SEARCHING. I FEEL LIKE I'VE BEEN *EVERYWHERE*...
"I'M EXHAUSTED...
"BEAUTIFUL PLANETS. STRANGE PLANETS. SOME ARE VAST AND EMPTY...AND OTHERS ARE FULL OF STRANGE AND BEAUTIFUL BEINGS.

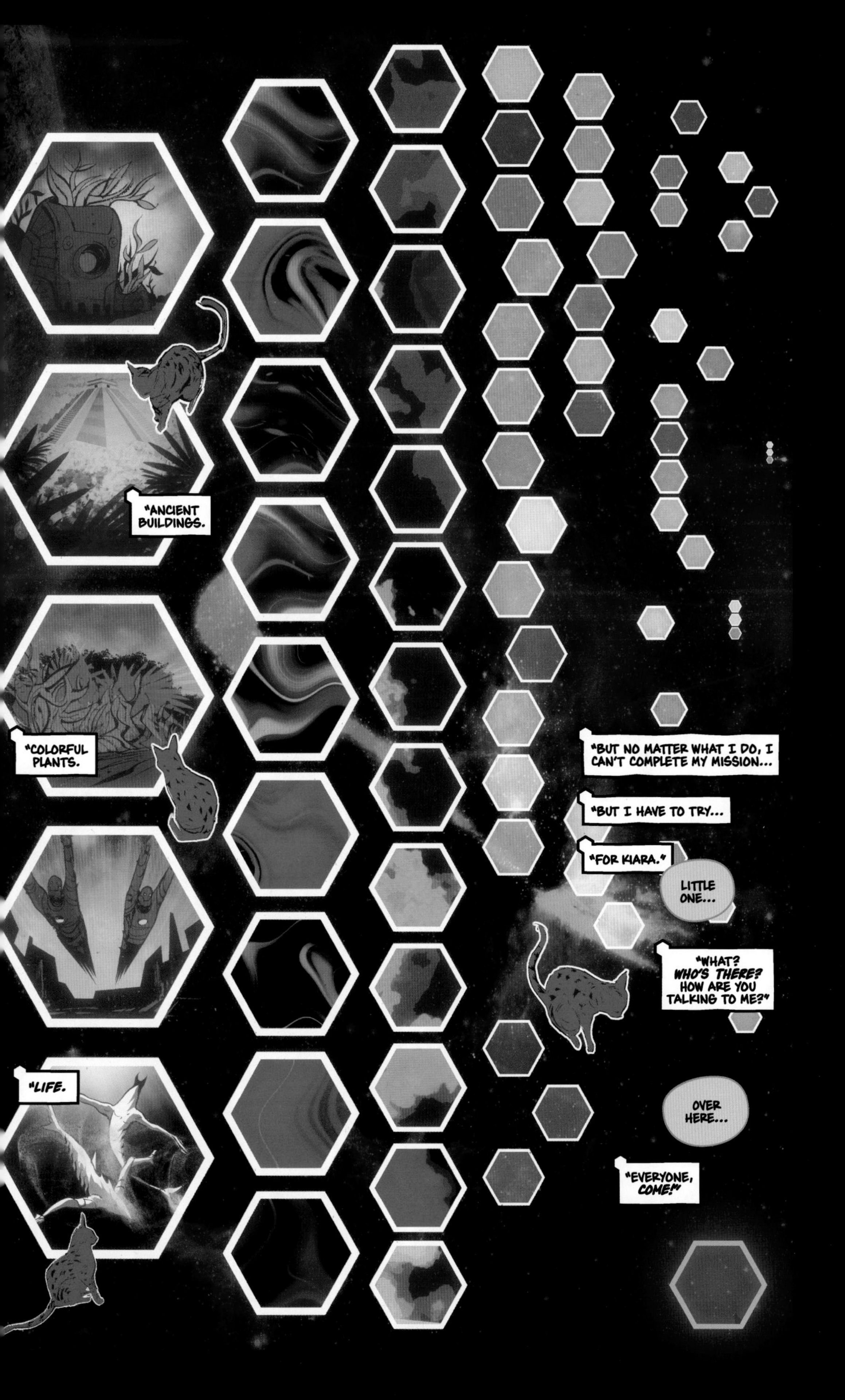

"ANCIENT BUILDINGS.
"COLORFUL PLANTS.
"LIFE.
"BUT NO MATTER WHAT I DO, I CAN'T COMPLETE MY MISSION...
"BUT I HAVE TO TRY...
"FOR KIARA."
LITTLE ONE...
"WHAT? *WHO'S THERE?* HOW ARE YOU TALKING TO ME?"
OVER HERE...
"EVERYONE, *COME!*"

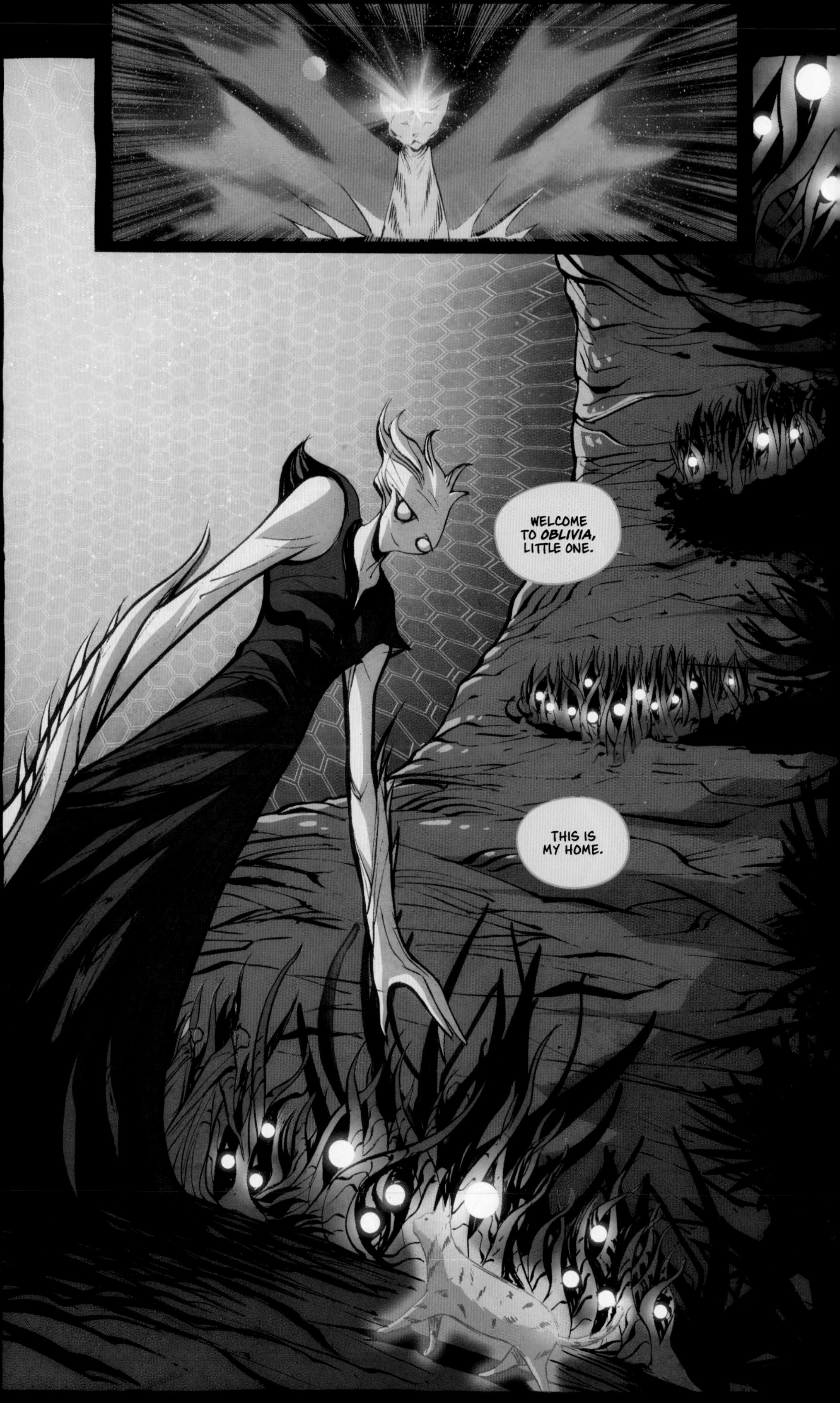
WELCOME TO *OBLIVIA*, LITTLE ONE.
THIS IS MY HOME.

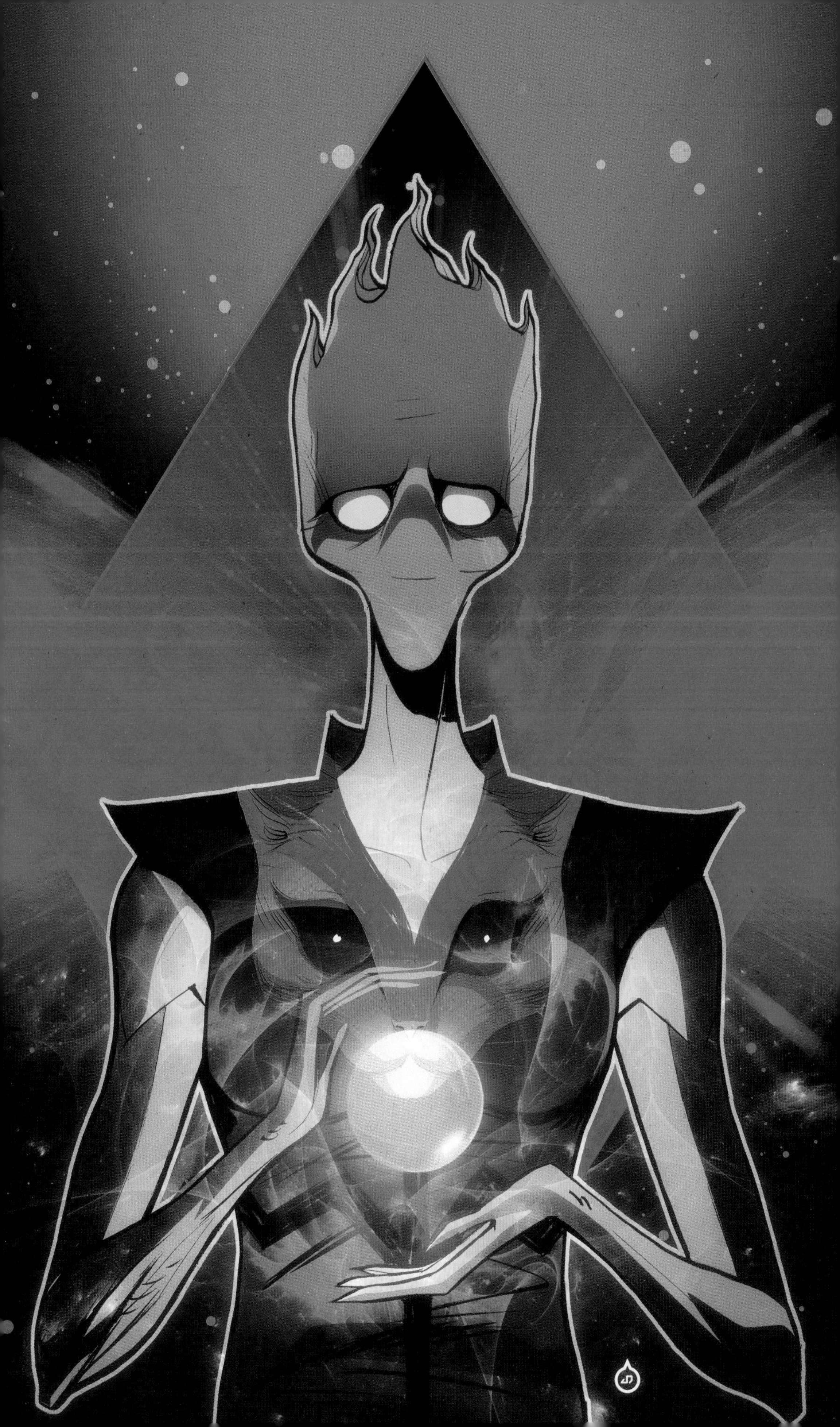

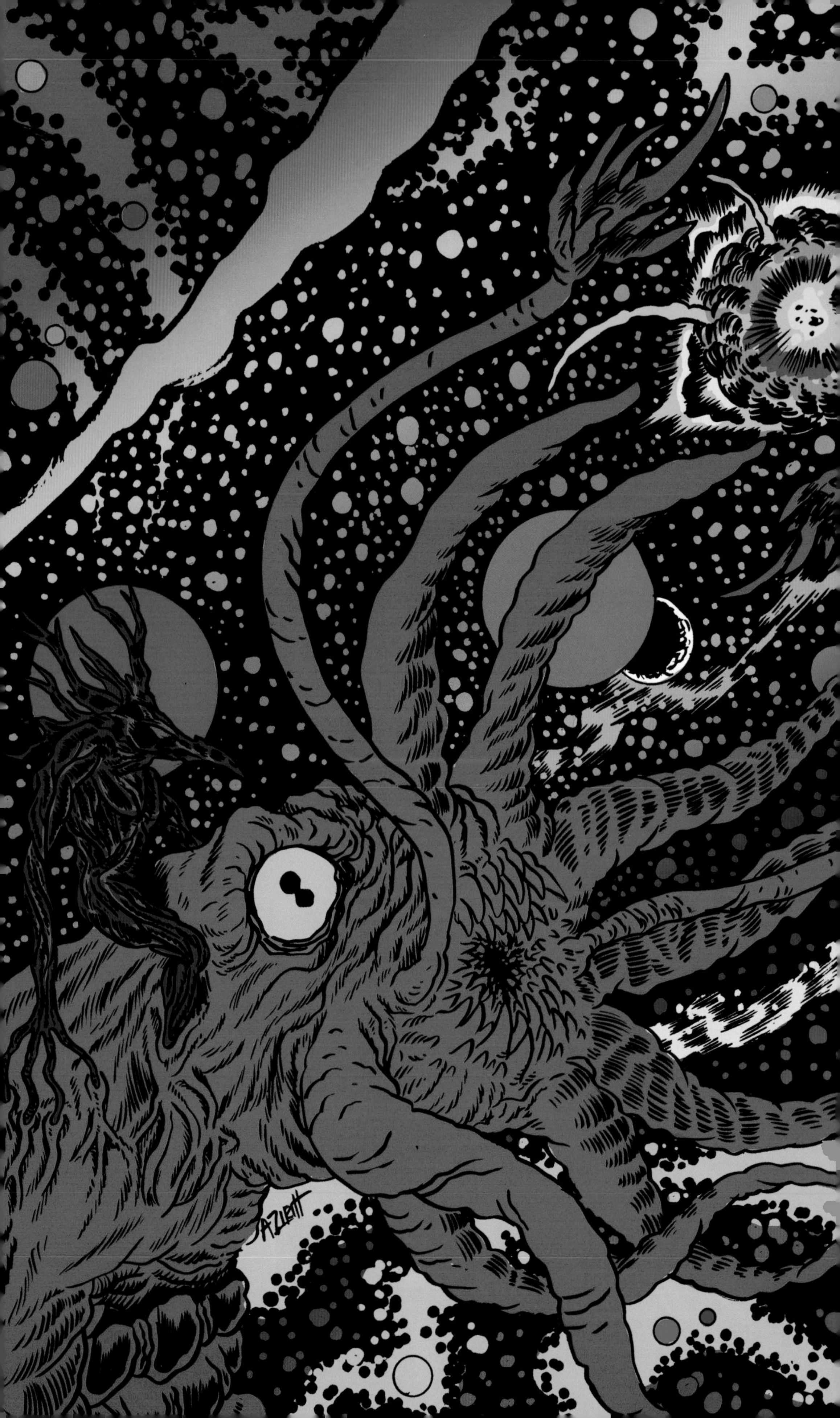

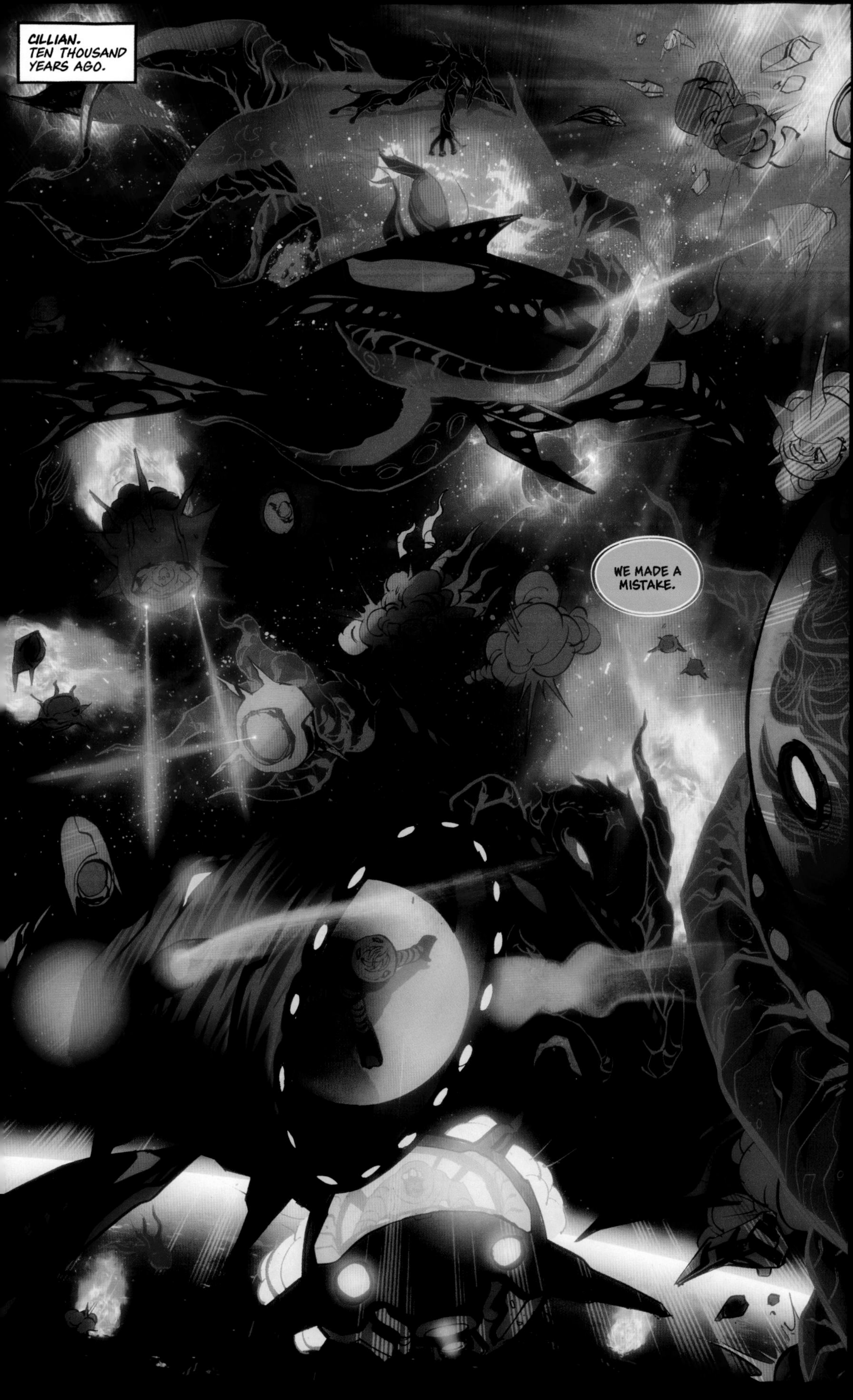
CILLIAN.
TEN THOUSAND
YEARS AGO.
WE MADE A
MISTAKE.

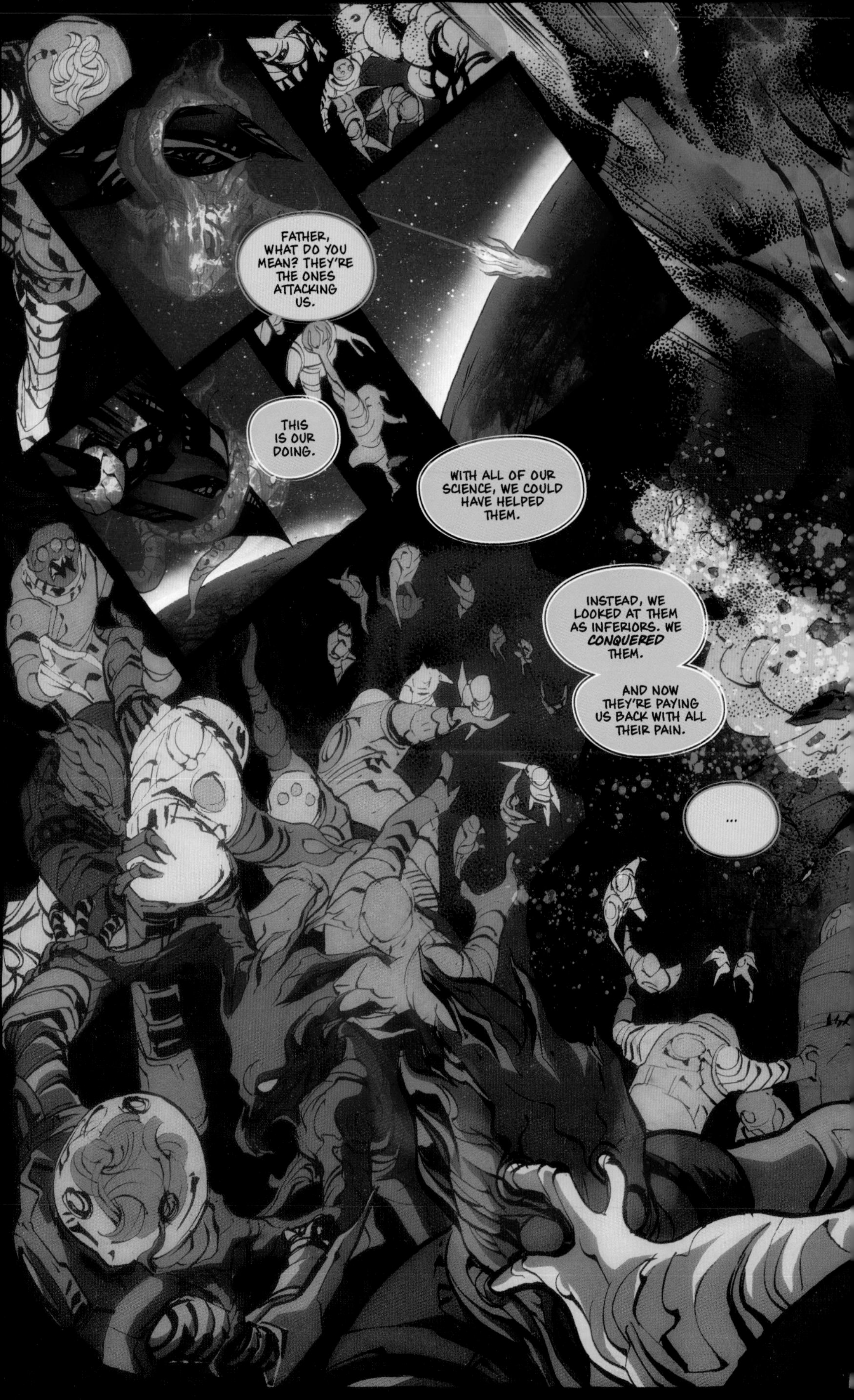
FATHER, WHAT DO YOU MEAN? THEY'RE THE ONES ATTACKING US.
THIS IS OUR DOING.
WITH ALL OF OUR SCIENCE, WE COULD HAVE HELPED THEM.
INSTEAD, WE LOOKED AT THEM AS INFERIORS. WE *CONQUERED* THEM.
AND NOW THEY'RE PAYING US BACK WITH ALL THEIR PAIN.
...

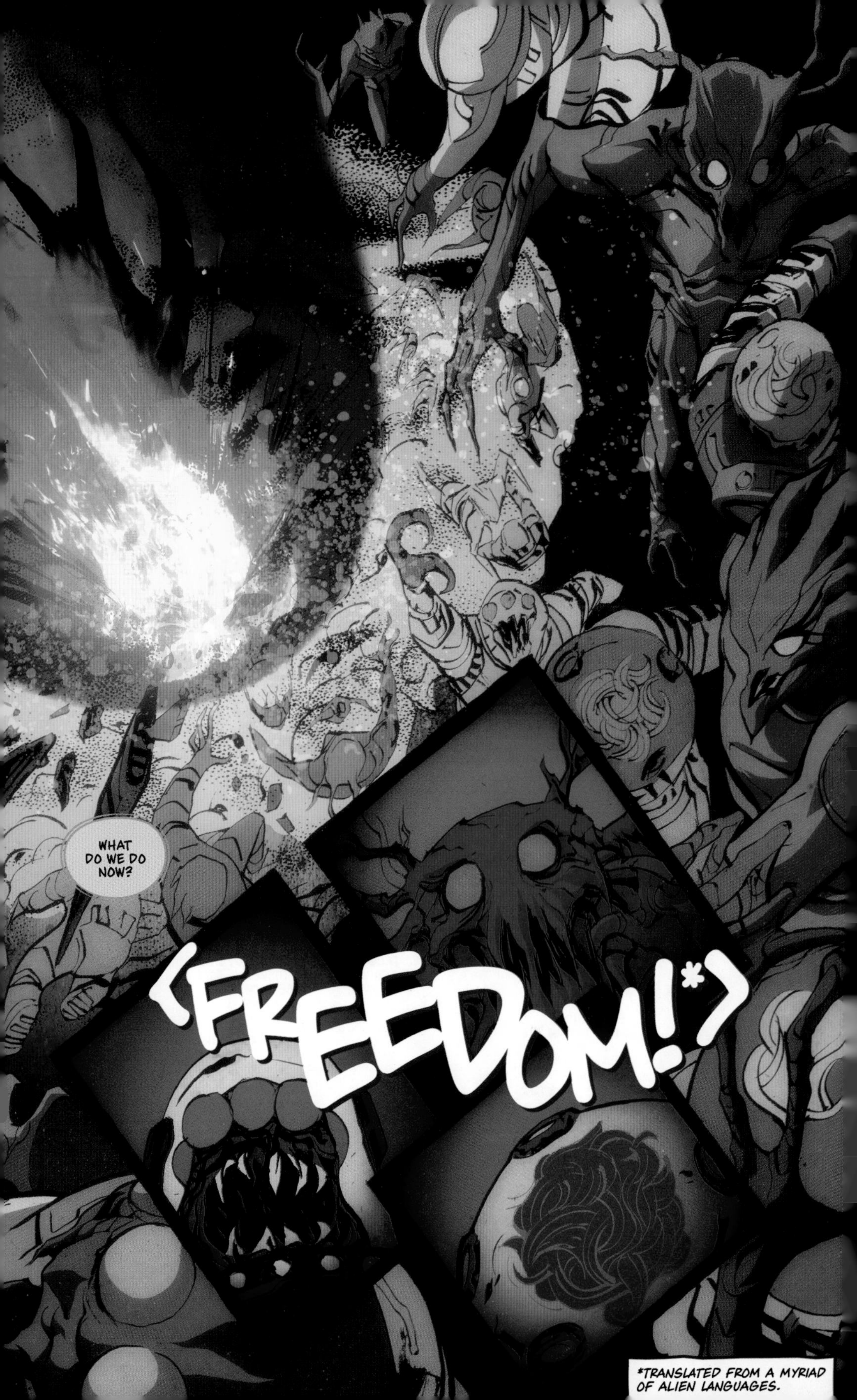
WHAT DO WE DO NOW?
<FREEDOM!*>
*TRANSLATED FROM A MYRIAD OF ALIEN LANGUAGES.

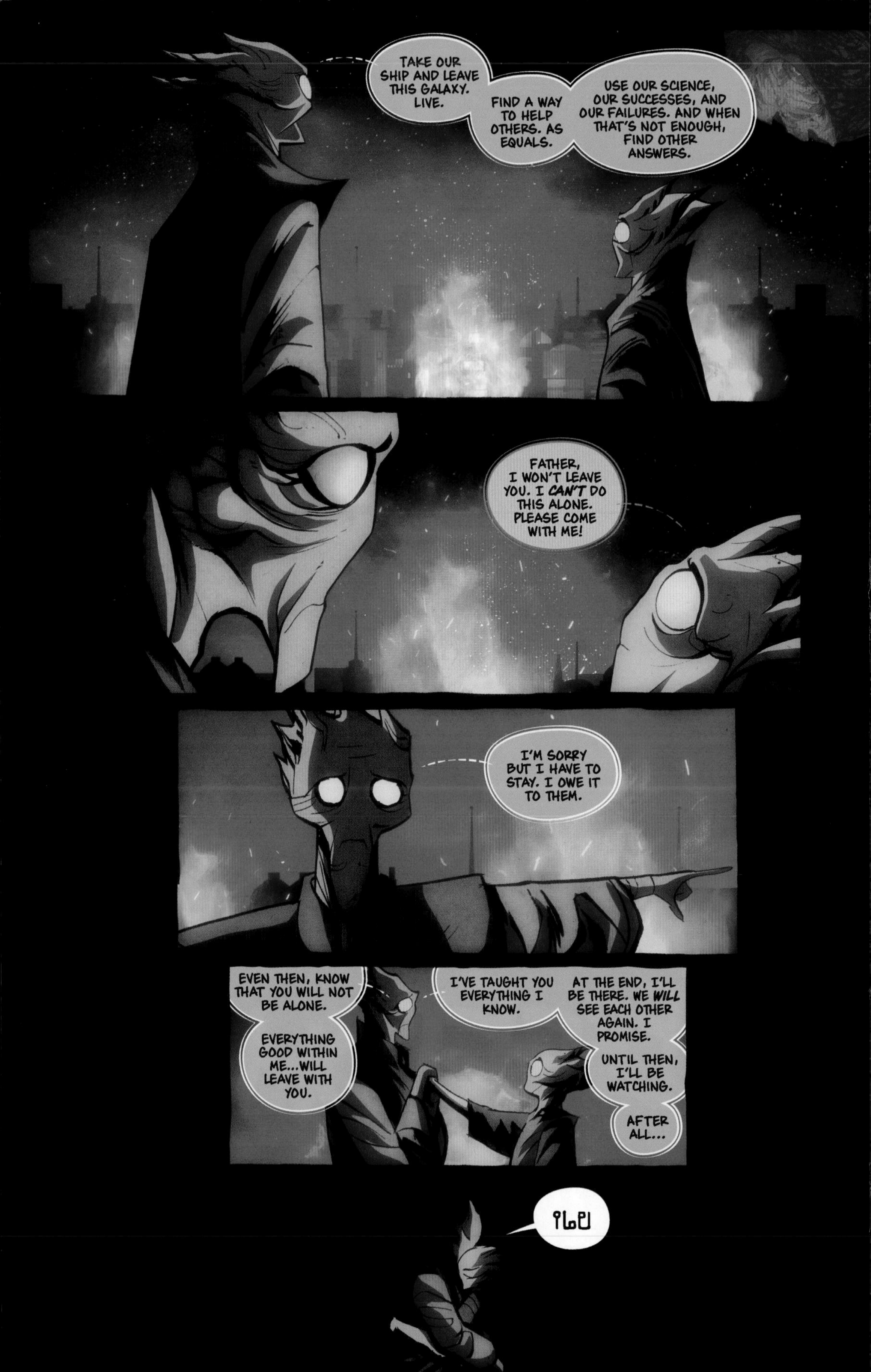
TAKE OUR SHIP AND LEAVE THIS GALAXY. LIVE.
FIND A WAY TO HELP OTHERS. AS EQUALS.
USE OUR SCIENCE, OUR SUCCESSES, AND OUR FAILURES. AND WHEN THAT'S NOT ENOUGH, FIND OTHER ANSWERS.
FATHER, I WON'T LEAVE YOU. I CAN'T DO THIS ALONE. PLEASE COME WITH ME!
I'M SORRY BUT I HAVE TO STAY. I OWE IT TO THEM.
EVEN THEN, KNOW THAT YOU WILL NOT BE ALONE.
EVERYTHING GOOD WITHIN ME...WILL LEAVE WITH YOU.
I'VE TAUGHT YOU EVERYTHING I KNOW.
AT THE END, I'LL BE THERE. WE WILL SEE EACH OTHER AGAIN. I PROMISE.
UNTIL THEN, I'LL BE WATCHING.
AFTER ALL...

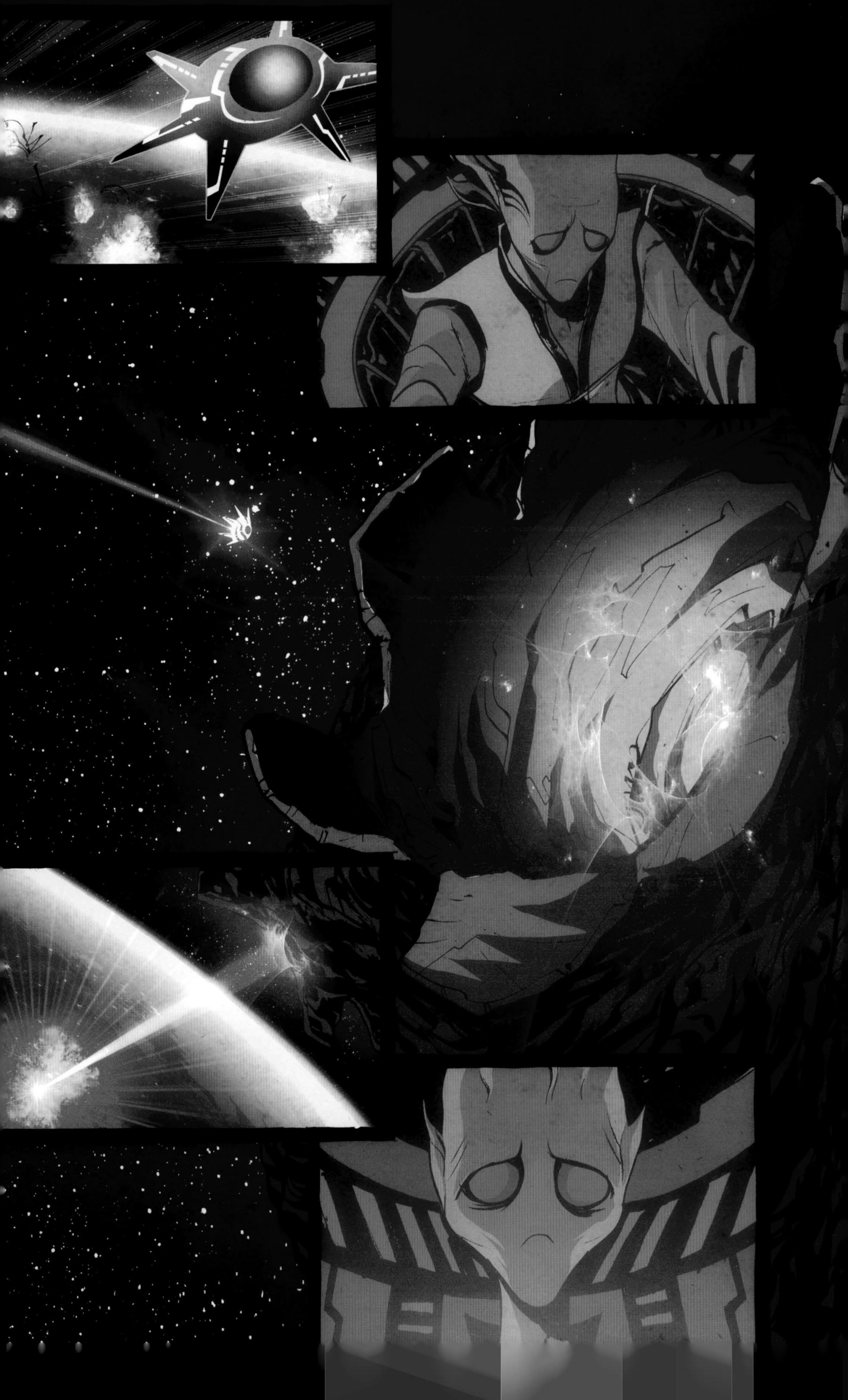

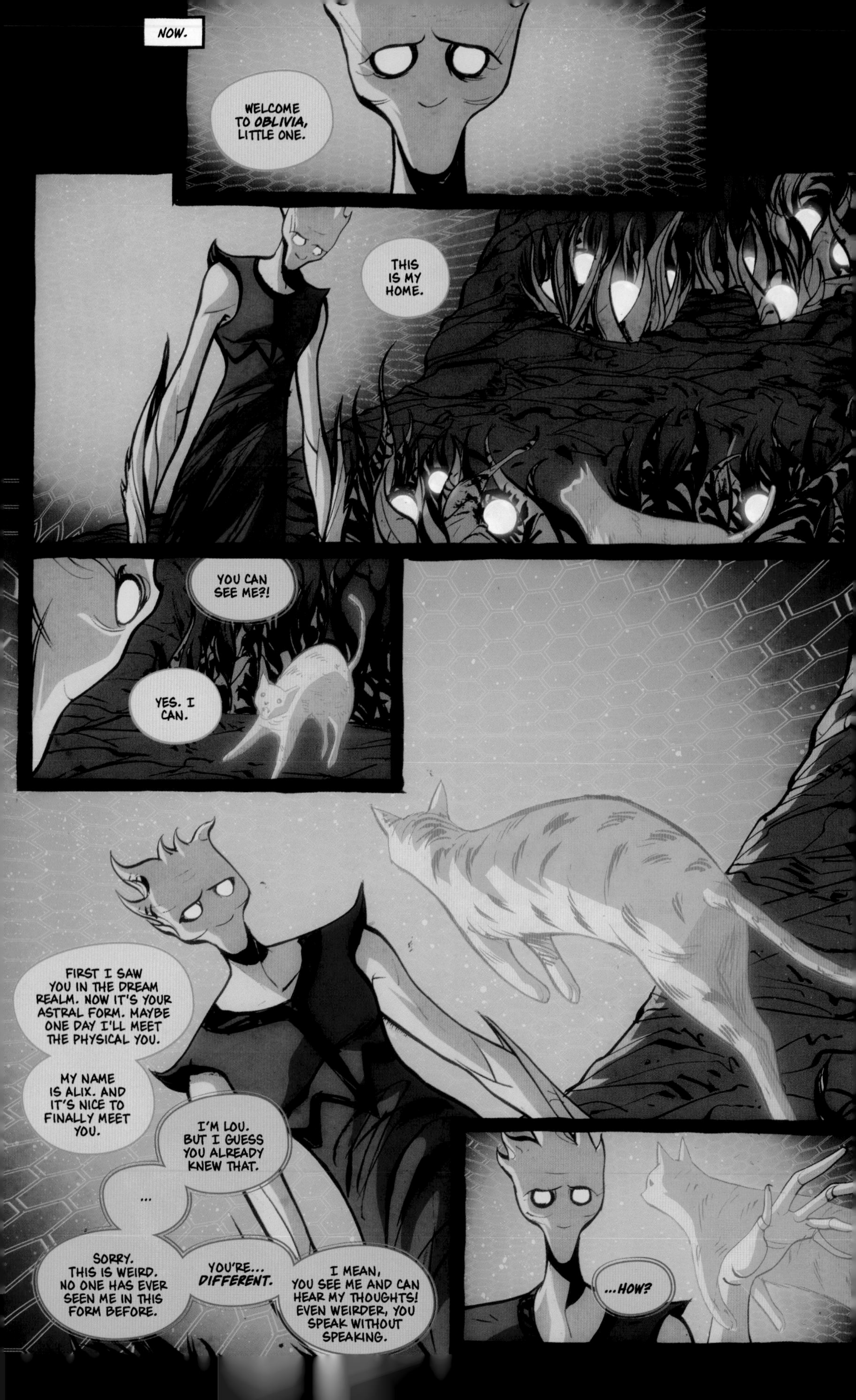
NOW.
WELCOME TO OBLIVIA, LITTLE ONE.
THIS IS MY HOME.
YOU CAN SEE ME?!
YES. I CAN.
FIRST I SAW YOU IN THE DREAM REALM. NOW IT'S YOUR ASTRAL FORM. MAYBE ONE DAY I'LL MEET THE PHYSICAL YOU.
MY NAME IS ALIX. AND IT'S NICE TO FINALLY MEET YOU.
I'M LOU. BUT I GUESS YOU ALREADY KNEW THAT.
...
SORRY. THIS IS WEIRD. NO ONE HAS EVER SEEN ME IN THIS FORM BEFORE.
YOU'RE... DIFFERENT.
I MEAN, YOU SEE ME AND CAN HEAR MY THOUGHTS! EVEN WEIRDER, YOU SPEAK WITHOUT SPEAKING.
...HOW?

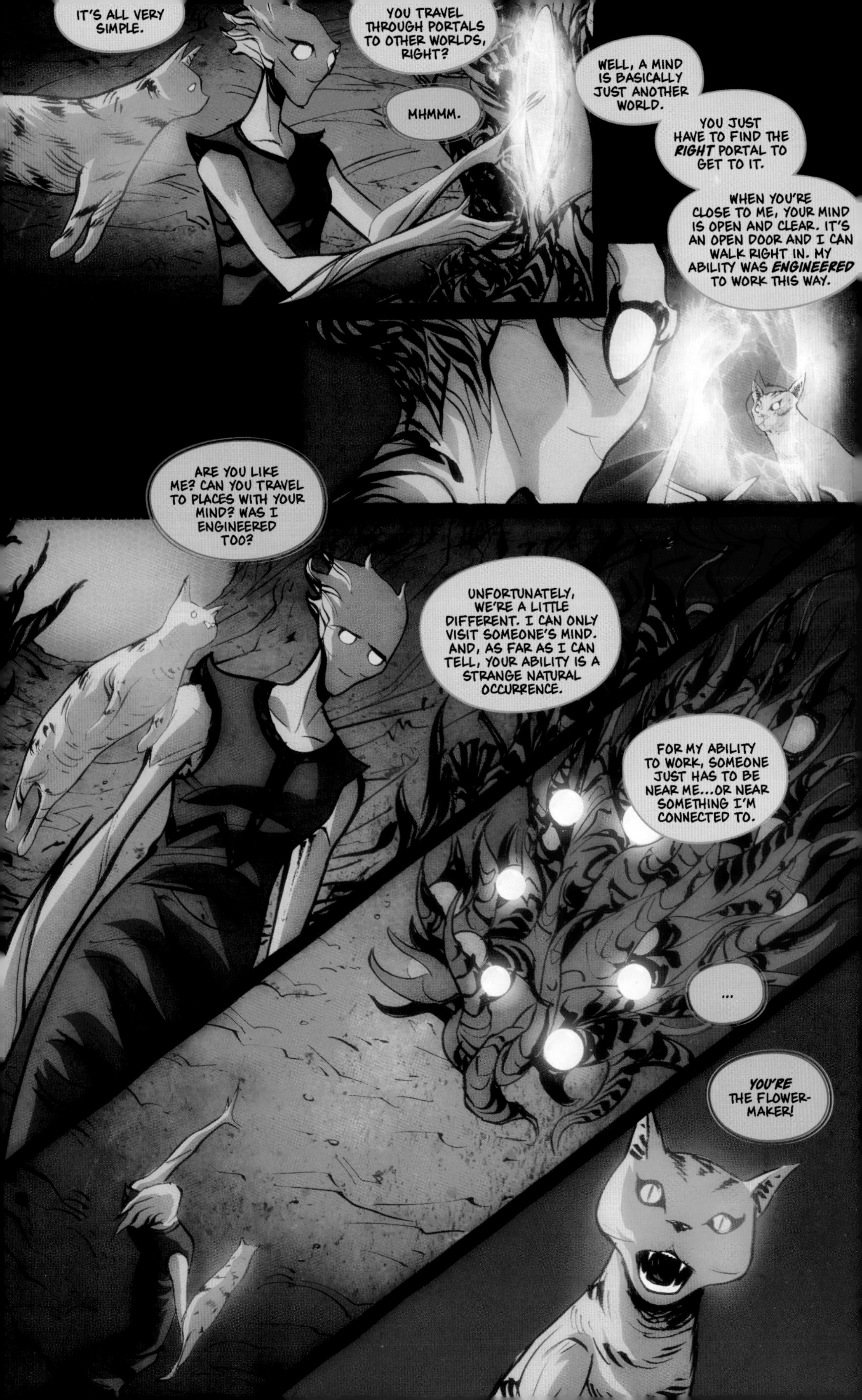
IT'S ALL VERY SIMPLE.
YOU TRAVEL THROUGH PORTALS TO OTHER WORLDS, RIGHT?
MHMMM.
WELL, A MIND IS BASICALLY JUST ANOTHER WORLD.
YOU JUST HAVE TO FIND THE RIGHT PORTAL TO GET TO IT.
WHEN YOU'RE CLOSE TO ME, YOUR MIND IS OPEN AND CLEAR. IT'S AN OPEN DOOR AND I CAN WALK RIGHT IN. MY ABILITY WAS ENGINEERED TO WORK THIS WAY.
ARE YOU LIKE ME? CAN YOU TRAVEL TO PLACES WITH YOUR MIND? WAS I ENGINEERED TOO?
UNFORTUNATELY, WE'RE A LITTLE DIFFERENT. I CAN ONLY VISIT SOMEONE'S MIND. AND, AS FAR AS I CAN TELL, YOUR ABILITY IS A STRANGE NATURAL OCCURRENCE.
FOR MY ABILITY TO WORK, SOMEONE JUST HAS TO BE NEAR ME...OR NEAR SOMETHING I'M CONNECTED TO.
...
YOU'RE THE FLOWER-MAKER!

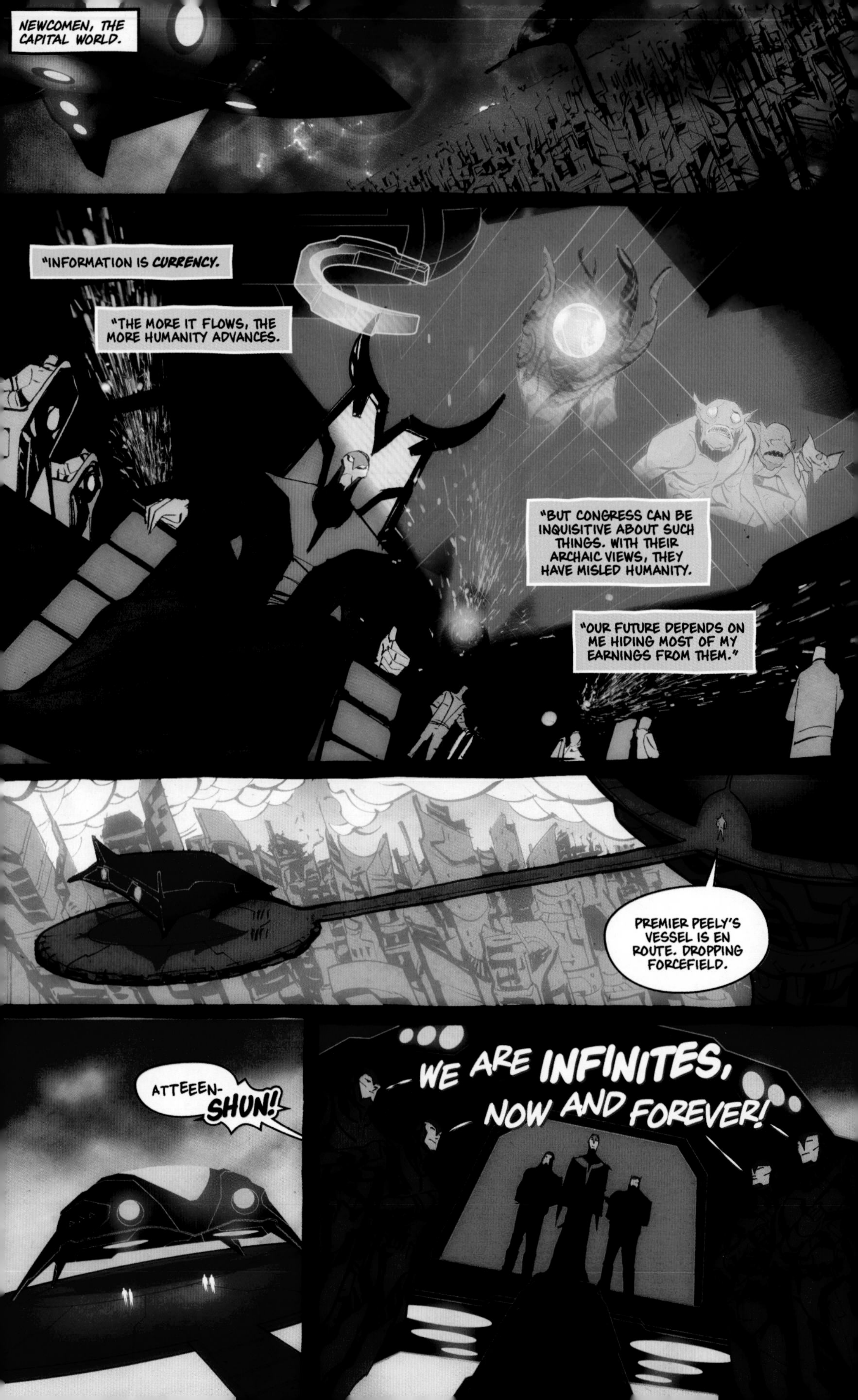
NEWCOMEN, THE CAPITAL WORLD.
"INFORMATION IS CURRENCY.
"THE MORE IT FLOWS, THE MORE HUMANITY ADVANCES.
"BUT CONGRESS CAN BE INQUISITIVE ABOUT SUCH THINGS. WITH THEIR ARCHAIC VIEWS, THEY HAVE MISLED HUMANITY.
"OUR FUTURE DEPENDS ON ME HIDING MOST OF MY EARNINGS FROM THEM."
PREMIER PEELY'S VESSEL IS EN ROUTE. DROPPING FORCEFIELD.
ATTEEEN-SHUN!
WE ARE INFINITES, NOW AND FOREVER!

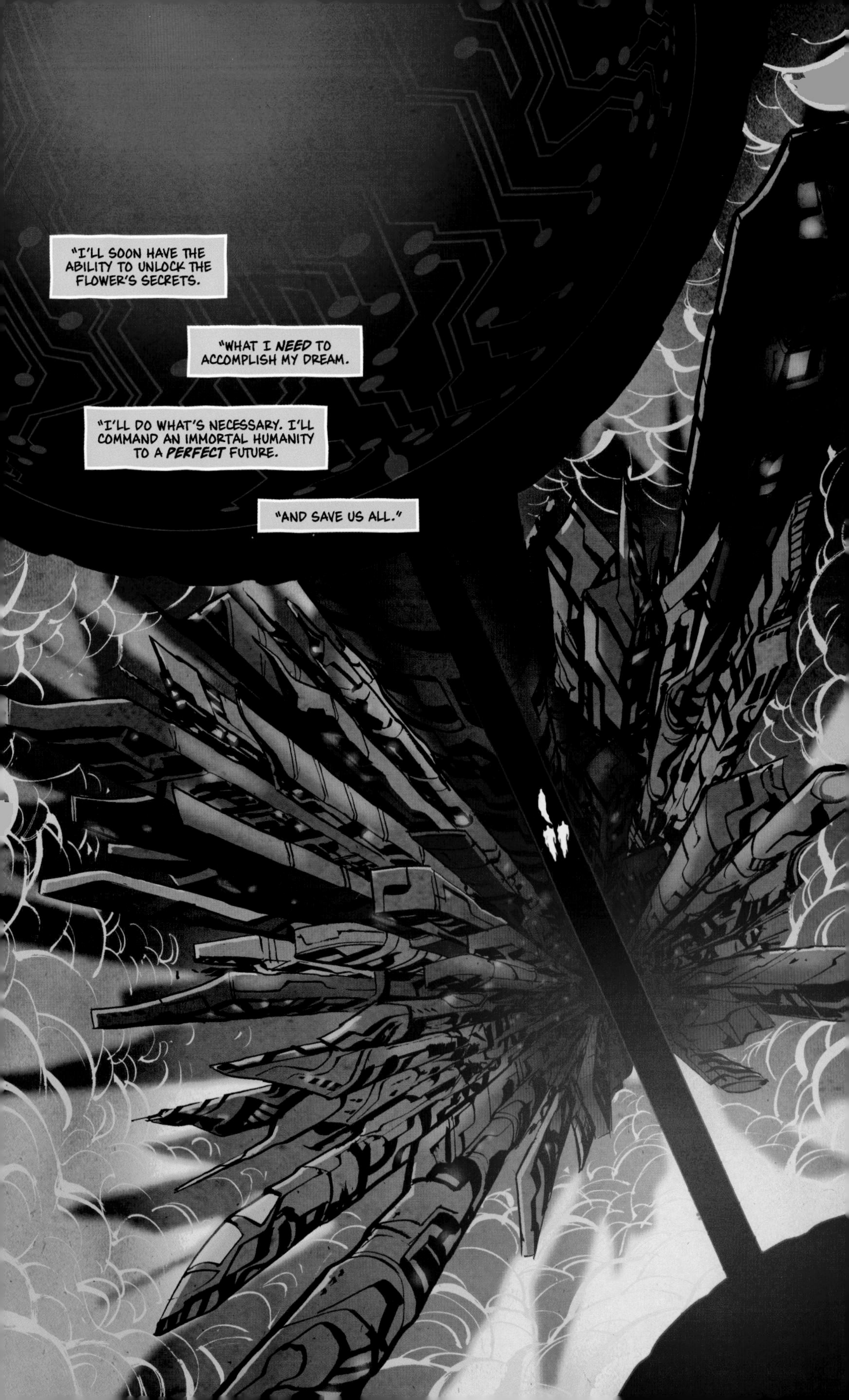
"I'LL SOON HAVE THE ABILITY TO UNLOCK THE FLOWER'S SECRETS.
"WHAT I *NEED* TO ACCOMPLISH MY DREAM.
"I'LL DO WHAT'S NECESSARY. I'LL COMMAND AN IMMORTAL HUMANITY TO A *PERFECT* FUTURE.
"AND SAVE US ALL."

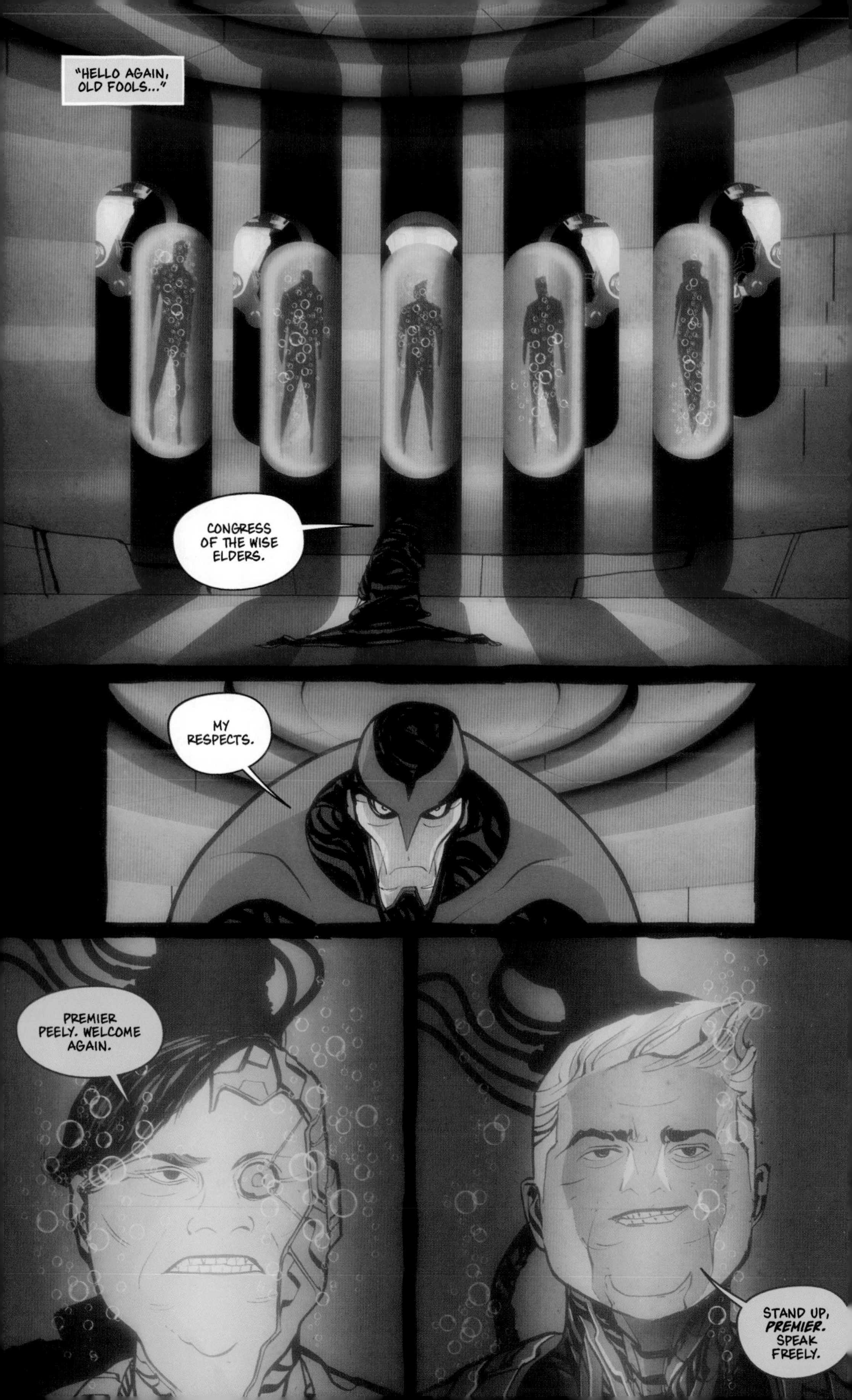
"HELLO AGAIN, OLD FOOLS..."
CONGRESS OF THE WISE ELDERS.
MY RESPECTS.
PREMIER PEELY. WELCOME AGAIN.
STAND UP, *PREMIER.* SPEAK FREELY.

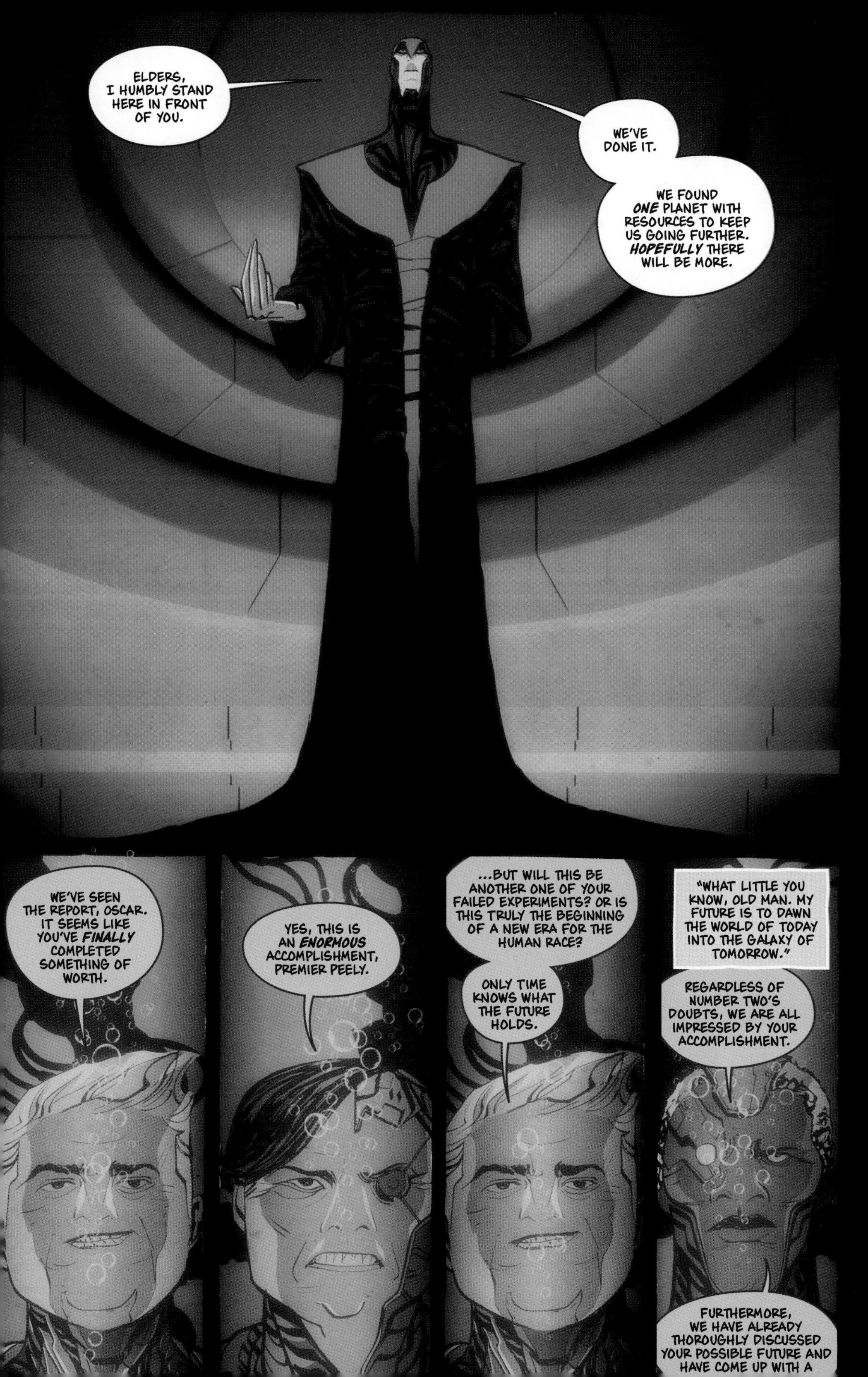
ELDERS, I HUMBLY STAND HERE IN FRONT OF YOU.
WE'VE DONE IT.
WE FOUND *ONE* PLANET WITH RESOURCES TO KEEP US GOING FURTHER. *HOPEFULLY* THERE WILL BE MORE.
WE'VE SEEN THE REPORT, OSCAR. IT SEEMS LIKE YOU'VE *FINALLY* COMPLETED SOMETHING OF WORTH.
YES, THIS IS AN *ENORMOUS* ACCOMPLISHMENT, PREMIER PEELY.
...BUT WILL THIS BE ANOTHER ONE OF YOUR FAILED EXPERIMENTS? OR IS THIS TRULY THE BEGINNING OF A NEW ERA FOR THE HUMAN RACE?
ONLY TIME KNOWS WHAT THE FUTURE HOLDS.
"WHAT LITTLE YOU KNOW, OLD MAN. MY FUTURE IS TO DAWN THE WORLD OF TODAY INTO THE GALAXY OF TOMORROW."
REGARDLESS OF NUMBER TWO'S DOUBTS, WE ARE ALL IMPRESSED BY YOUR ACCOMPLISHMENT.
FURTHERMORE, WE HAVE ALREADY THOROUGHLY DISCUSSED YOUR POSSIBLE FUTURE AND HAVE COME UP WITH A

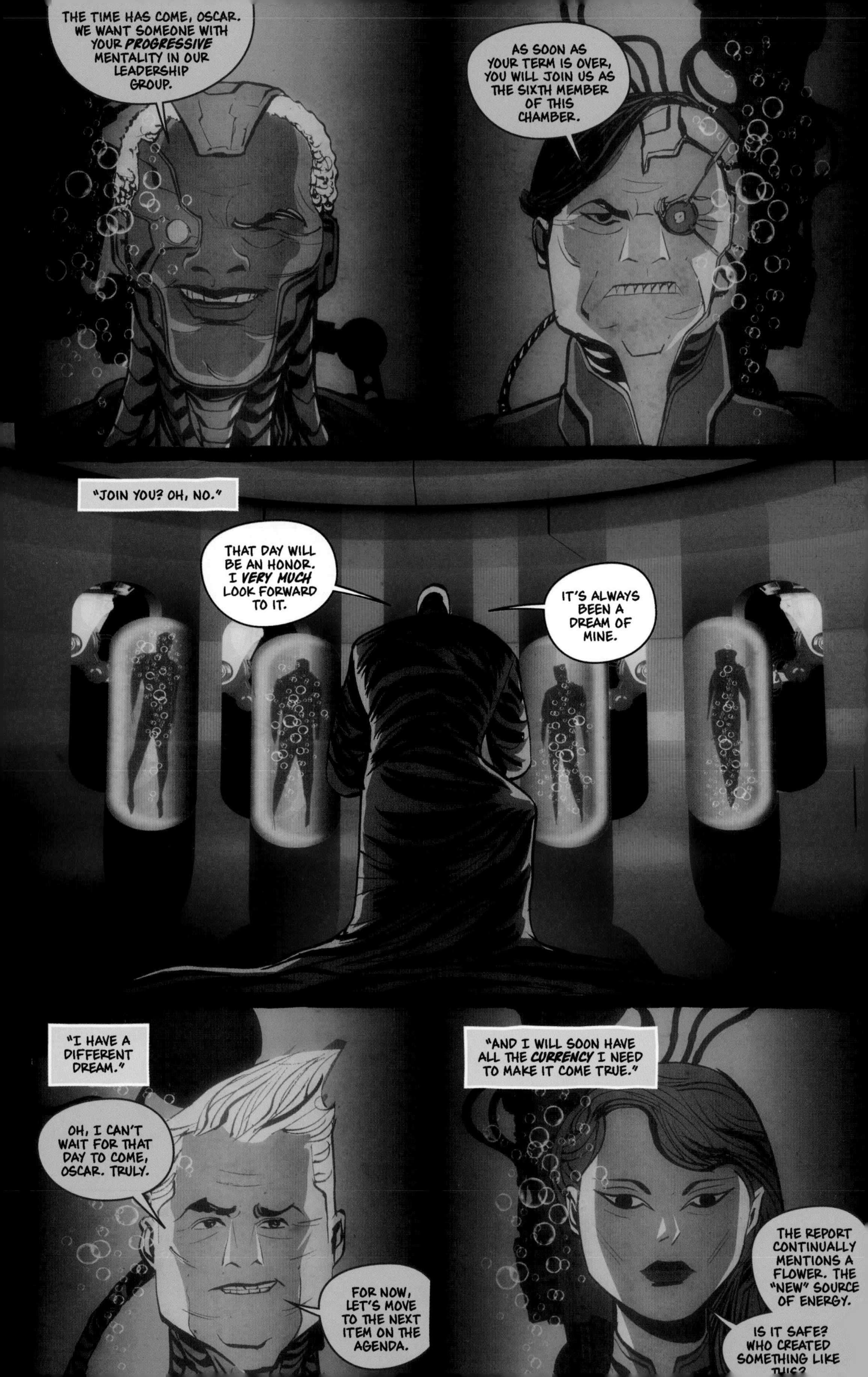
THE TIME HAS COME, OSCAR. WE WANT SOMEONE WITH YOUR PROGRESSIVE MENTALITY IN OUR LEADERSHIP GROUP.
AS SOON AS YOUR TERM IS OVER, YOU WILL JOIN US AS THE SIXTH MEMBER OF THIS CHAMBER.
"JOIN YOU? OH, NO."
THAT DAY WILL BE AN HONOR. I VERY MUCH LOOK FORWARD TO IT.
IT'S ALWAYS BEEN A DREAM OF MINE.
"I HAVE A DIFFERENT DREAM."
OH, I CAN'T WAIT FOR THAT DAY TO COME, OSCAR. TRULY.
FOR NOW, LET'S MOVE TO THE NEXT ITEM ON THE AGENDA.
"AND I WILL SOON HAVE ALL THE CURRENCY I NEED TO MAKE IT COME TRUE."
THE REPORT CONTINUALLY MENTIONS A FLOWER. THE "NEW" SOURCE OF ENERGY.
IS IT SAFE? WHO CREATED SOMETHING LIKE

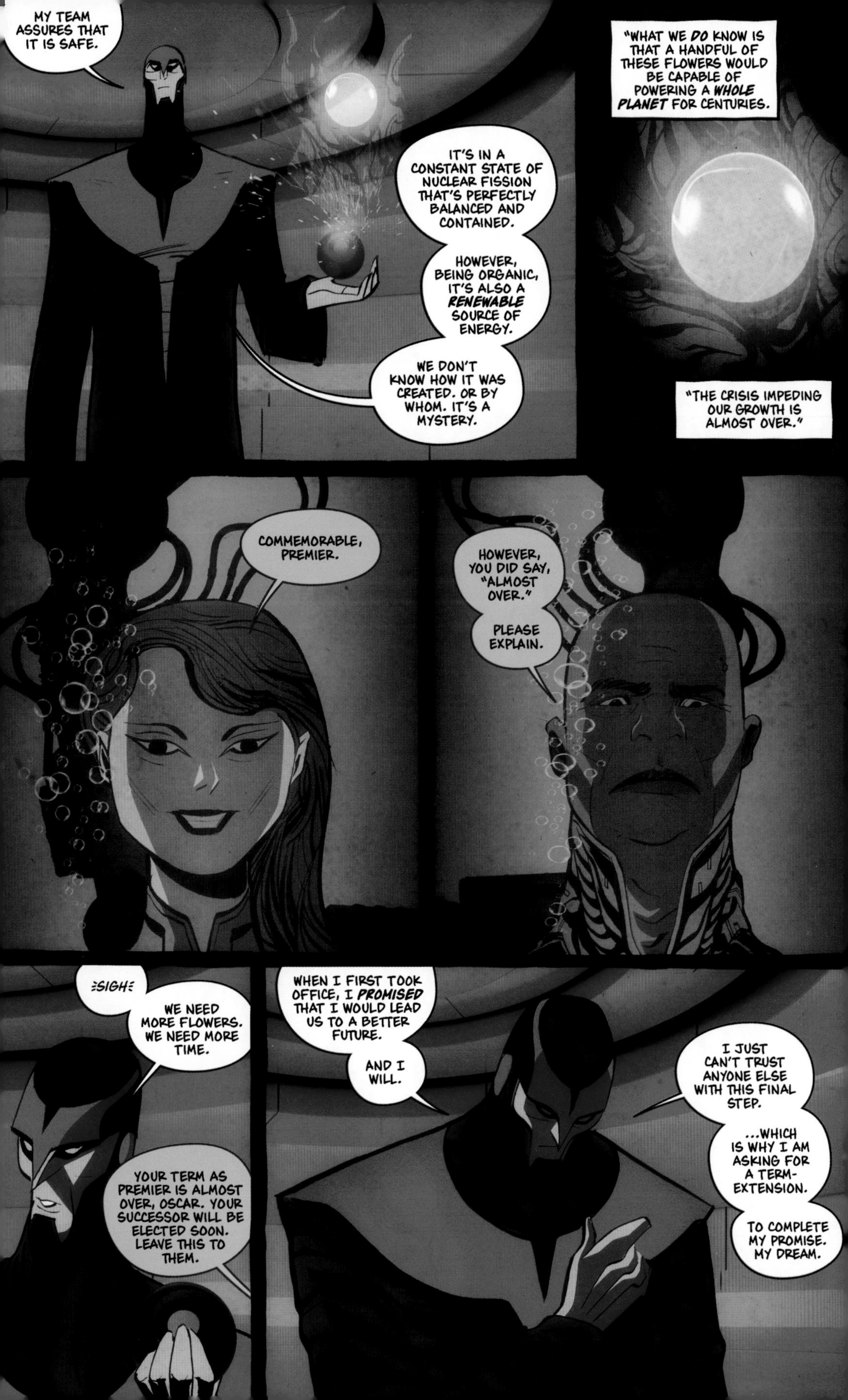
MY TEAM ASSURES THAT IT IS SAFE.
IT'S IN A CONSTANT STATE OF NUCLEAR FISSION THAT'S PERFECTLY BALANCED AND CONTAINED.
HOWEVER, BEING ORGANIC, IT'S ALSO A *RENEWABLE* SOURCE OF ENERGY.
WE DON'T KNOW HOW IT WAS CREATED. OR BY WHOM. IT'S A MYSTERY.
"WHAT WE *DO* KNOW IS THAT A HANDFUL OF THESE FLOWERS WOULD BE CAPABLE OF POWERING A *WHOLE PLANET* FOR CENTURIES.
"THE CRISIS IMPEDING OUR GROWTH IS ALMOST OVER."
COMMEMORABLE, PREMIER.
HOWEVER, YOU DID SAY, "ALMOST OVER."
PLEASE EXPLAIN.
SIGH
WE NEED MORE FLOWERS. WE NEED MORE TIME.
YOUR TERM AS PREMIER IS ALMOST OVER, OSCAR. YOUR SUCCESSOR WILL BE ELECTED SOON. LEAVE THIS TO THEM.
WHEN I FIRST TOOK OFFICE, I *PROMISED* THAT I WOULD LEAD US TO A BETTER FUTURE.
AND I WILL.
I JUST CAN'T TRUST ANYONE ELSE WITH THIS FINAL STEP.
...WHICH IS WHY I AM ASKING FOR A TERM-EXTENSION.
TO COMPLETE MY PROMISE. MY DREAM.

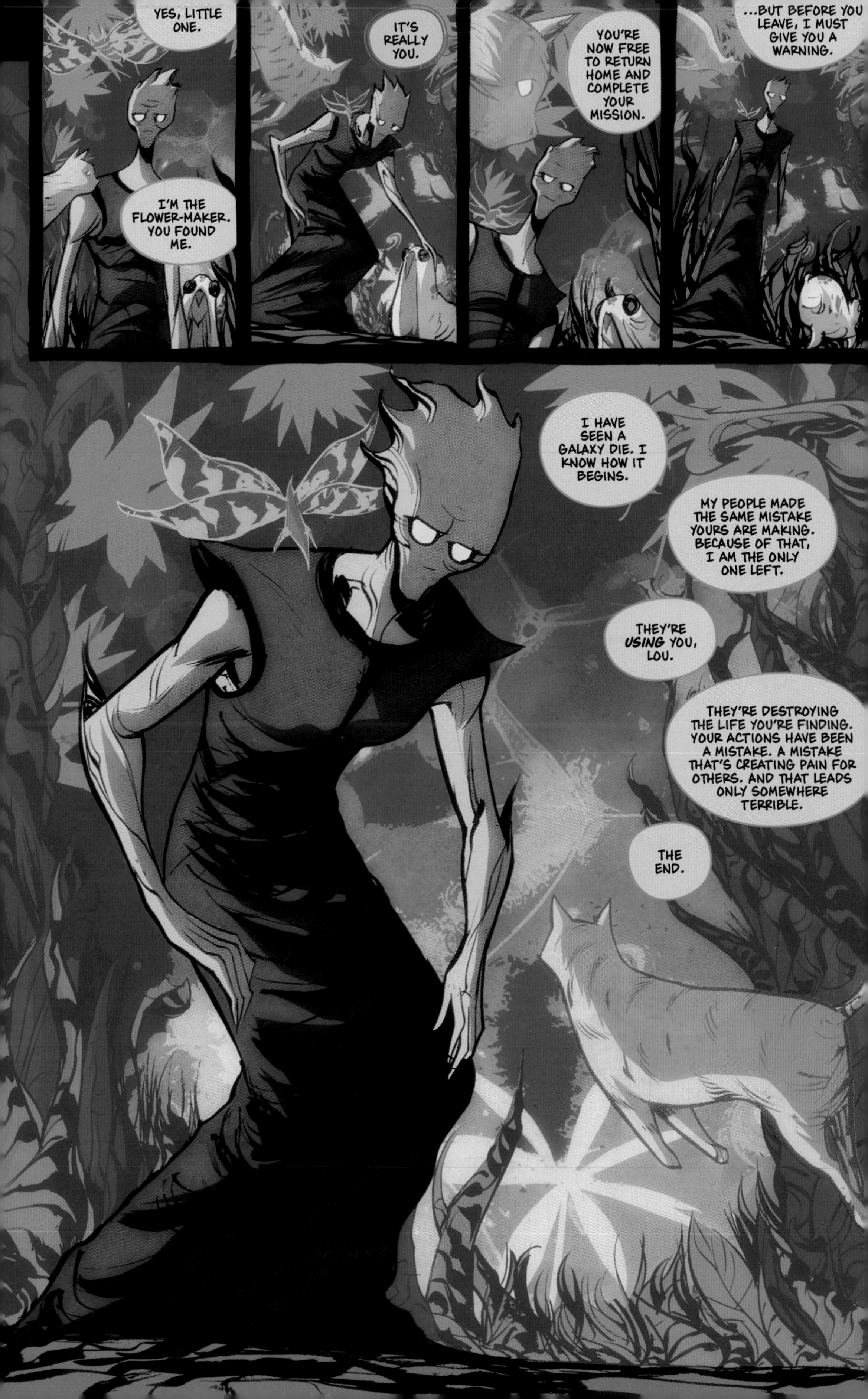
YES, LITTLE ONE.
I'M THE FLOWER-MAKER. YOU FOUND ME.
IT'S REALLY YOU.
YOU'RE NOW FREE TO RETURN HOME AND COMPLETE YOUR MISSION.
...BUT BEFORE YOU LEAVE, I MUST GIVE YOU A WARNING.
I HAVE SEEN A GALAXY DIE. I KNOW HOW IT BEGINS.
MY PEOPLE MADE THE SAME MISTAKE YOURS ARE MAKING. BECAUSE OF THAT, I AM THE ONLY ONE LEFT.
THEY'RE *USING* YOU, LOU.
THEY'RE DESTROYING THE LIFE YOU'RE FINDING. YOUR ACTIONS HAVE BEEN A MISTAKE. A MISTAKE THAT'S CREATING PAIN FOR OTHERS. AND THAT LEADS ONLY SOMEWHERE TERRIBLE.
THE END.

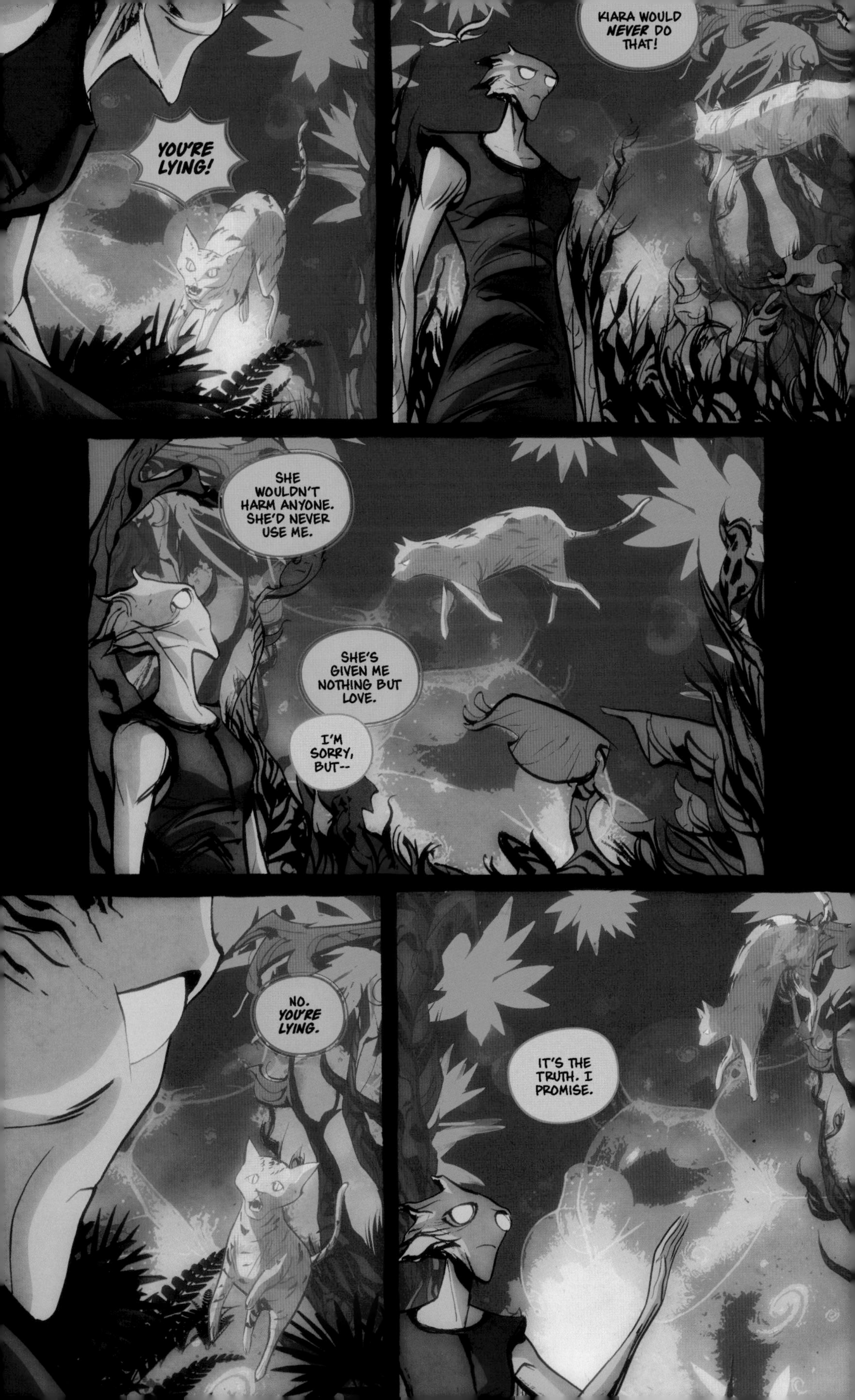
YOU'RE LYING!
KIARA WOULD NEVER DO THAT!
SHE WOULDN'T HARM ANYONE. SHE'D NEVER USE ME.
SHE'S GIVEN ME NOTHING BUT LOVE.
I'M SORRY, BUT--
NO. YOU'RE LYING.
IT'S THE TRUTH. I PROMISE.

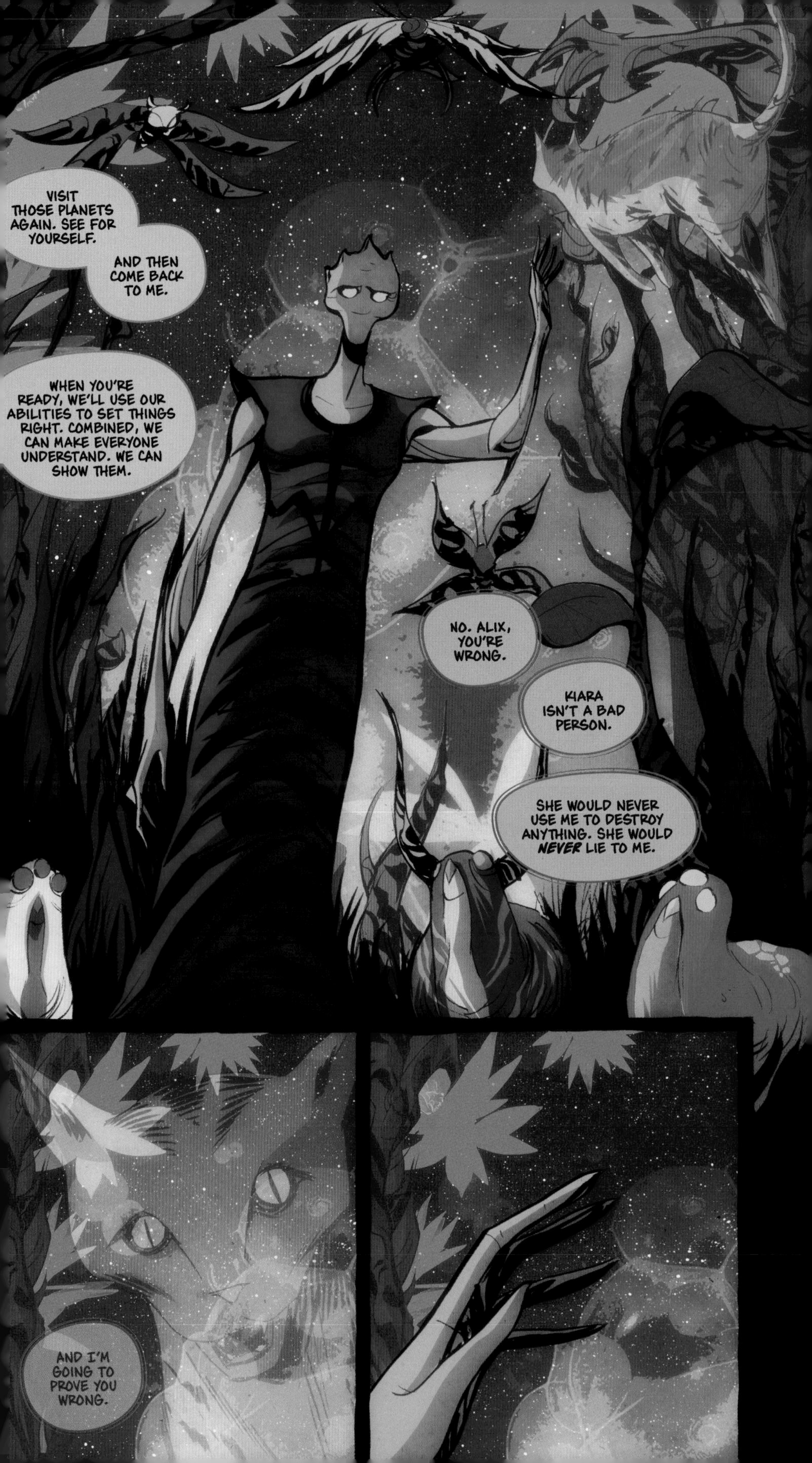
VISIT THOSE PLANETS AGAIN. SEE FOR YOURSELF.
AND THEN COME BACK TO ME.
WHEN YOU'RE READY, WE'LL USE OUR ABILITIES TO SET THINGS RIGHT. COMBINED, WE CAN MAKE EVERYONE UNDERSTAND. WE CAN SHOW THEM.
NO. ALIX, YOU'RE WRONG.
KIARA ISN'T A BAD PERSON.
SHE WOULD NEVER USE ME TO DESTROY ANYTHING. SHE WOULD *NEVER* LIE TO ME.
AND I'M GOING TO PROVE YOU WRONG.

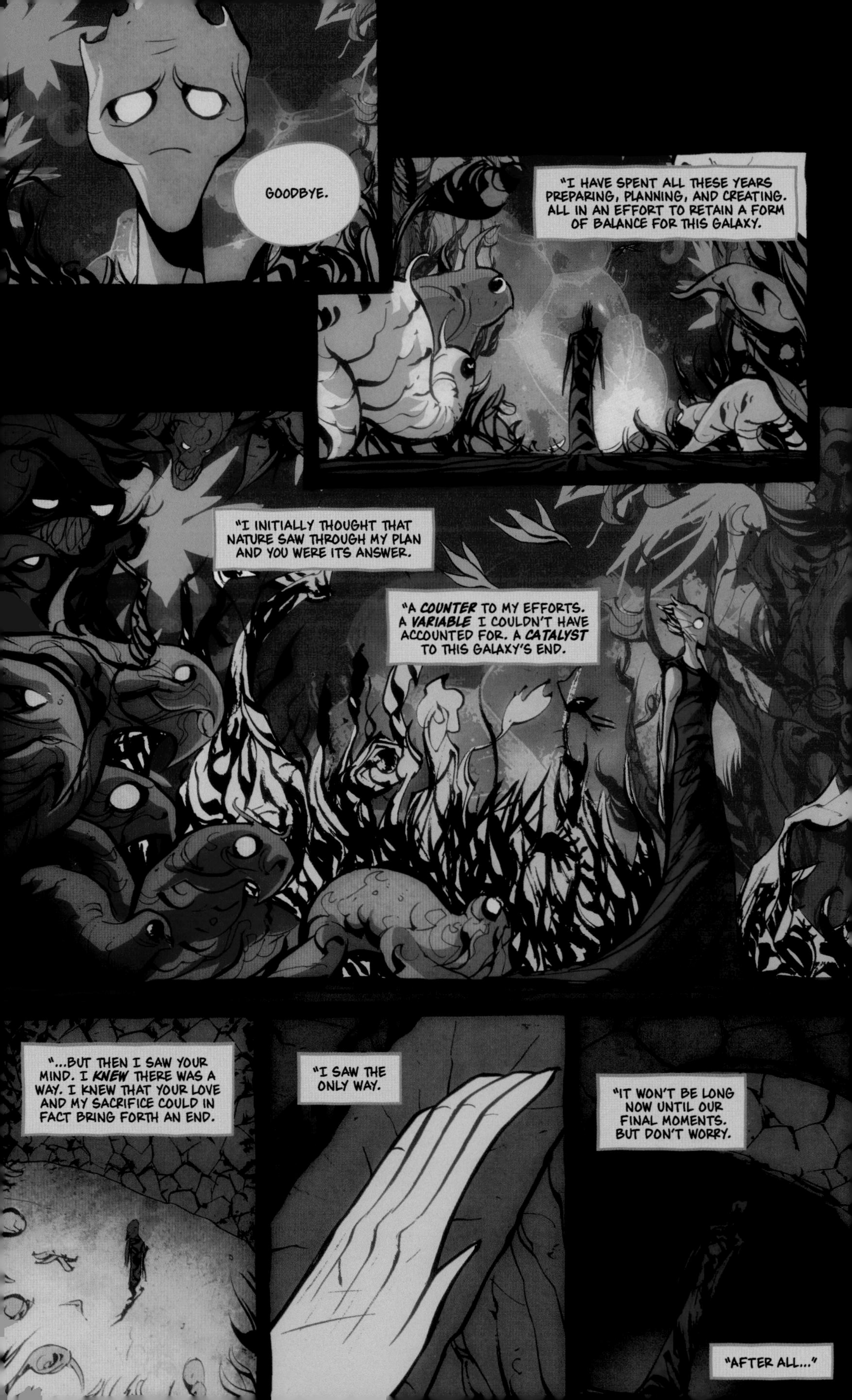
GOODBYE.
"I HAVE SPENT ALL THESE YEARS PREPARING, PLANNING, AND CREATING. ALL IN AN EFFORT TO RETAIN A FORM OF BALANCE FOR THIS GALAXY.
"I INITIALLY THOUGHT THAT NATURE SAW THROUGH MY PLAN AND YOU WERE ITS ANSWER.
"A COUNTER TO MY EFFORTS. A VARIABLE I COULDN'T HAVE ACCOUNTED FOR. A CATALYST TO THIS GALAXY'S END.
"...BUT THEN I SAW YOUR MIND. I KNEW THERE WAS A WAY. I KNEW THAT YOUR LOVE AND MY SACRIFICE COULD IN FACT BRING FORTH AN END.
"I SAW THE ONLY WAY.
"IT WON'T BE LONG NOW UNTIL OUR FINAL MOMENTS. BUT DON'T WORRY.
"AFTER ALL..."

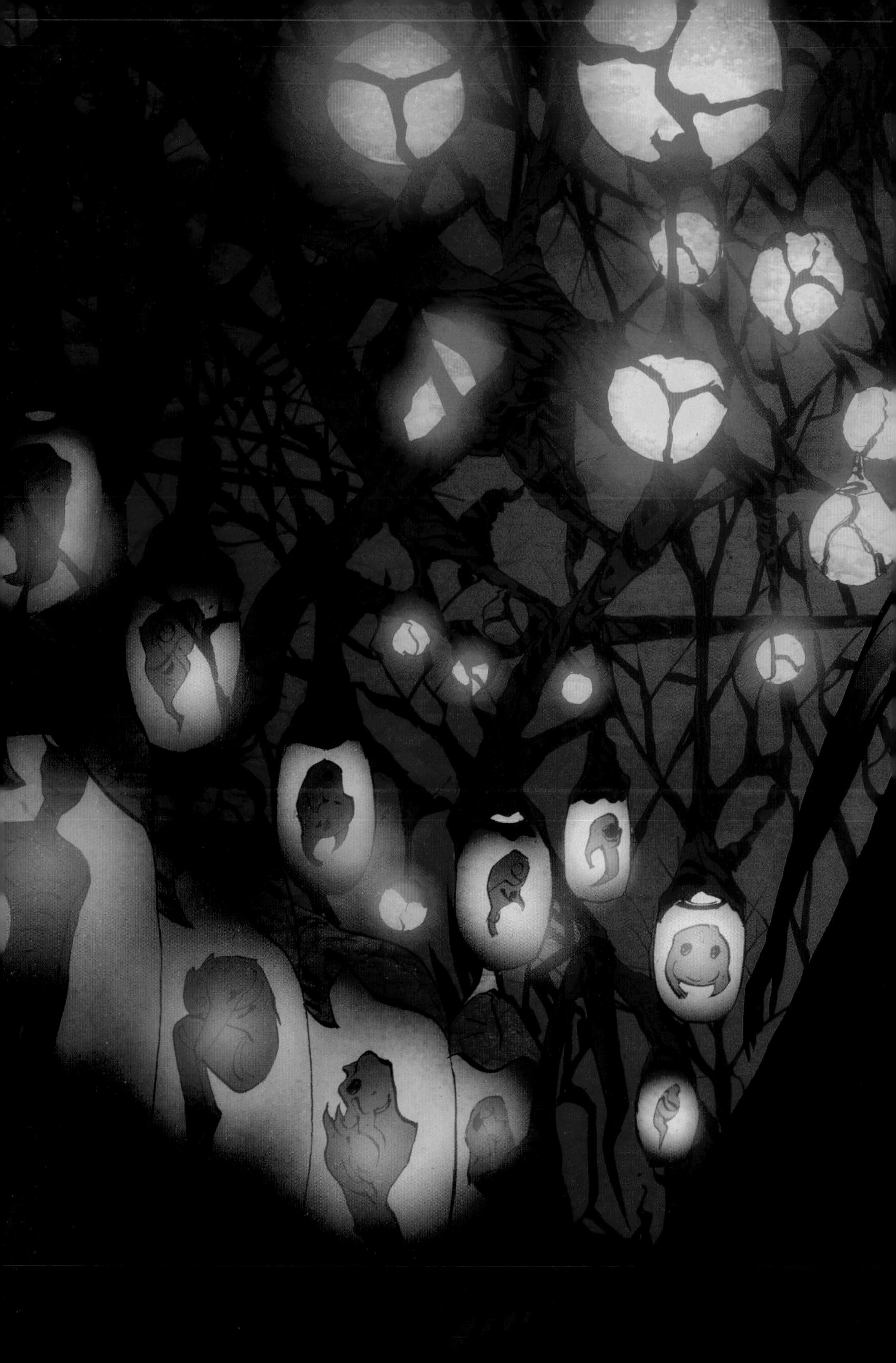

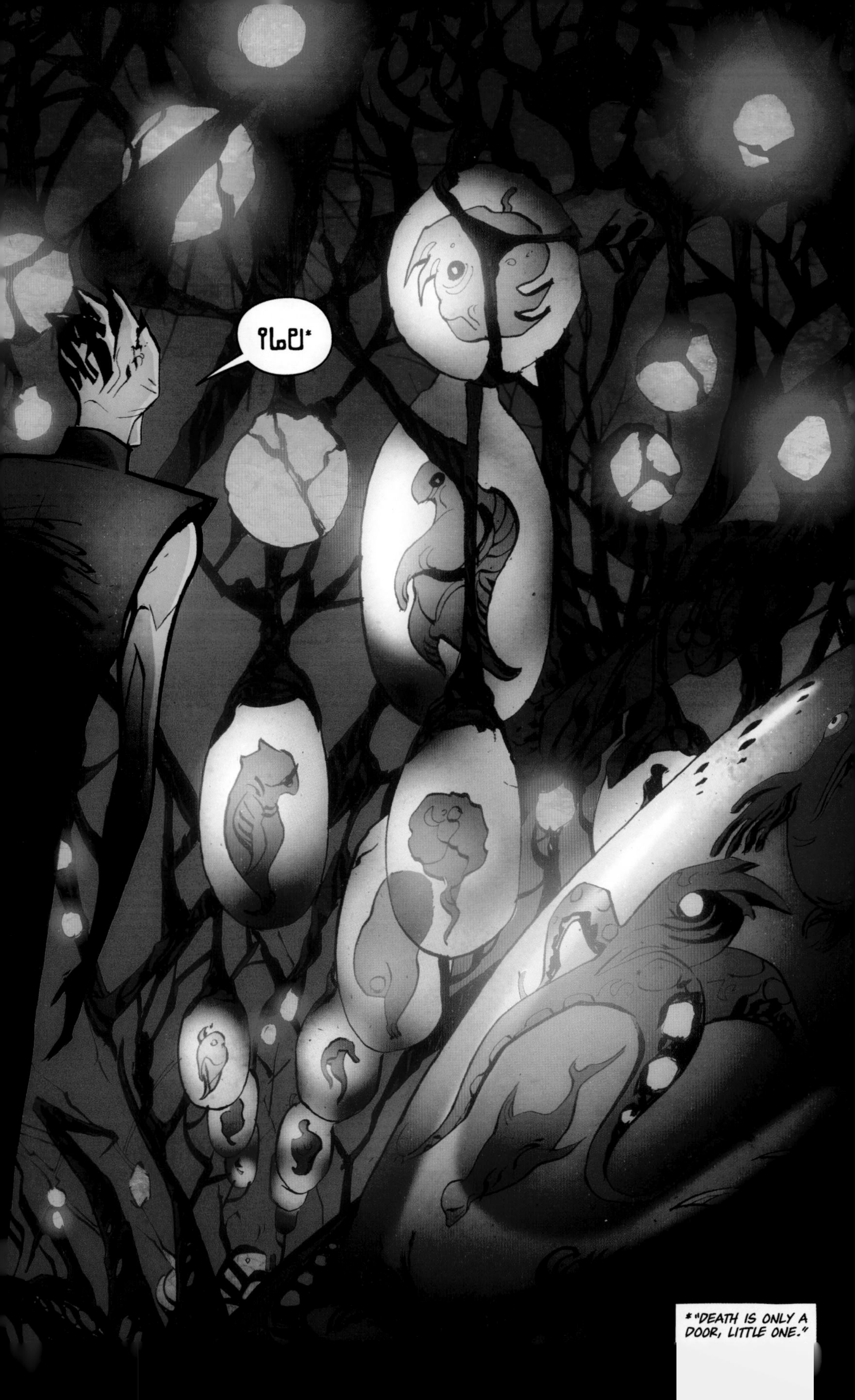
*"DEATH IS ONLY A DOOR, LITTLE ONE."

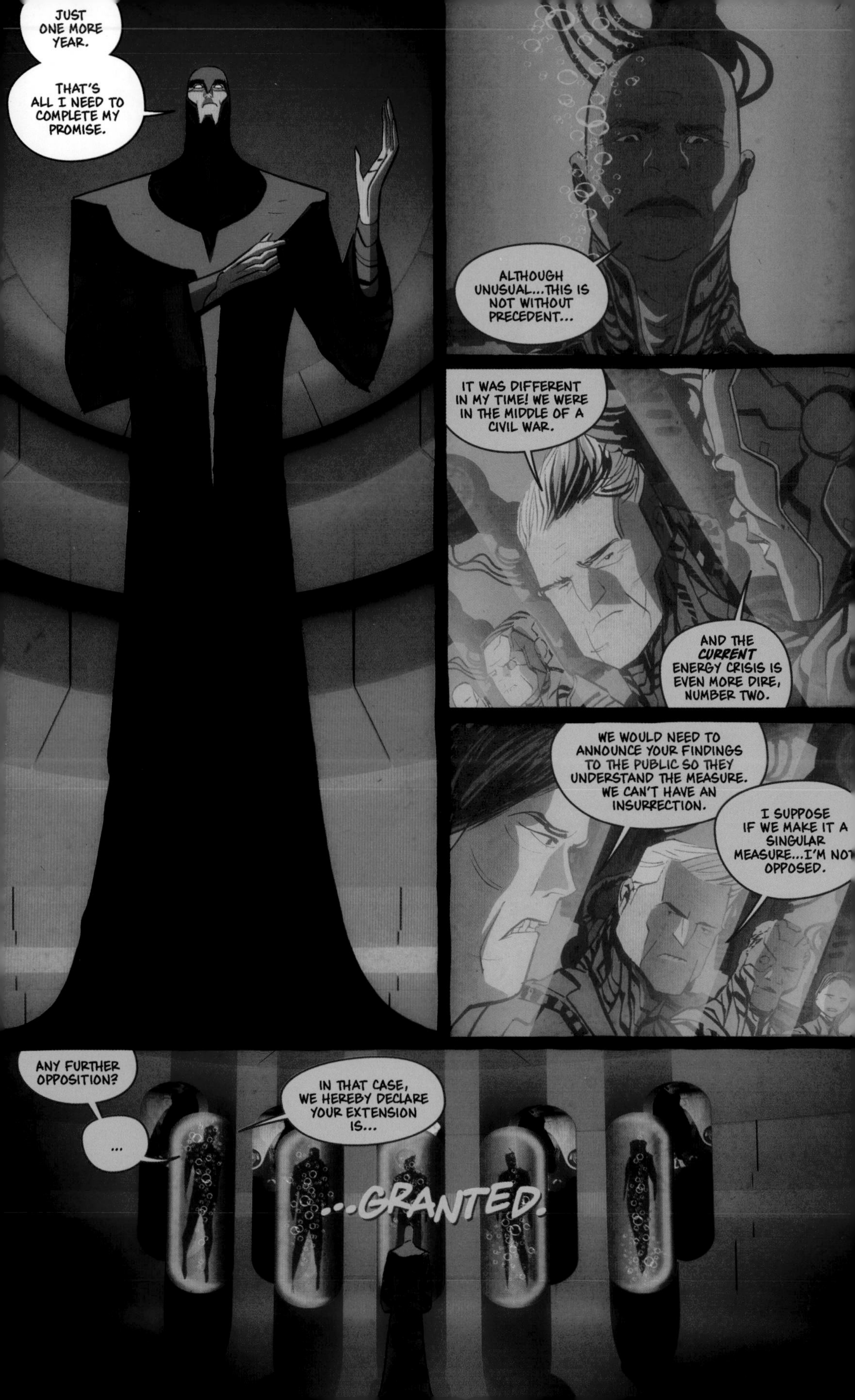
JUST ONE MORE YEAR.
THAT'S ALL I NEED TO COMPLETE MY PROMISE.
ALTHOUGH UNUSUAL...THIS IS NOT WITHOUT PRECEDENT...
IT WAS DIFFERENT IN MY TIME! WE WERE IN THE MIDDLE OF A CIVIL WAR.
AND THE CURRENT ENERGY CRISIS IS EVEN MORE DIRE, NUMBER TWO.
WE WOULD NEED TO ANNOUNCE YOUR FINDINGS TO THE PUBLIC SO THEY UNDERSTAND THE MEASURE. WE CAN'T HAVE AN INSURRECTION.
I SUPPOSE IF WE MAKE IT A SINGULAR MEASURE...I'M NOT OPPOSED.
ANY FURTHER OPPOSITION?
...
IN THAT CASE, WE HEREBY DECLARE YOUR EXTENSION IS...
...GRANTED.

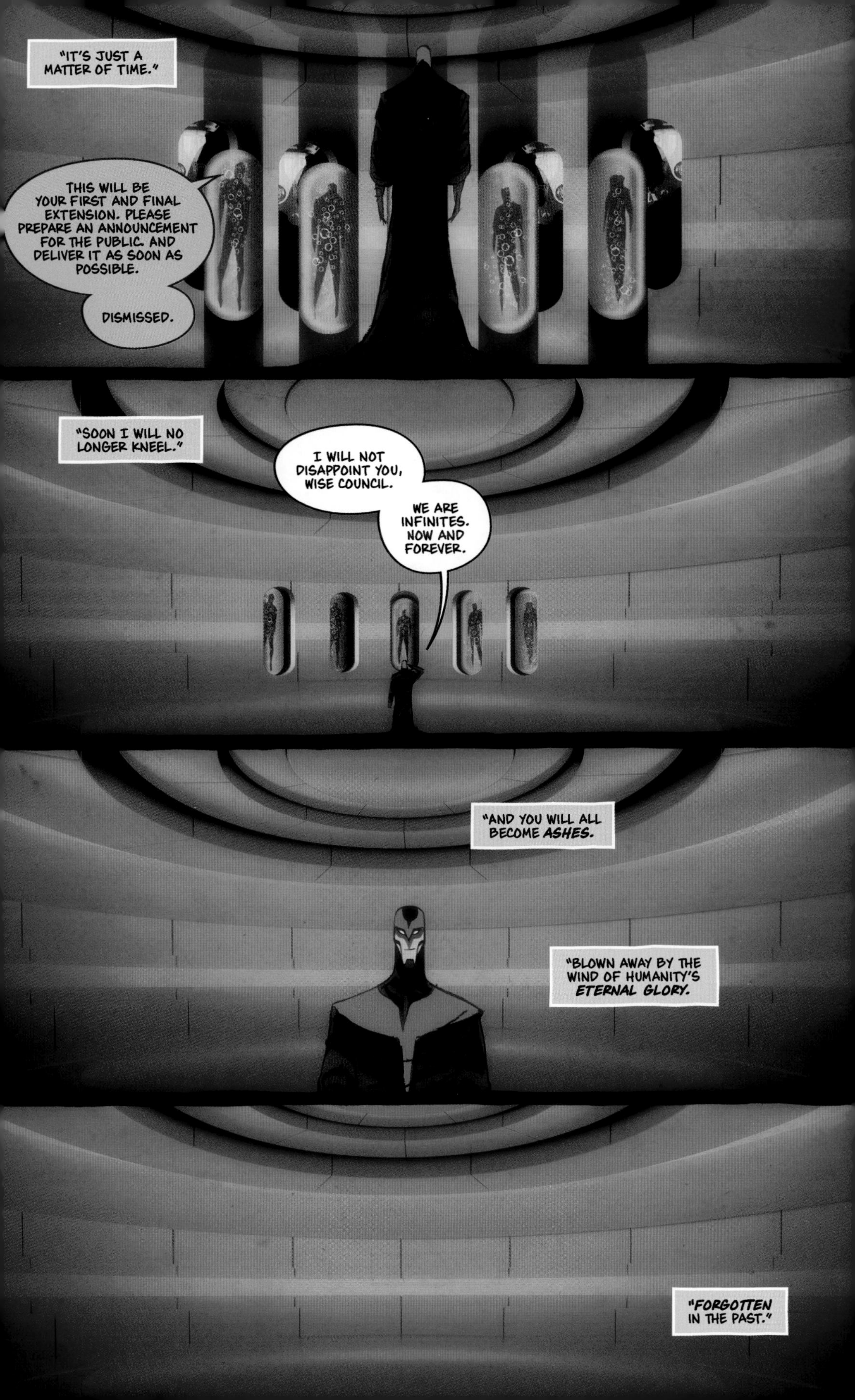
"IT'S JUST A MATTER OF TIME."
THIS WILL BE YOUR FIRST AND FINAL EXTENSION. PLEASE PREPARE AN ANNOUNCEMENT FOR THE PUBLIC. AND DELIVER IT AS SOON AS POSSIBLE.
DISMISSED.
"SOON I WILL NO LONGER KNEEL."
I WILL NOT DISAPPOINT YOU, WISE COUNCIL.
WE ARE INFINITES. NOW AND FOREVER.
"AND YOU WILL ALL BECOME *ASHES.*
"BLOWN AWAY BY THE WIND OF HUMANITY'S *ETERNAL GLORY.*
"*FORGOTTEN* IN THE PAST."

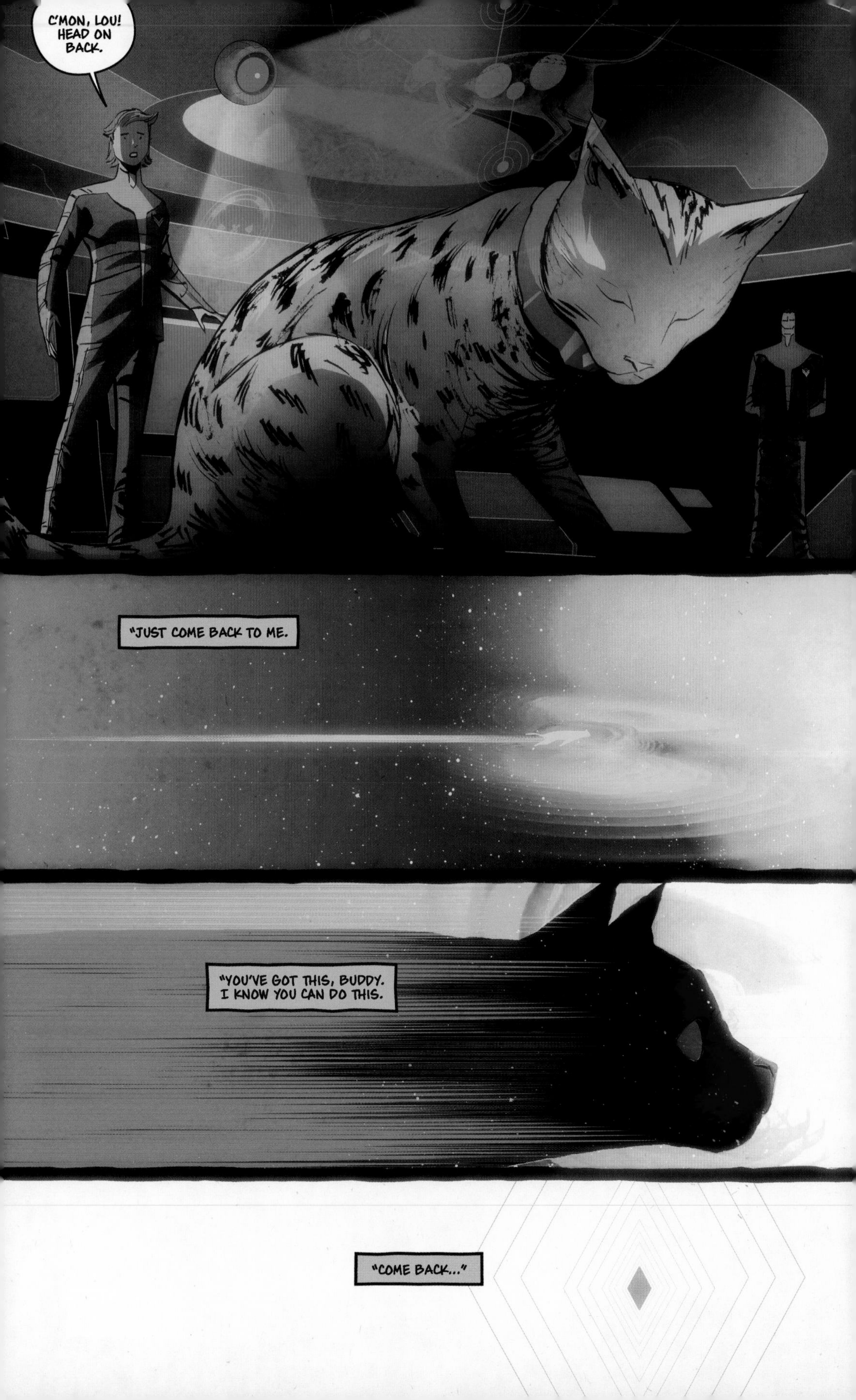
C'MON, LOU! HEAD ON BACK.
"JUST COME BACK TO ME.
"YOU'VE GOT THIS, BUDDY. I KNOW YOU CAN DO THIS.
"COME BACK..."

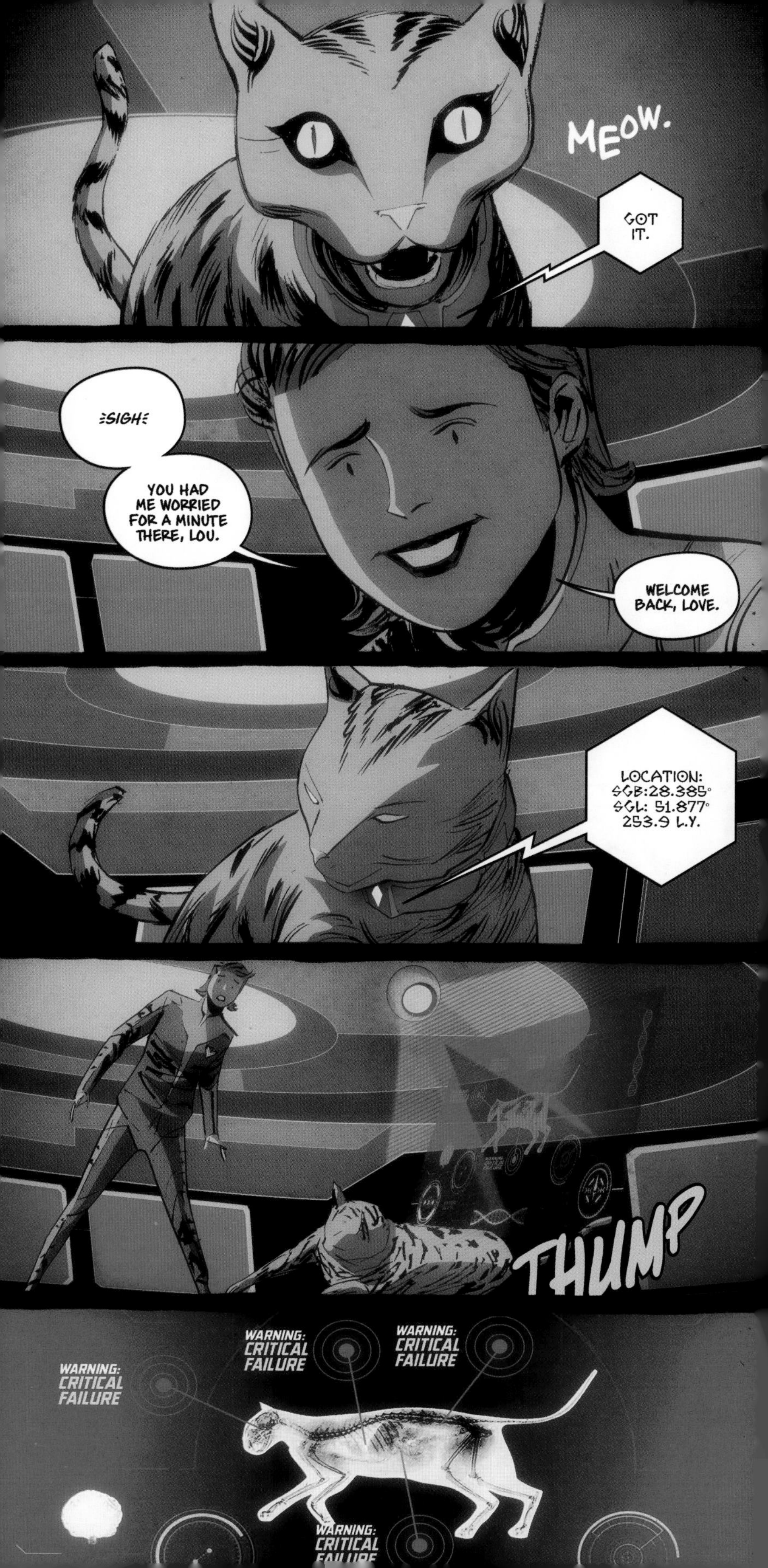
MEOW.
GOT IT.
SIGH
YOU HAD ME WORRIED FOR A MINUTE THERE, LOU.
WELCOME BACK, LOVE.
LOCATION: SGB:28.385° SGL: 51.877° 253.9 L.Y.
THUMP
WARNING: CRITICAL FAILURE
WARNING: CRITICAL FAILURE
WARNING: CRITICAL FAILURE
WARNING: CRITICAL

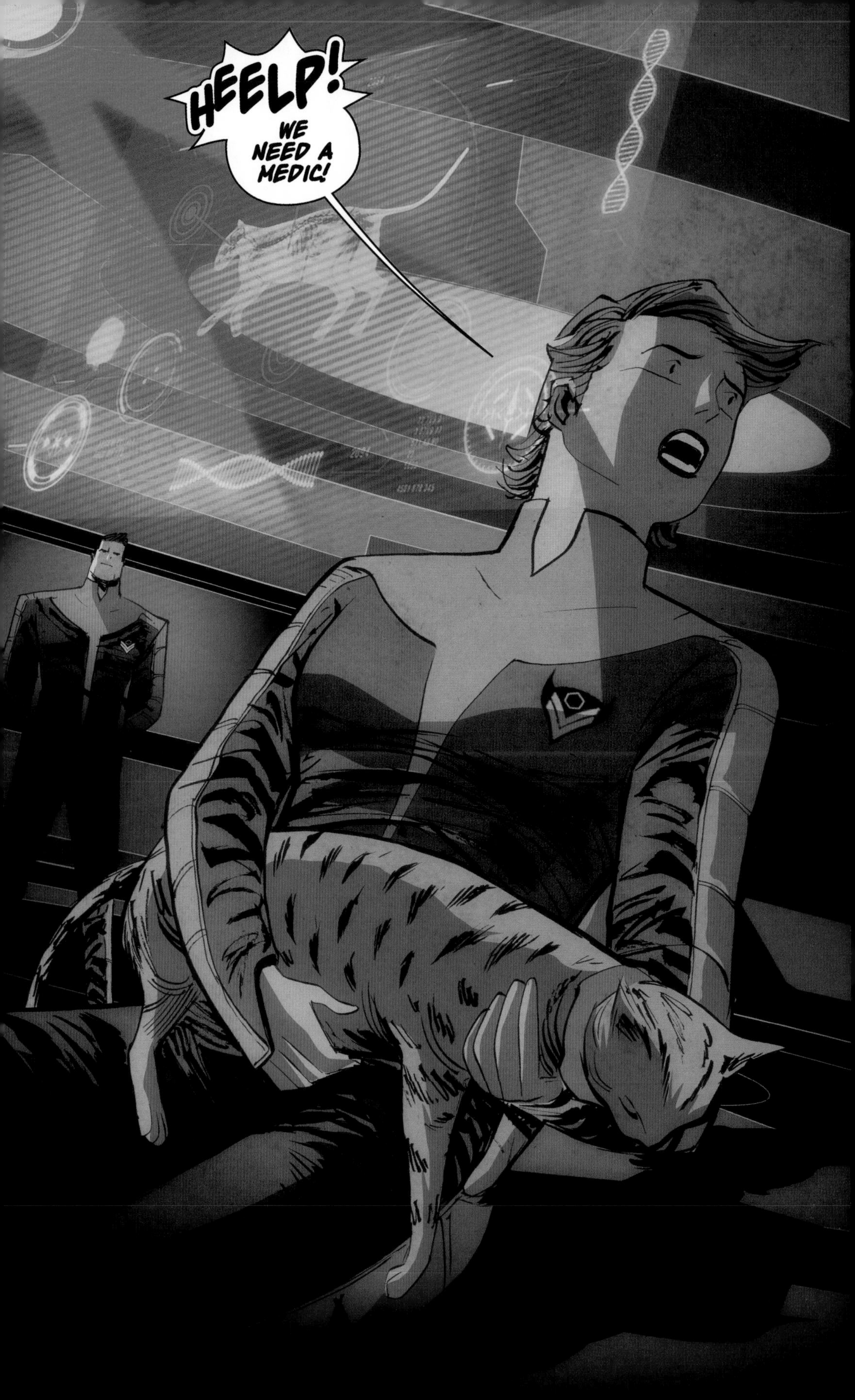
HEELP!
WE NEED A MEDIC!

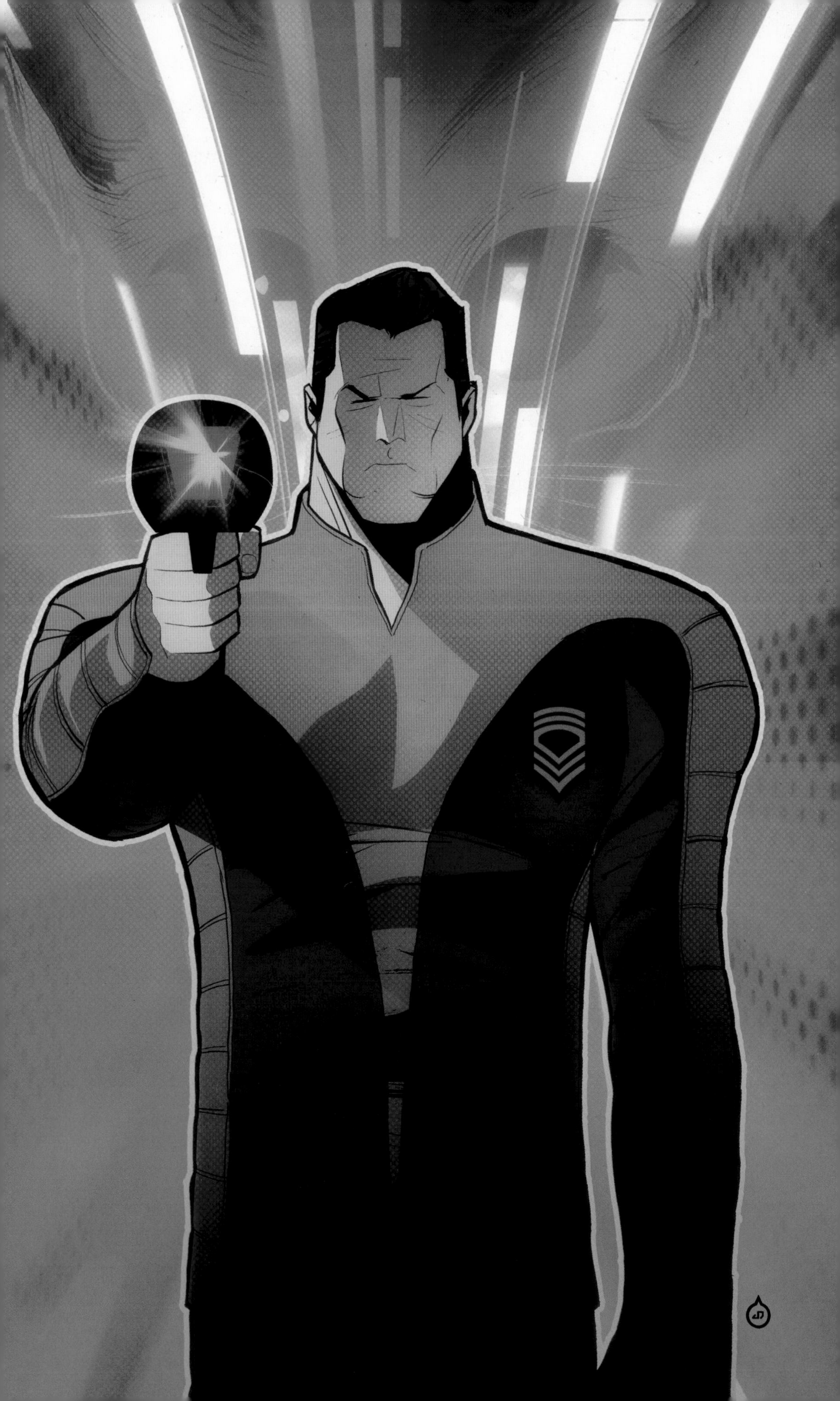

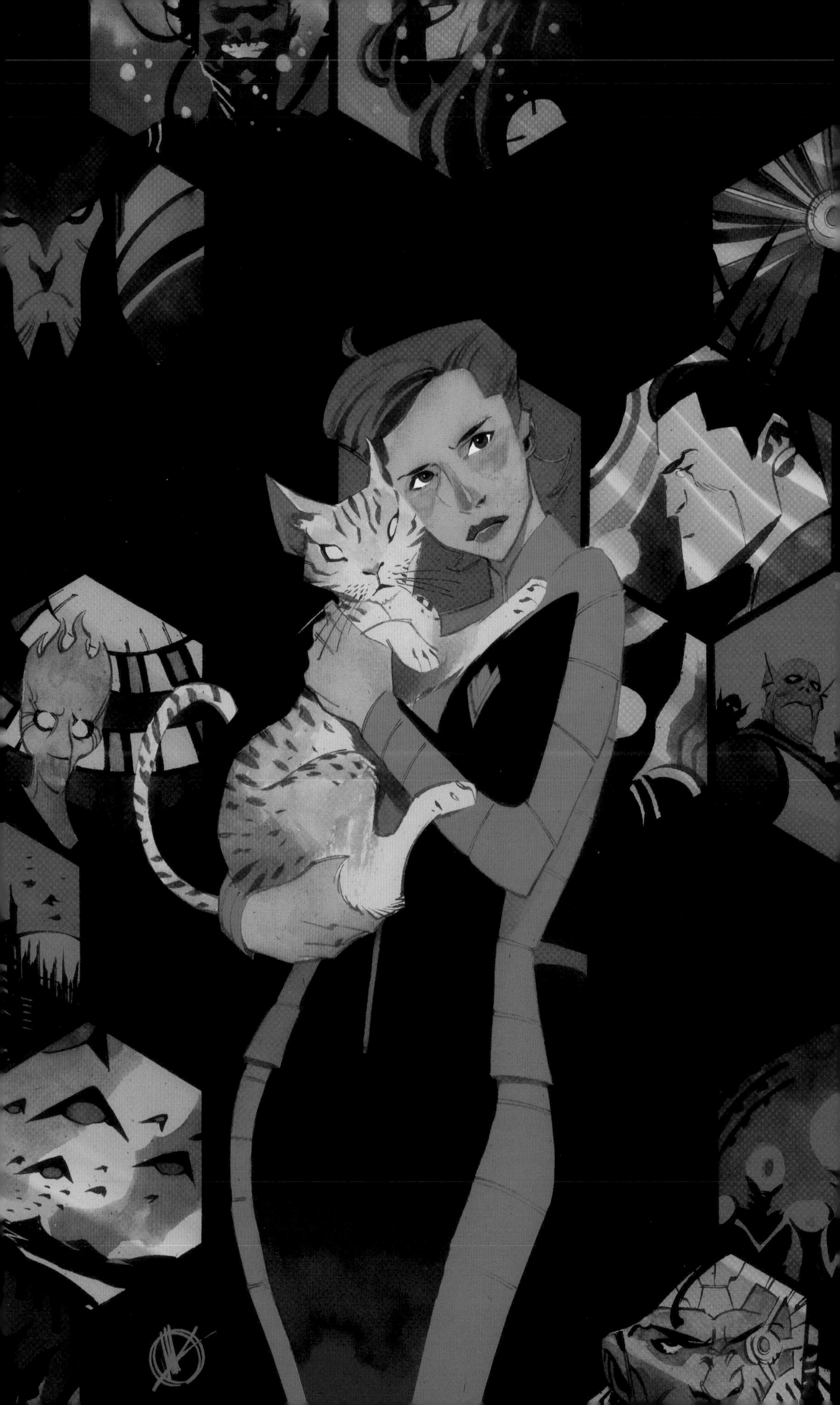

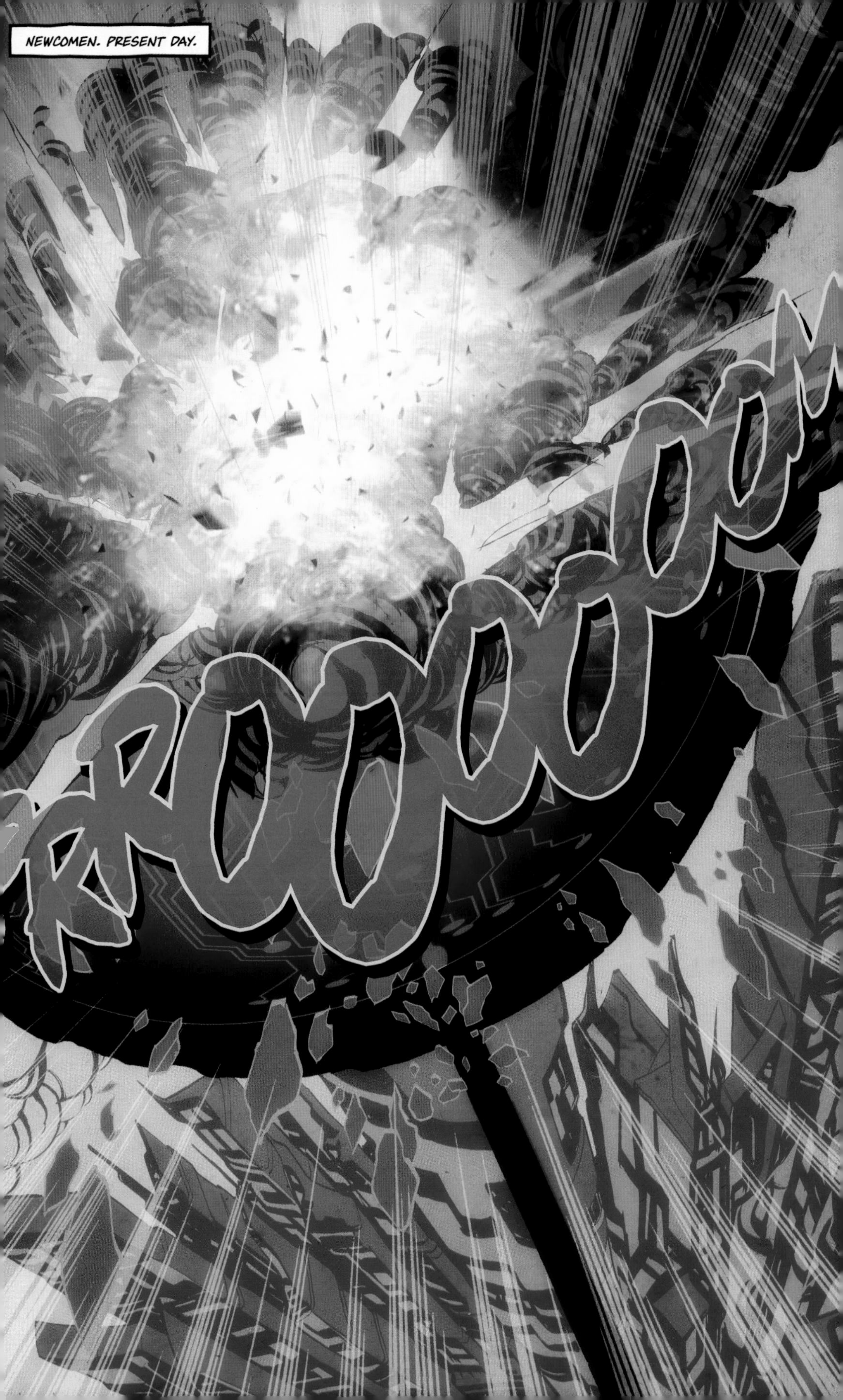
NEWCOMEN. PRESENT DAY.
KROOOOOOM

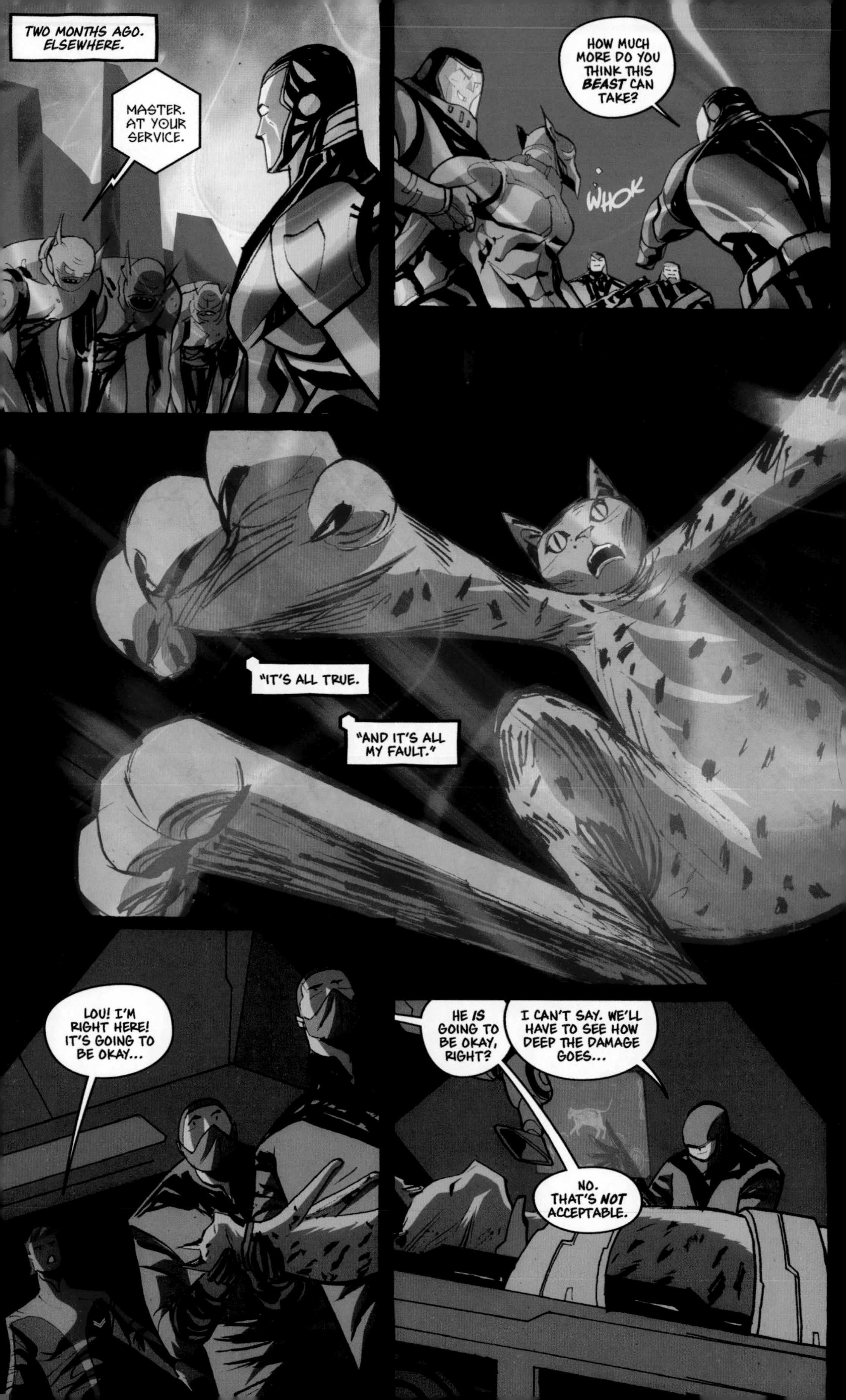
TWO MONTHS AGO. ELSEWHERE.
MASTER. AT YOUR SERVICE.
HOW MUCH MORE DO YOU THINK THIS BEAST CAN TAKE?
WHOK
"IT'S ALL TRUE.
"AND IT'S ALL MY FAULT."
LOU! I'M RIGHT HERE! IT'S GOING TO BE OKAY...
HE IS GOING TO BE OKAY, RIGHT?
I CAN'T SAY. WE'LL HAVE TO SEE HOW DEEP THE DAMAGE GOES...
NO. THAT'S NOT ACCEPTABLE.

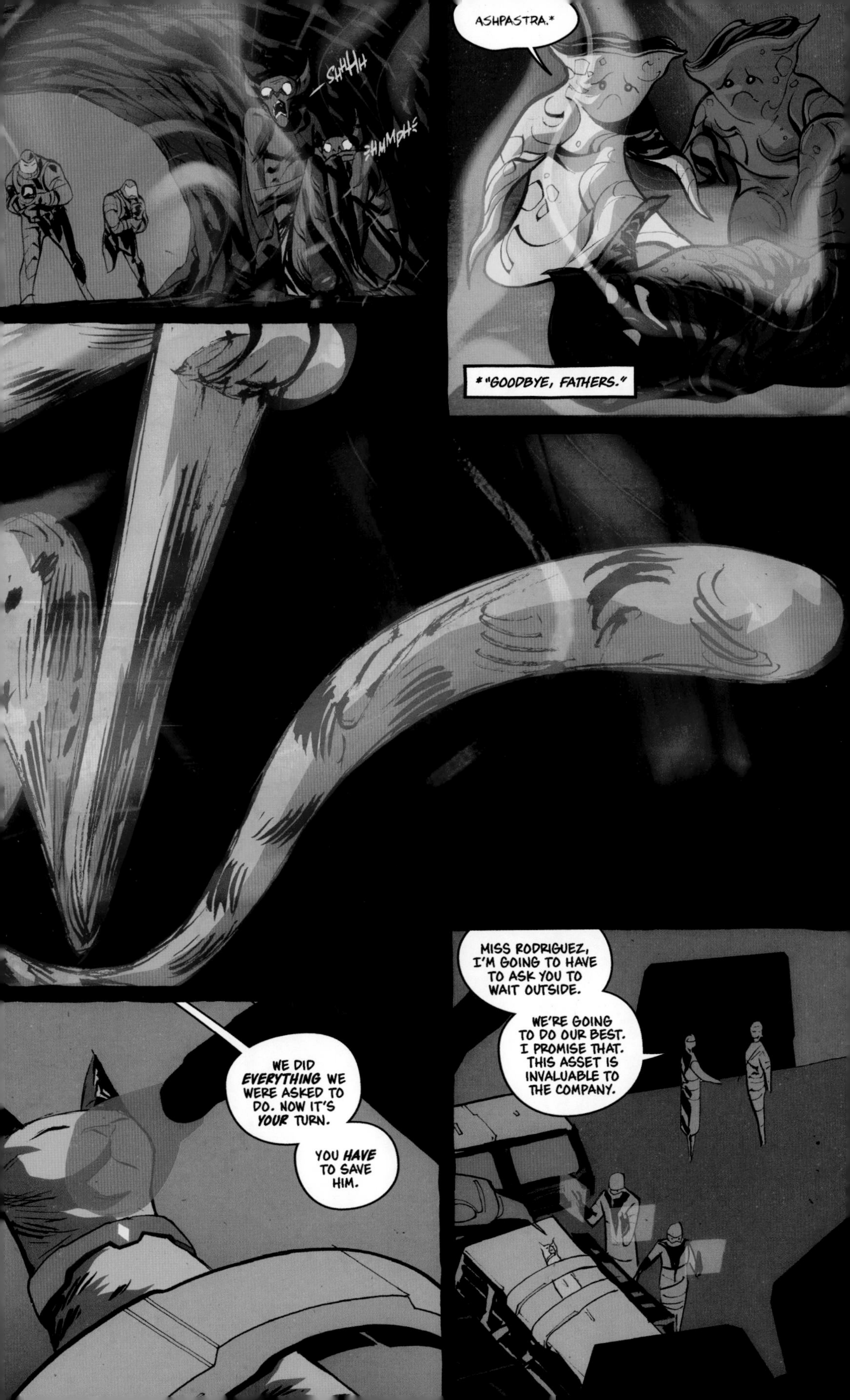
SHHHH
HMMPH
ASHPASTRA.*
*"GOODBYE, FATHERS."
WE DID EVERYTHING WE WERE ASKED TO DO. NOW IT'S YOUR TURN.
YOU HAVE TO SAVE HIM.
MISS RODRIGUEZ, I'M GOING TO HAVE TO ASK YOU TO WAIT OUTSIDE.
WE'RE GOING TO DO OUR BEST. I PROMISE THAT. THIS ASSET IS INVALUABLE TO THE COMPANY.

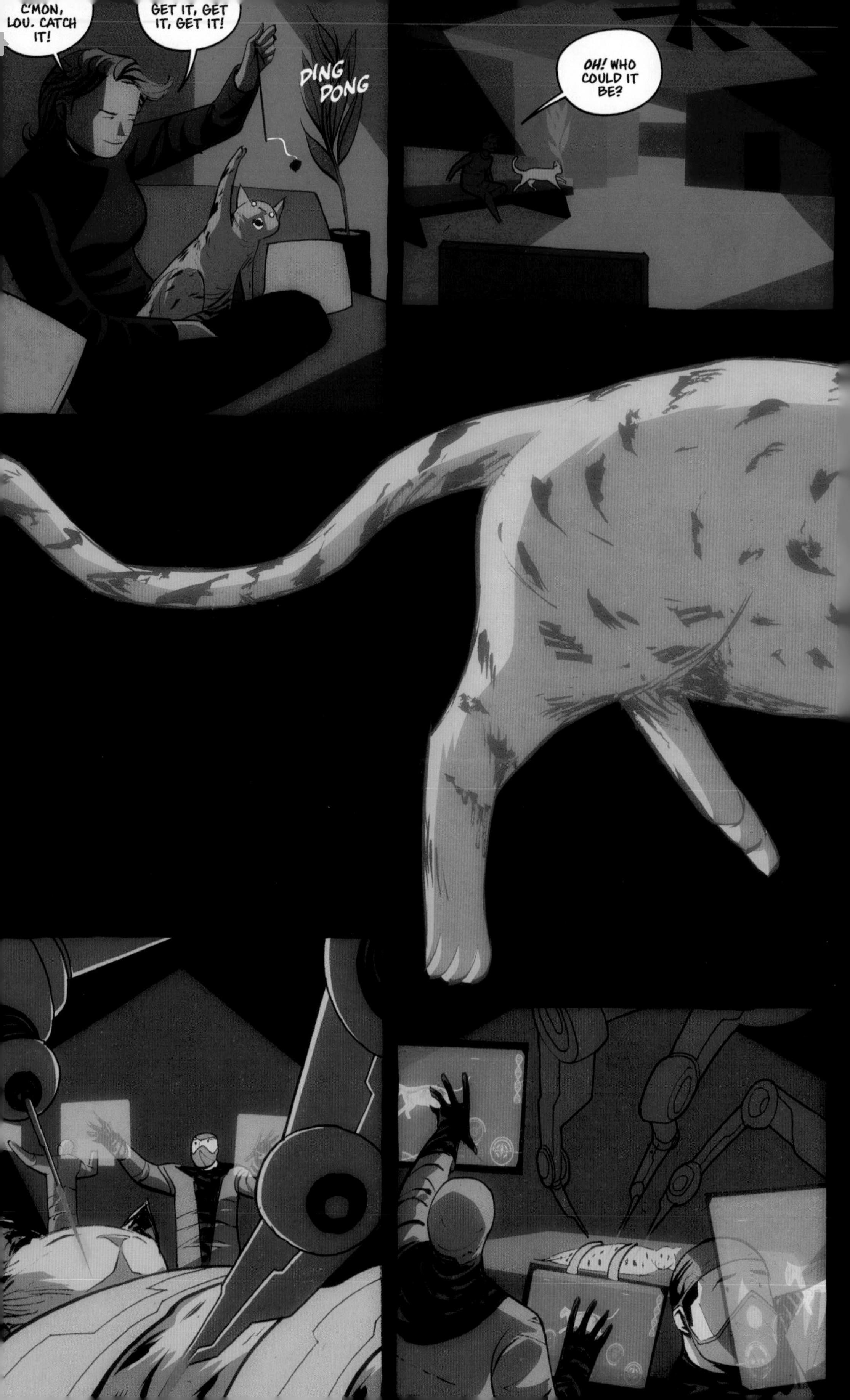
C'MON, LOU. CATCH IT!
GET IT, GET IT, GET IT!
DING DONG
OH! WHO COULD IT BE?

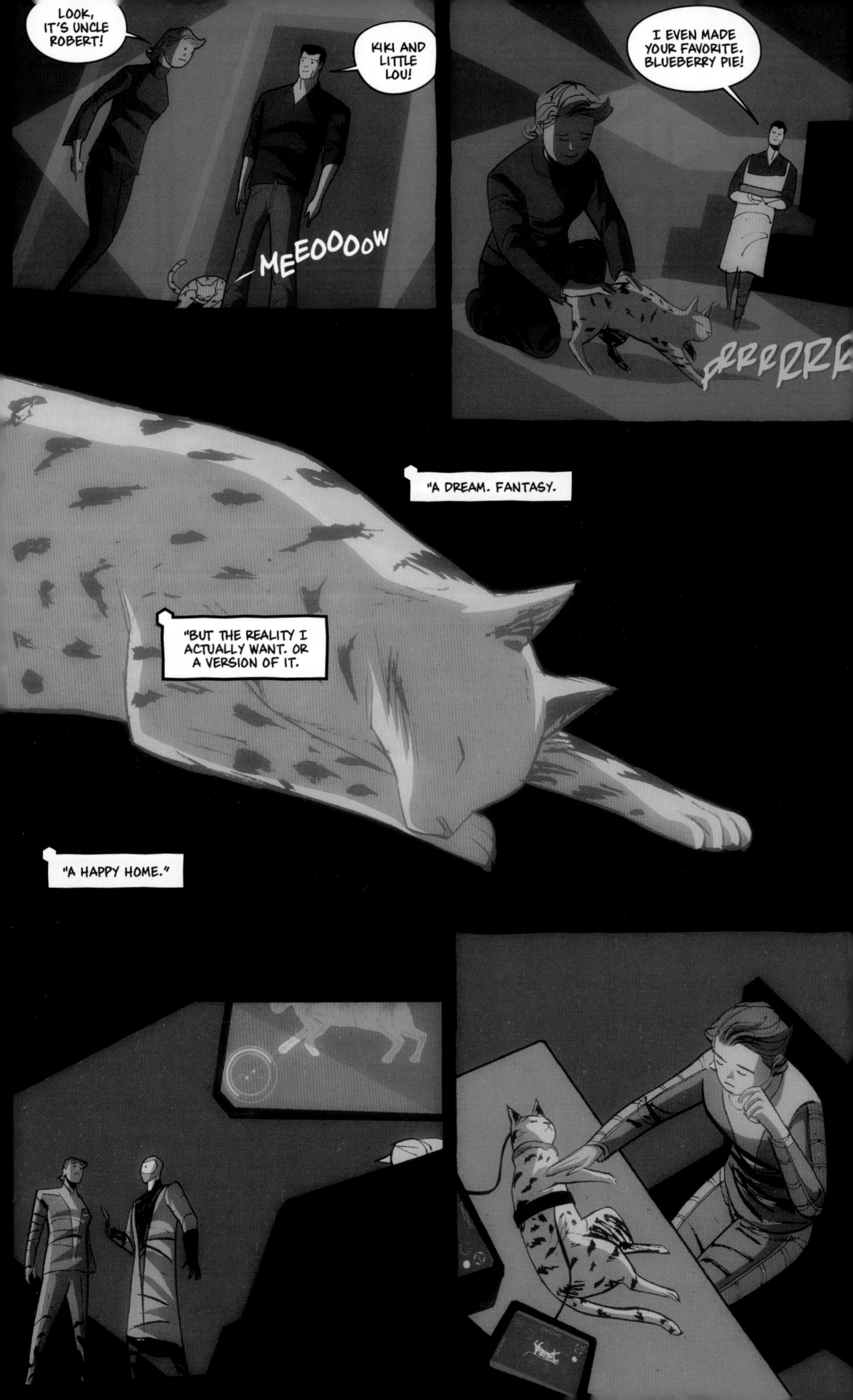
LOOK, IT'S UNCLE ROBERT!
KIKI AND LITTLE LOU!
MEEOOOOW
I EVEN MADE YOUR FAVORITE. BLUEBERRY PIE!
RRRRRR
"A DREAM. FANTASY.
"BUT THE REALITY I ACTUALLY WANT. OR A VERSION OF IT.
"A HAPPY HOME."

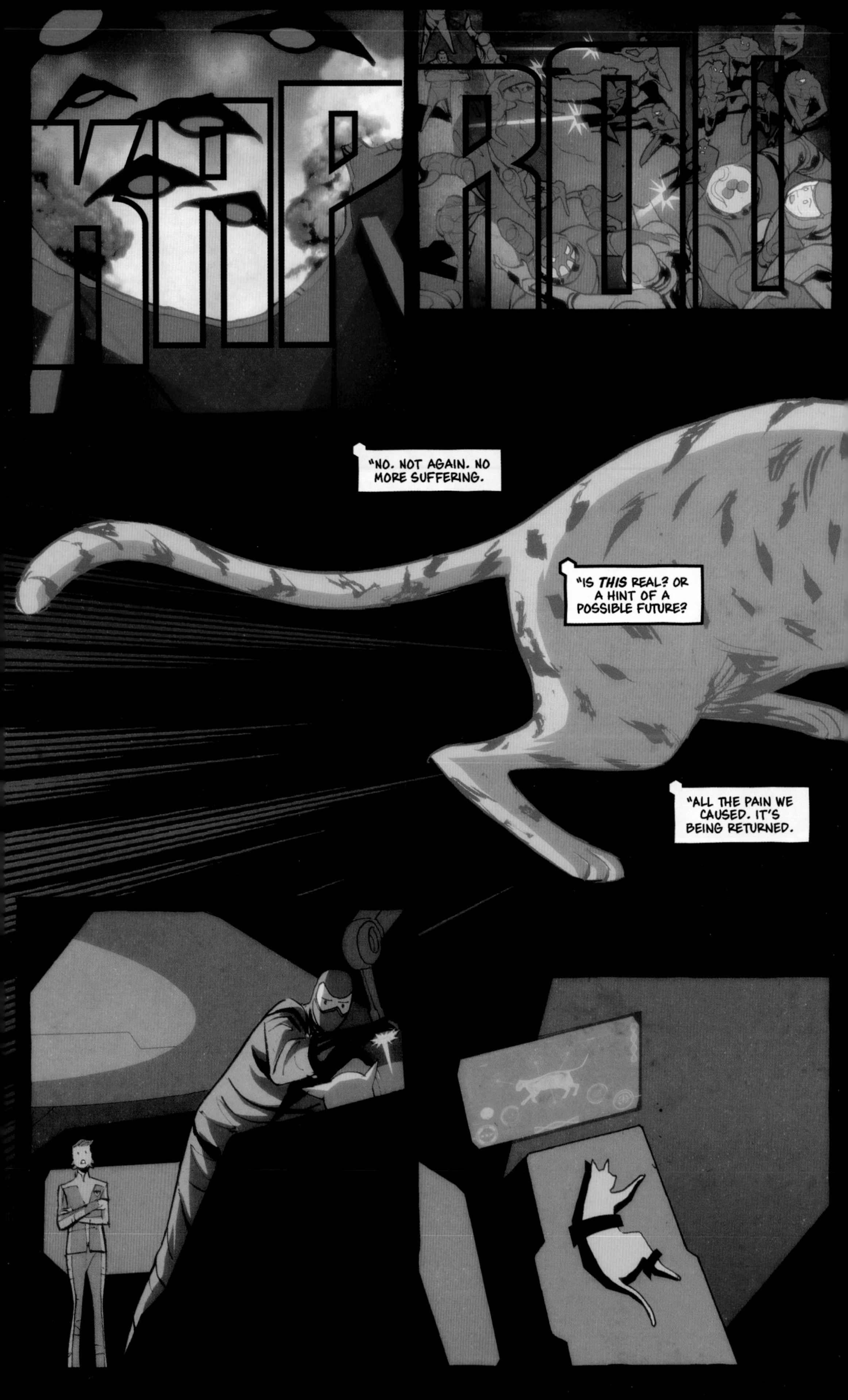
"NO. NOT AGAIN. NO MORE SUFFERING.
"IS *THIS* REAL? OR A HINT OF A POSSIBLE FUTURE?
"ALL THE PAIN WE CAUSED. IT'S BEING RETURNED.

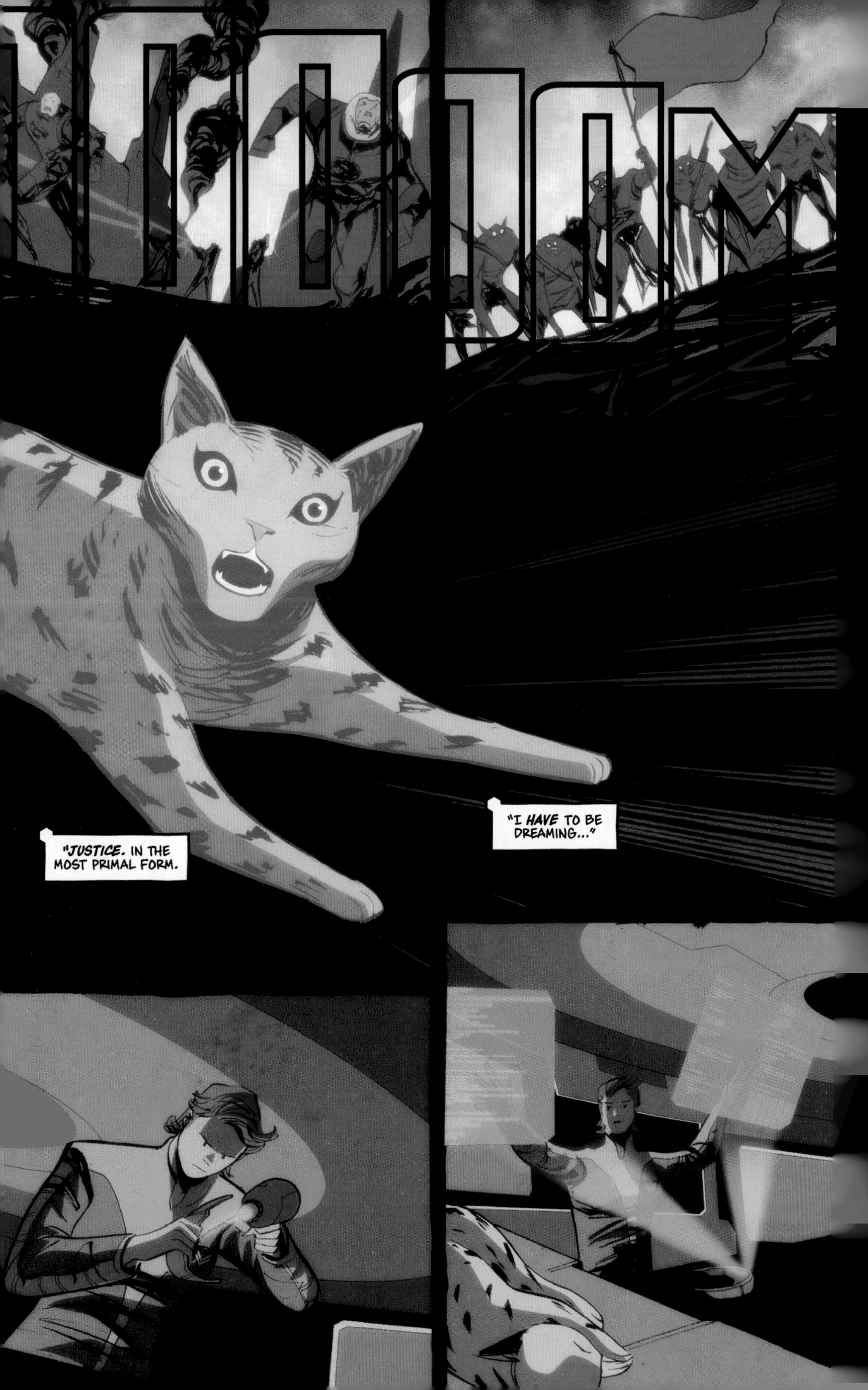
"JUSTICE. IN THE MOST PRIMAL FORM.
"I HAVE TO BE DREAMING..."

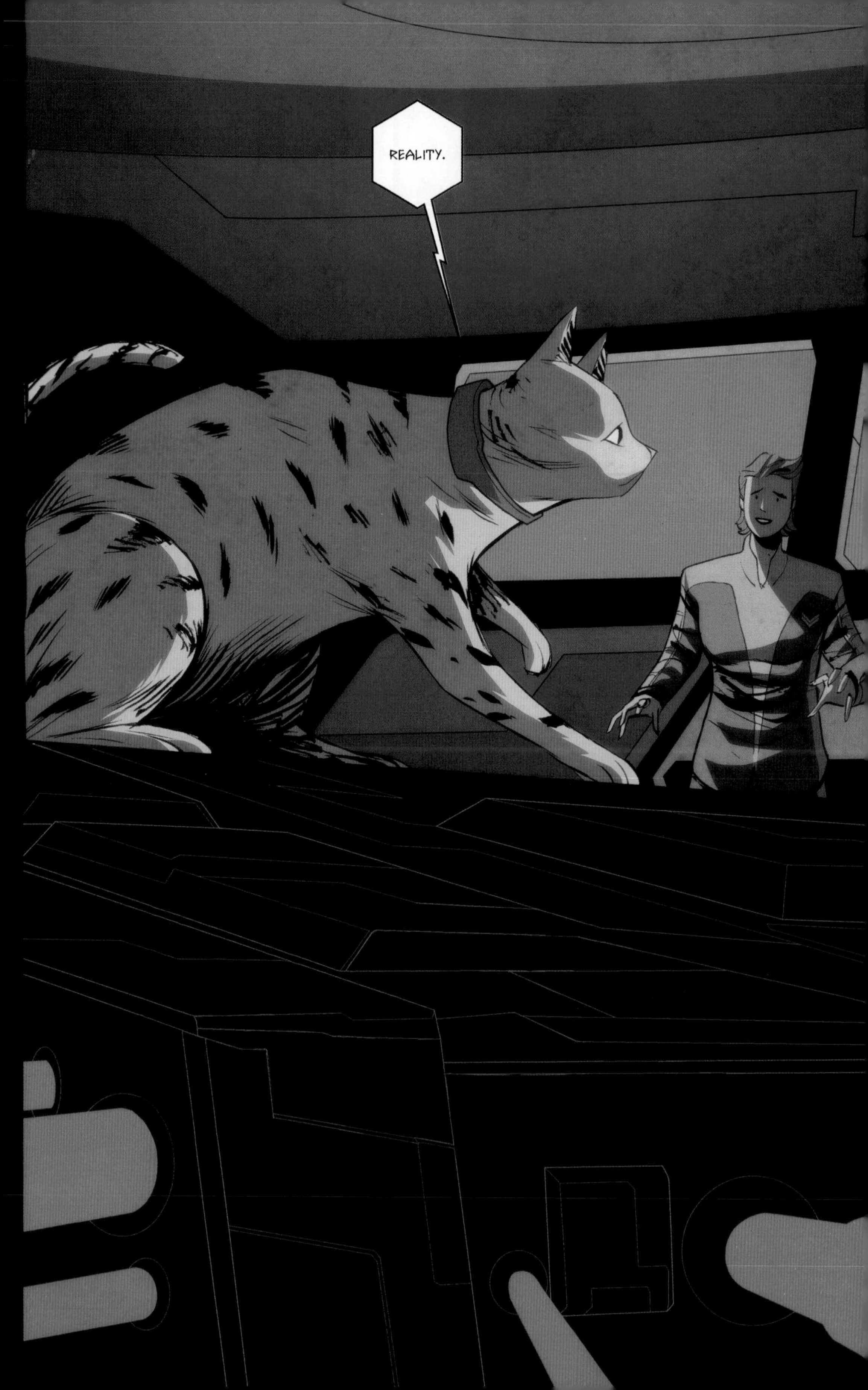
REALITY.

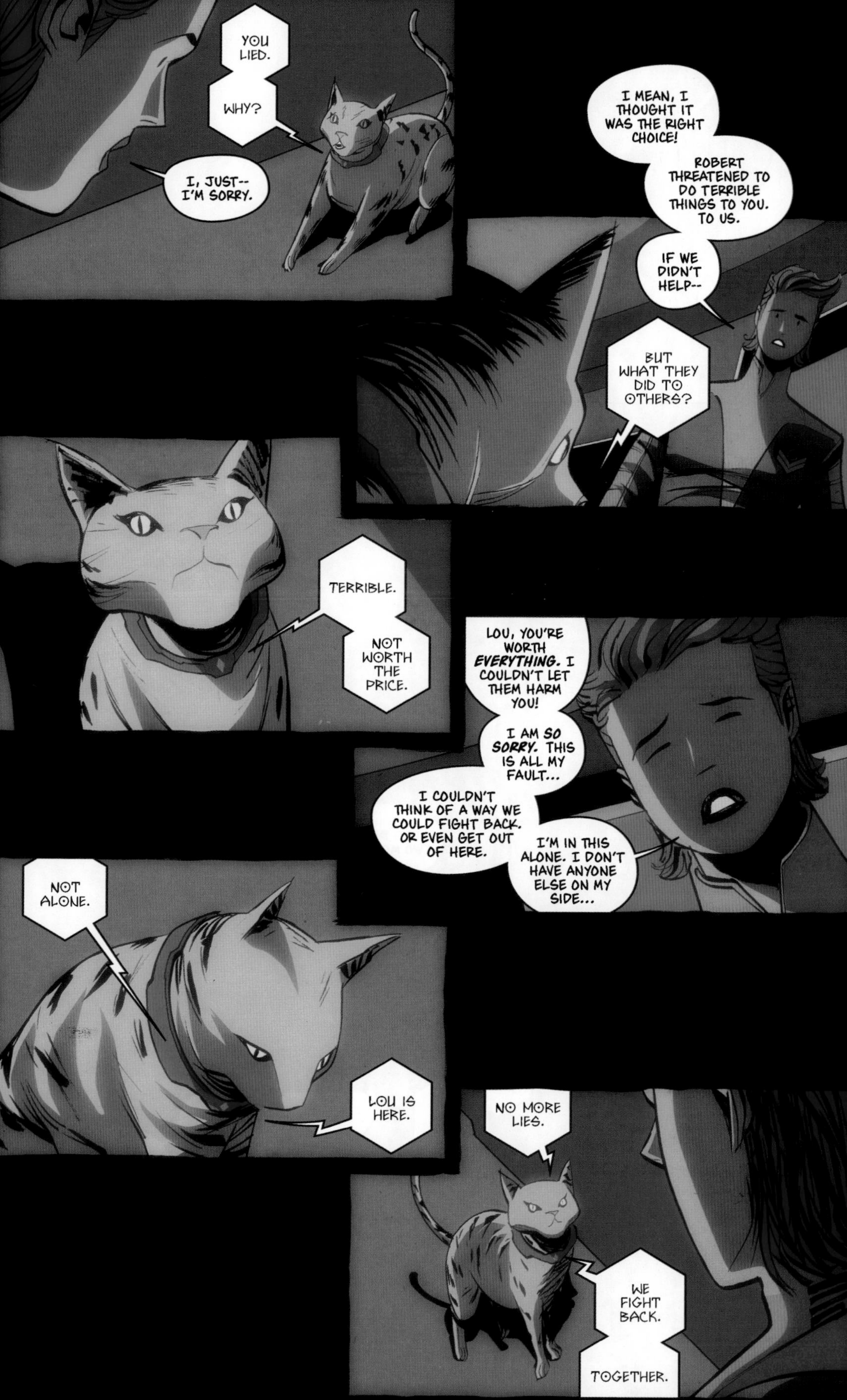
YOU LIED.
WHY?
I, JUST-- I'M SORRY.
I MEAN, I THOUGHT IT WAS THE RIGHT CHOICE!
ROBERT THREATENED TO DO TERRIBLE THINGS TO YOU. TO US.
IF WE DIDN'T HELP--
BUT WHAT THEY DID TO OTHERS?
TERRIBLE.
NOT WORTH THE PRICE.
LOU, YOU'RE WORTH *EVERYTHING.* I COULDN'T LET THEM HARM YOU!
I AM *SO SORRY.* THIS IS ALL MY FAULT...
I COULDN'T THINK OF A WAY WE COULD FIGHT BACK. OR EVEN GET OUT OF HERE.
I'M IN THIS ALONE. I DON'T HAVE ANYONE ELSE ON MY SIDE...
NOT ALONE.
LOU IS HERE.
NO MORE LIES.
WE FIGHT BACK.
TOGETHER.

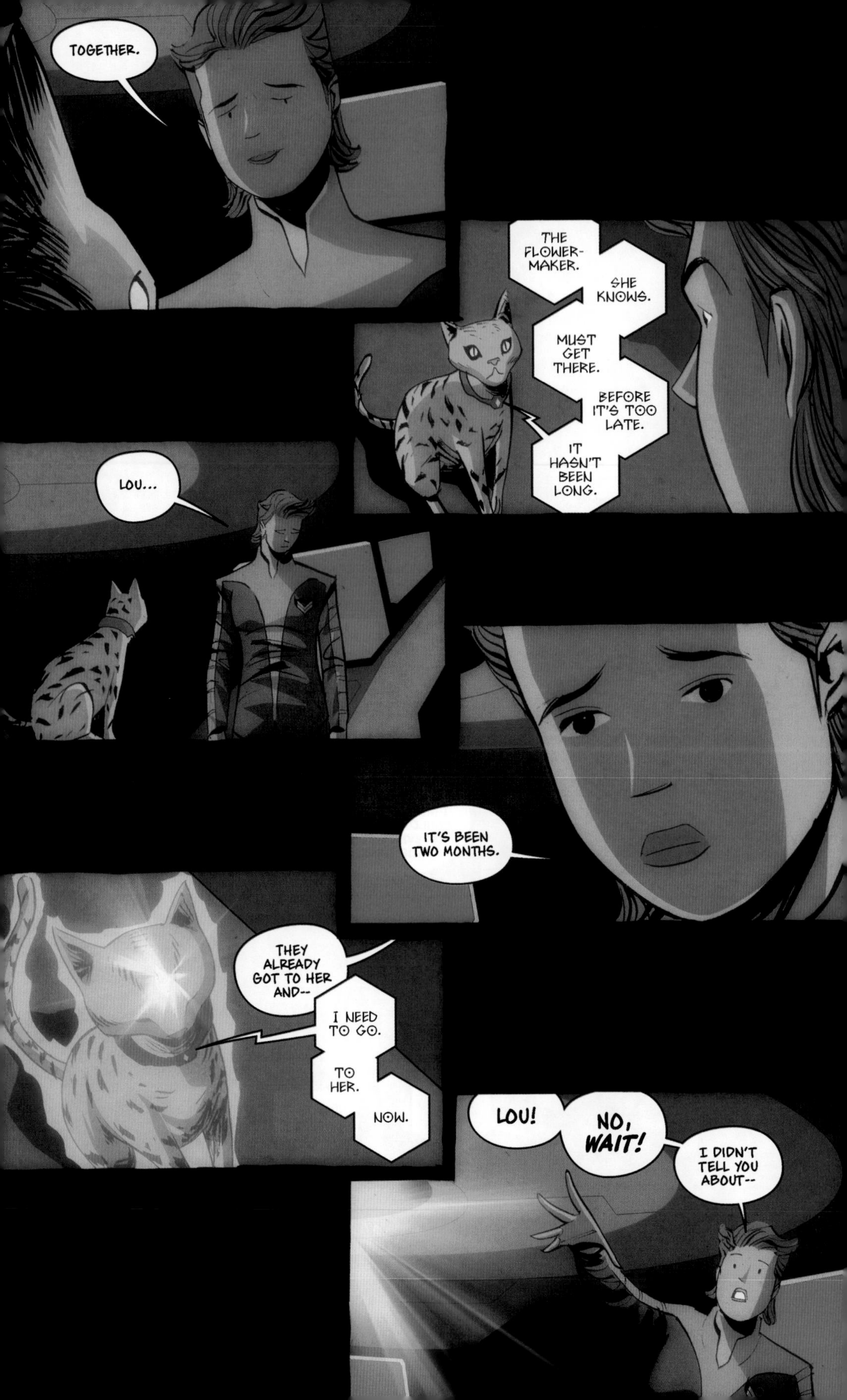
TOGETHER.
THE FLOWER-MAKER.
SHE KNOWS.
MUST GET THERE.
BEFORE IT'S TOO LATE.
IT HASN'T BEEN LONG.
LOU...
IT'S BEEN TWO MONTHS.
THEY ALREADY GOT TO HER AND--
I NEED TO GO.
TO HER.
NOW.
LOU!
NO, WAIT!
I DIDN'T TELL YOU ABOUT--

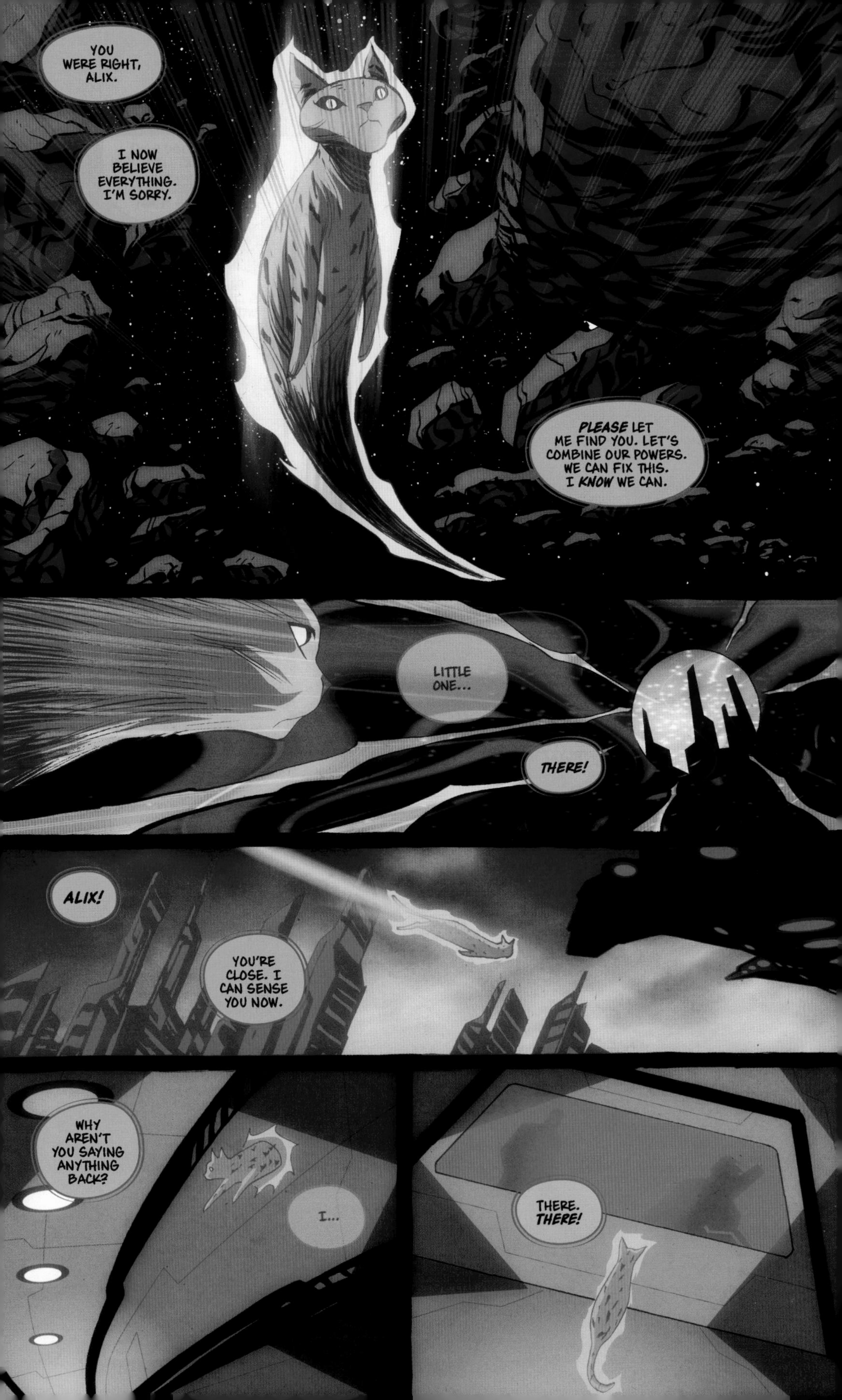

YOU WERE RIGHT, ALIX.
I NOW BELIEVE EVERYTHING. I'M SORRY.
PLEASE LET ME FIND YOU. LET'S COMBINE OUR POWERS. WE CAN FIX THIS. I KNOW WE CAN.
LITTLE ONE...
THERE!
ALIX!
YOU'RE CLOSE. I CAN SENSE YOU NOW.
WHY AREN'T YOU SAYING ANYTHING BACK?
I...
THERE. THERE!

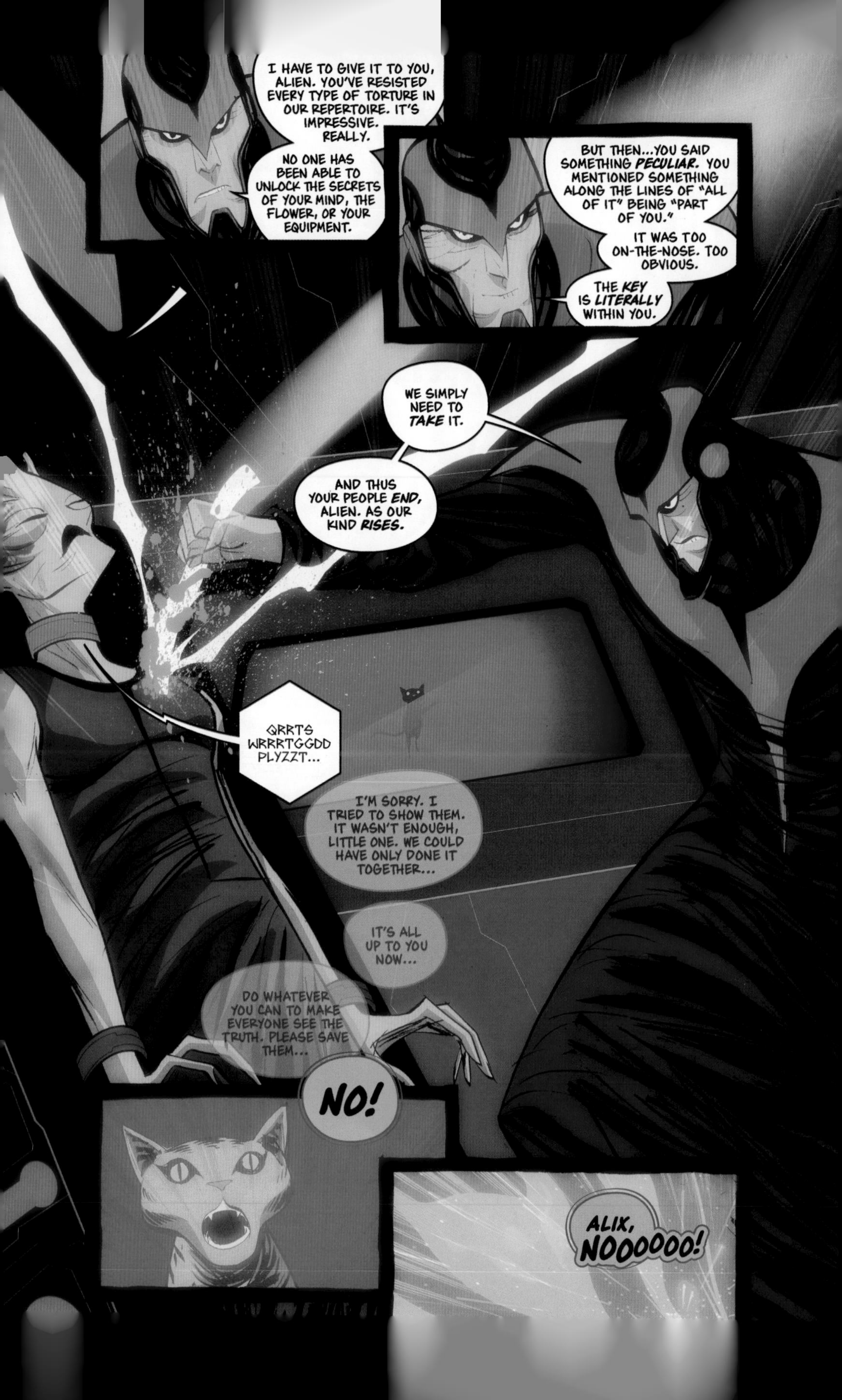
I HAVE TO GIVE IT TO YOU, ALIEN. YOU'VE RESISTED EVERY TYPE OF TORTURE IN OUR REPERTOIRE. IT'S IMPRESSIVE. REALLY.
NO ONE HAS BEEN ABLE TO UNLOCK THE SECRETS OF YOUR MIND, THE FLOWER, OR YOUR EQUIPMENT.
BUT THEN...YOU SAID SOMETHING PECULIAR. YOU MENTIONED SOMETHING ALONG THE LINES OF "ALL OF IT" BEING "PART OF YOU."
IT WAS TOO ON-THE-NOSE. TOO OBVIOUS.
THE KEY IS LITERALLY WITHIN YOU.
WE SIMPLY NEED TO TAKE IT.
AND THUS YOUR PEOPLE END, ALIEN. AS OUR KIND RISES.
QRRTS WRRRTGGDD PLYZZT...
I'M SORRY. I TRIED TO SHOW THEM. IT WASN'T ENOUGH, LITTLE ONE. WE COULD HAVE ONLY DONE IT TOGETHER...
IT'S ALL UP TO YOU NOW...
DO WHATEVER YOU CAN TO MAKE EVERYONE SEE THE TRUTH. PLEASE SAVE THEM...
NO!
ALIX, NOOOOOO!

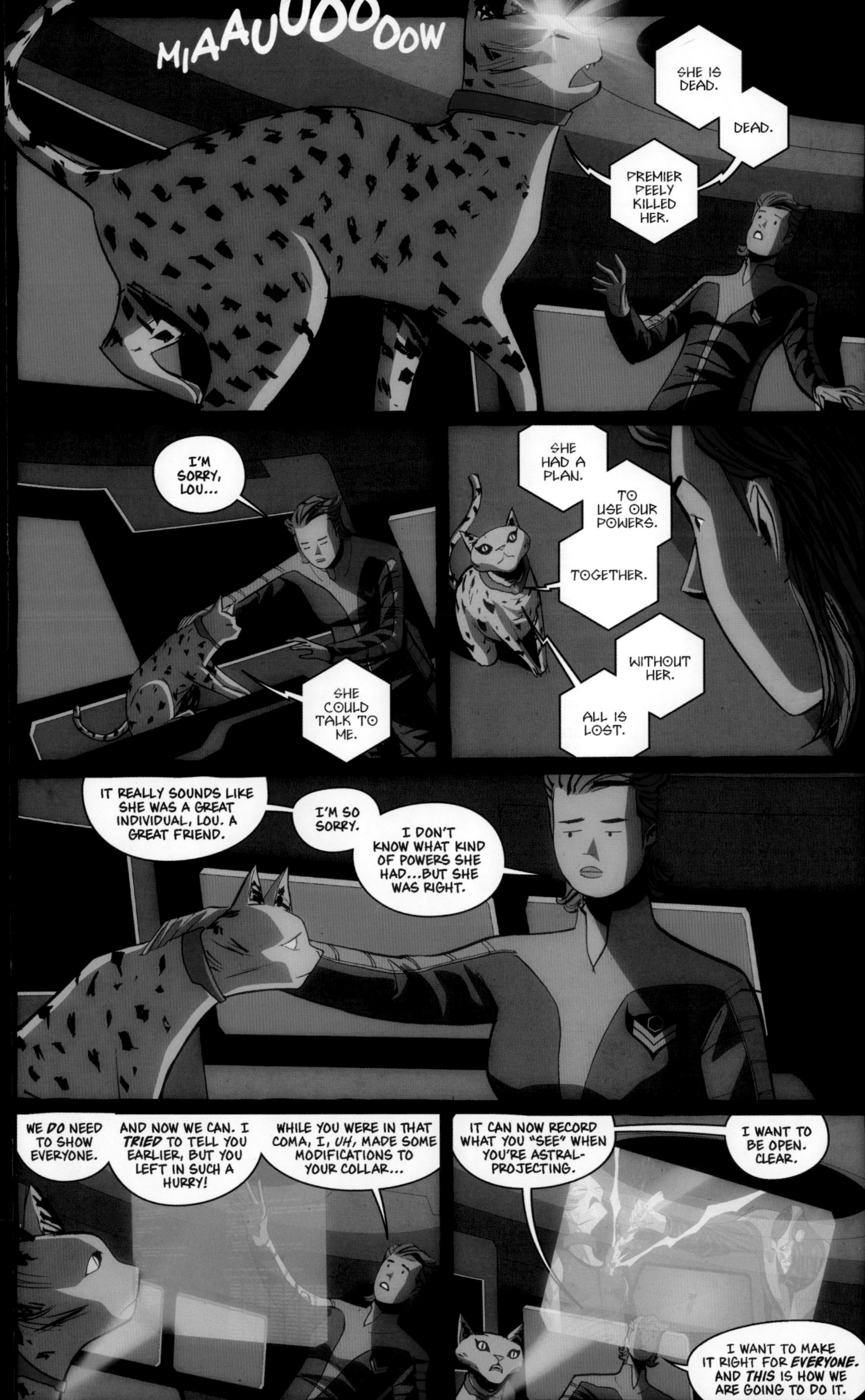
MIAAUOOOOOW
SHE IS DEAD.
DEAD.
PREMIER PEELY KILLED HER.
I'M SORRY, LOU...
SHE COULD TALK TO ME.
SHE HAD A PLAN.
TO USE OUR POWERS.
TOGETHER.
WITHOUT HER.
ALL IS LOST.
IT REALLY SOUNDS LIKE SHE WAS A GREAT INDIVIDUAL, LOU. A GREAT FRIEND.
I'M SO SORRY.
I DON'T KNOW WHAT KIND OF POWERS SHE HAD...BUT SHE WAS RIGHT.
WE *DO* NEED TO SHOW EVERYONE.
AND NOW WE CAN. I *TRIED* TO TELL YOU EARLIER, BUT YOU LEFT IN SUCH A HURRY!
WHILE YOU WERE IN THAT COMA, I, *UH*, MADE SOME MODIFICATIONS TO YOUR COLLAR...
IT CAN NOW RECORD WHAT YOU "SEE" WHEN YOU'RE ASTRAL-PROJECTING.
I WANT TO BE OPEN. CLEAR.
I WANT TO MAKE IT RIGHT FOR *EVERYONE*. AND *THIS* IS HOW WE ARE GOING TO DO IT.

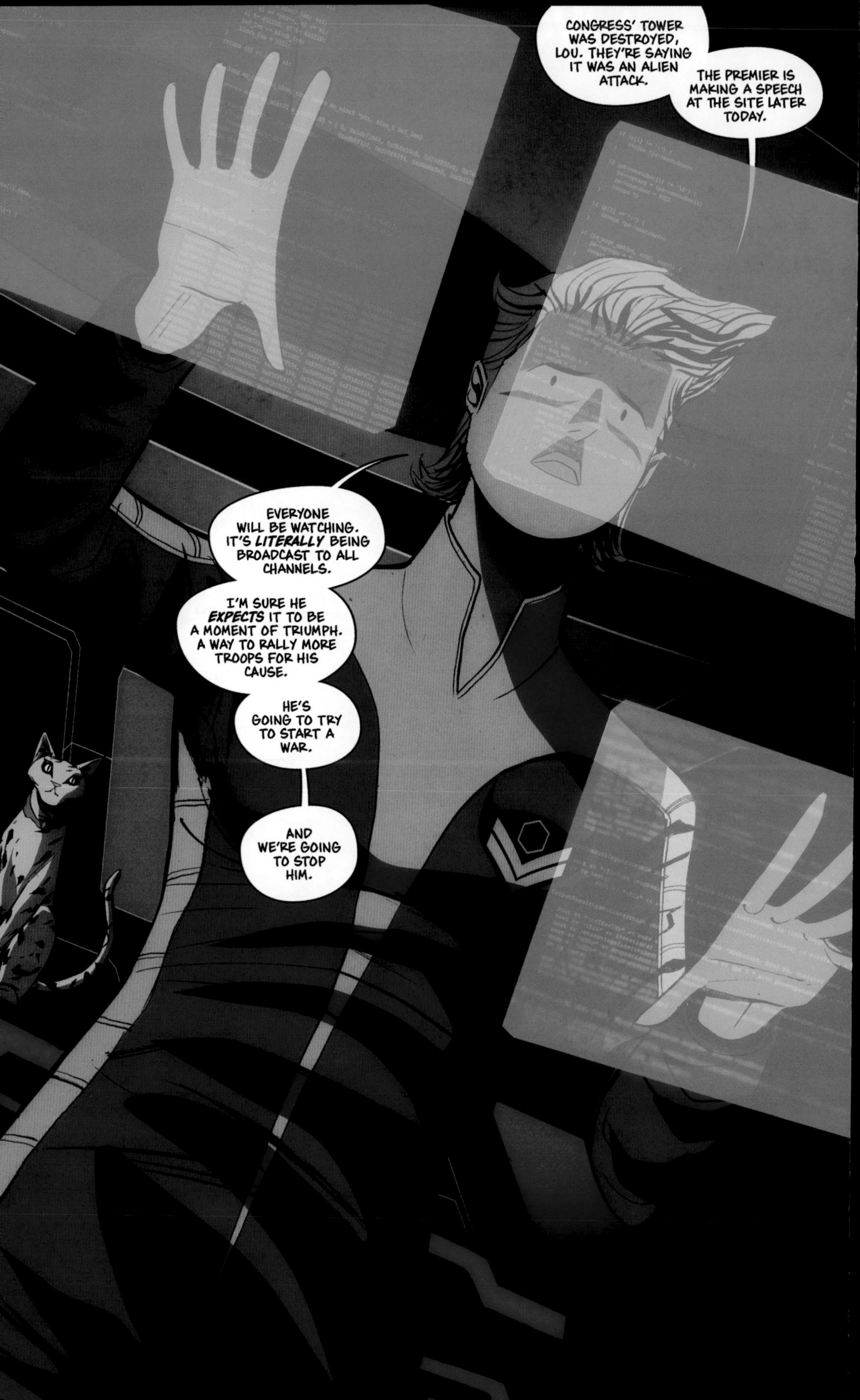
CONGRESS' TOWER WAS DESTROYED, LOU. THEY'RE SAYING IT WAS AN ALIEN ATTACK.
THE PREMIER IS MAKING A SPEECH AT THE SITE LATER TODAY.
EVERYONE WILL BE WATCHING. IT'S *LITERALLY* BEING BROADCAST TO ALL CHANNELS.
I'M SURE HE *EXPECTS* IT TO BE A MOMENT OF TRIUMPH. A WAY TO RALLY MORE TROOPS FOR HIS CAUSE.
HE'S GOING TO TRY TO START A WAR.
AND WE'RE GOING TO STOP HIM.

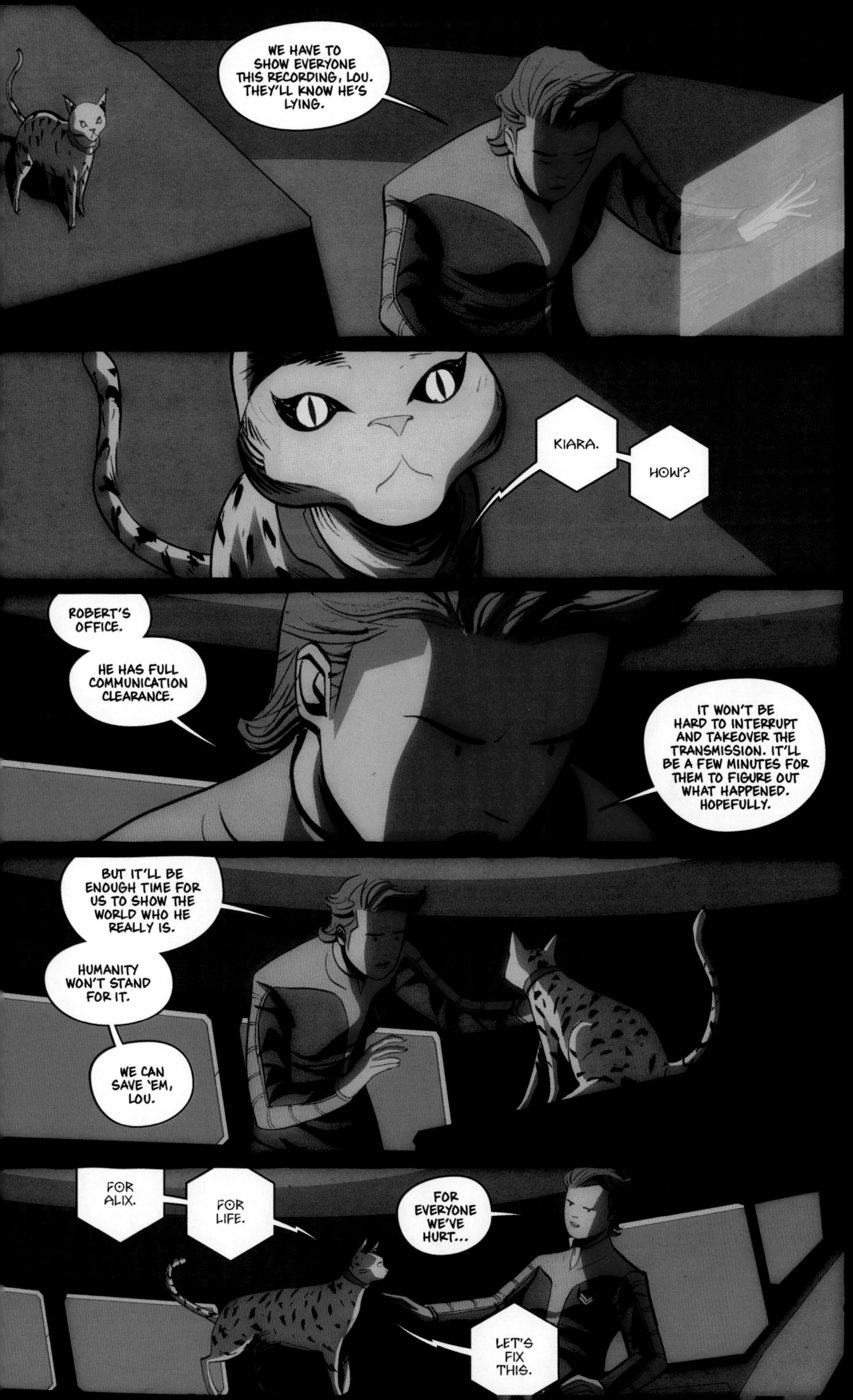
WE HAVE TO SHOW EVERYONE THIS RECORDING, LOU. THEY'LL KNOW HE'S LYING.
KIARA.
HOW?
ROBERT'S OFFICE.
HE HAS FULL COMMUNICATION CLEARANCE.
IT WON'T BE HARD TO INTERRUPT AND TAKEOVER THE TRANSMISSION. IT'LL BE A FEW MINUTES FOR THEM TO FIGURE OUT WHAT HAPPENED. HOPEFULLY.
BUT IT'LL BE ENOUGH TIME FOR US TO SHOW THE WORLD WHO HE REALLY IS.
HUMANITY WON'T STAND FOR IT.
WE CAN SAVE 'EM, LOU.
FOR ALIX.
FOR LIFE.
FOR EVERYONE WE'VE HURT...
LET'S FIX THIS.

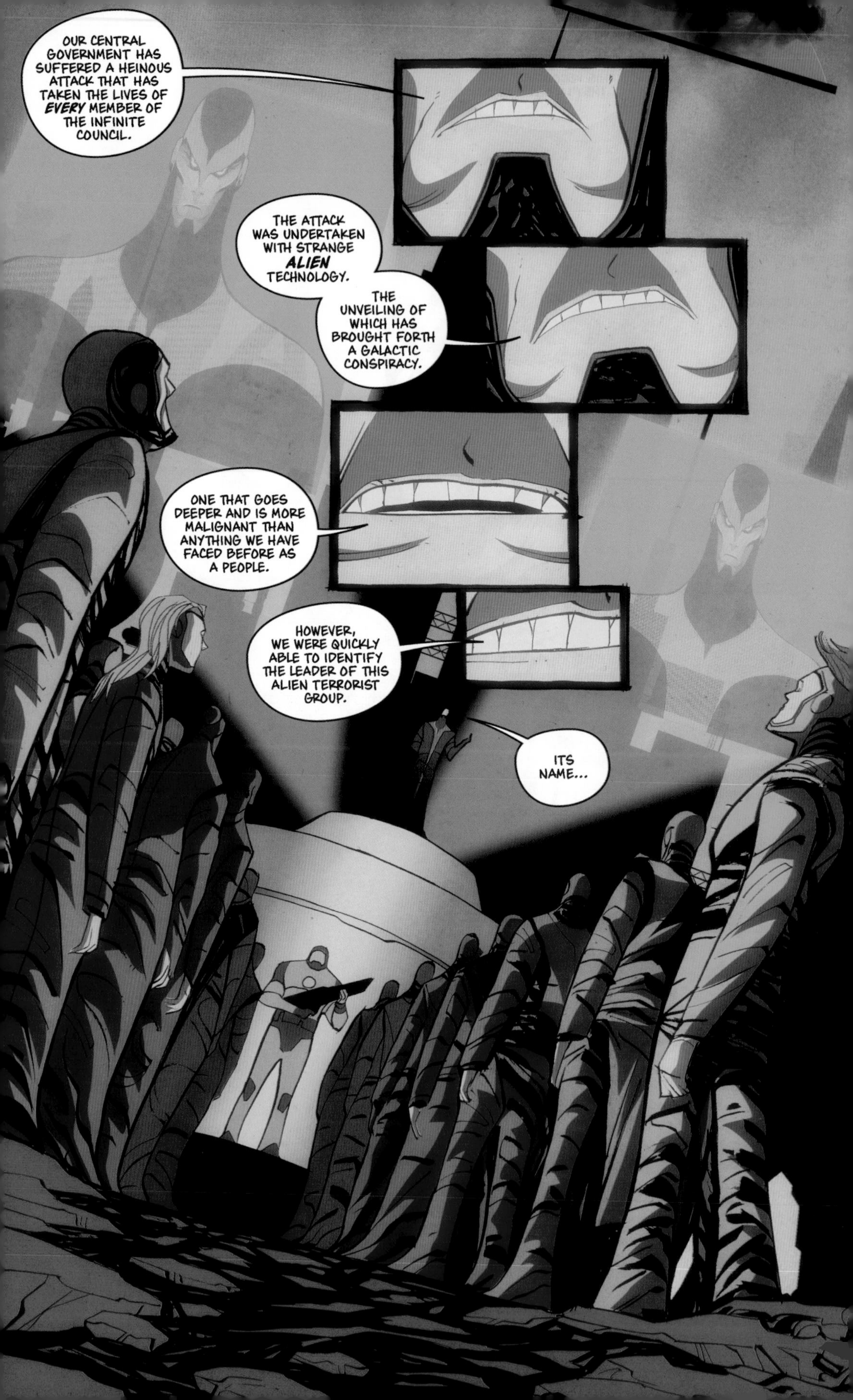
OUR CENTRAL GOVERNMENT HAS SUFFERED A HEINOUS ATTACK THAT HAS TAKEN THE LIVES OF EVERY MEMBER OF THE INFINITE COUNCIL.
THE ATTACK WAS UNDERTAKEN WITH STRANGE ALIEN TECHNOLOGY.
THE UNVEILING OF WHICH HAS BROUGHT FORTH A GALACTIC CONSPIRACY.
ONE THAT GOES DEEPER AND IS MORE MALIGNANT THAN ANYTHING WE HAVE FACED BEFORE AS A PEOPLE.
HOWEVER, WE WERE QUICKLY ABLE TO IDENTIFY THE LEADER OF THIS ALIEN TERRORIST GROUP.
ITS NAME...

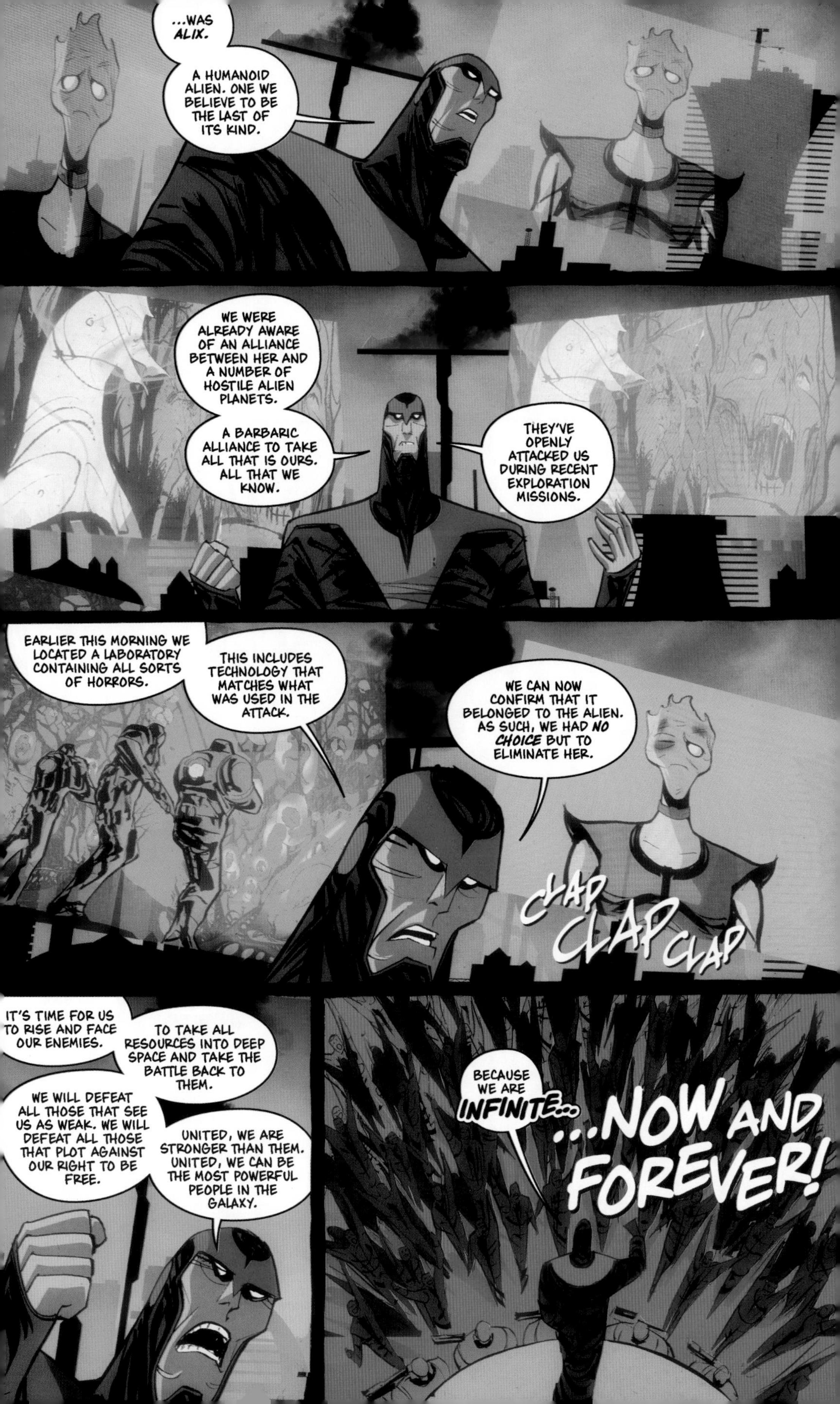
...WAS ALIX.
A HUMANOID ALIEN. ONE WE BELIEVE TO BE THE LAST OF ITS KIND.
WE WERE ALREADY AWARE OF AN ALLIANCE BETWEEN HER AND A NUMBER OF HOSTILE ALIEN PLANETS.
A BARBARIC ALLIANCE TO TAKE ALL THAT IS OURS. ALL THAT WE KNOW.
THEY'VE OPENLY ATTACKED US DURING RECENT EXPLORATION MISSIONS.
EARLIER THIS MORNING WE LOCATED A LABORATORY CONTAINING ALL SORTS OF HORRORS.
THIS INCLUDES TECHNOLOGY THAT MATCHES WHAT WAS USED IN THE ATTACK.
WE CAN NOW CONFIRM THAT IT BELONGED TO THE ALIEN. AS SUCH, WE HAD NO CHOICE BUT TO ELIMINATE HER.
CLAP CLAP CLAP
IT'S TIME FOR US TO RISE AND FACE OUR ENEMIES.
TO TAKE ALL RESOURCES INTO DEEP SPACE AND TAKE THE BATTLE BACK TO THEM.
WE WILL DEFEAT ALL THOSE THAT SEE US AS WEAK. WE WILL DEFEAT ALL THOSE THAT PLOT AGAINST OUR RIGHT TO BE FREE.
UNITED, WE ARE STRONGER THAN THEM. UNITED, WE CAN BE THE MOST POWERFUL PEOPLE IN THE GALAXY.
BECAUSE WE ARE INFINITE...
...NOW AND FOREVER!

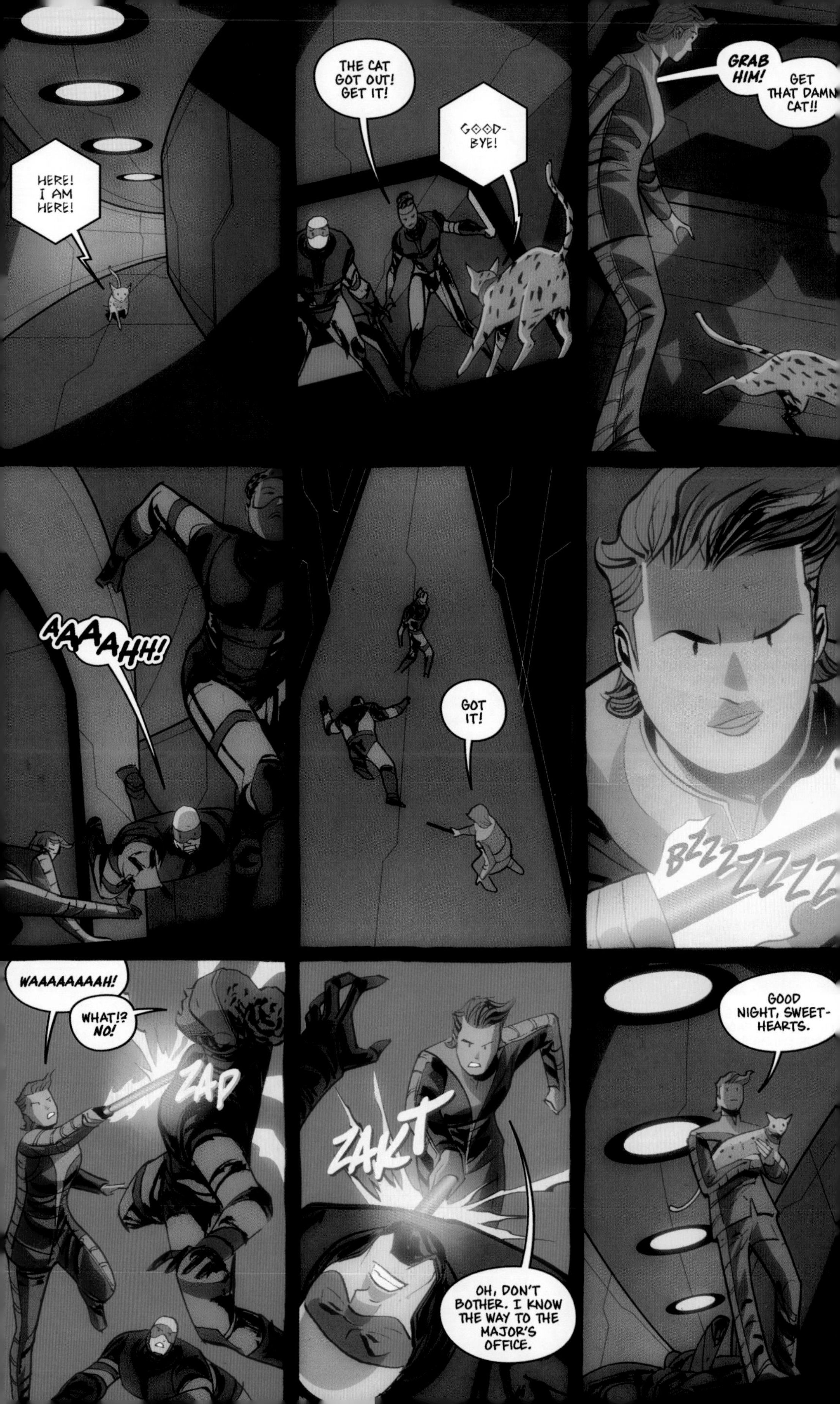
HERE! I AM HERE!
THE CAT GOT OUT! GET IT!
GOOD-BYE!
GRAB HIM!
GET THAT DAMN CAT!!
AAAAHH!
GOT IT!
BZZZZZZZ
WAAAAAAAAH!
WHAT!? NO!
ZAP
ZAKT
OH, DON'T BOTHER. I KNOW THE WAY TO THE MAJOR'S OFFICE.
GOOD NIGHT, SWEET-HEARTS.

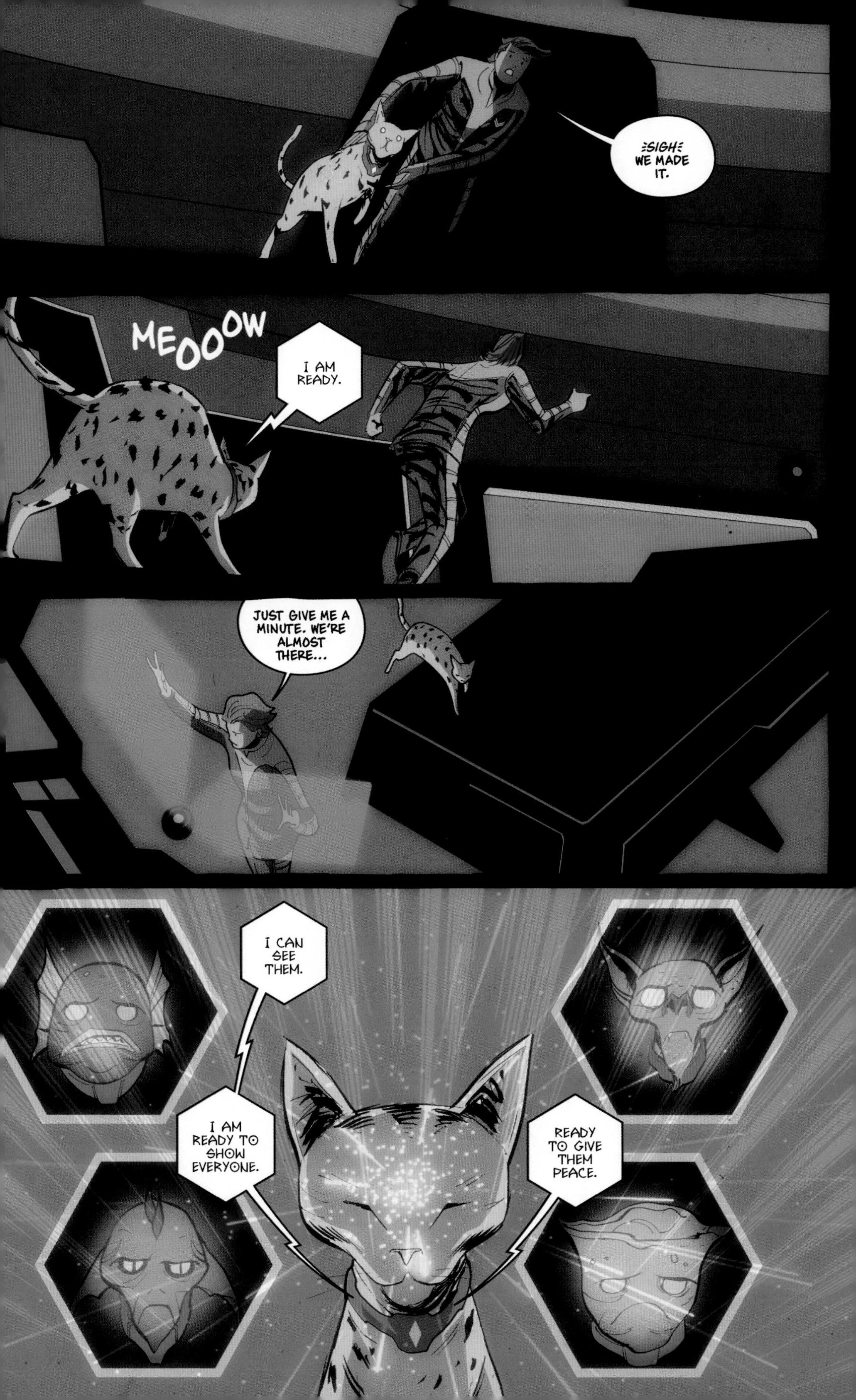
≡SIGH≡ WE MADE IT.
MEOOOW
I AM READY.
JUST GIVE ME A MINUTE. WE'RE ALMOST THERE...
I CAN SEE THEM.
I AM READY TO SHOW EVERYONE.
READY TO GIVE THEM PEACE.

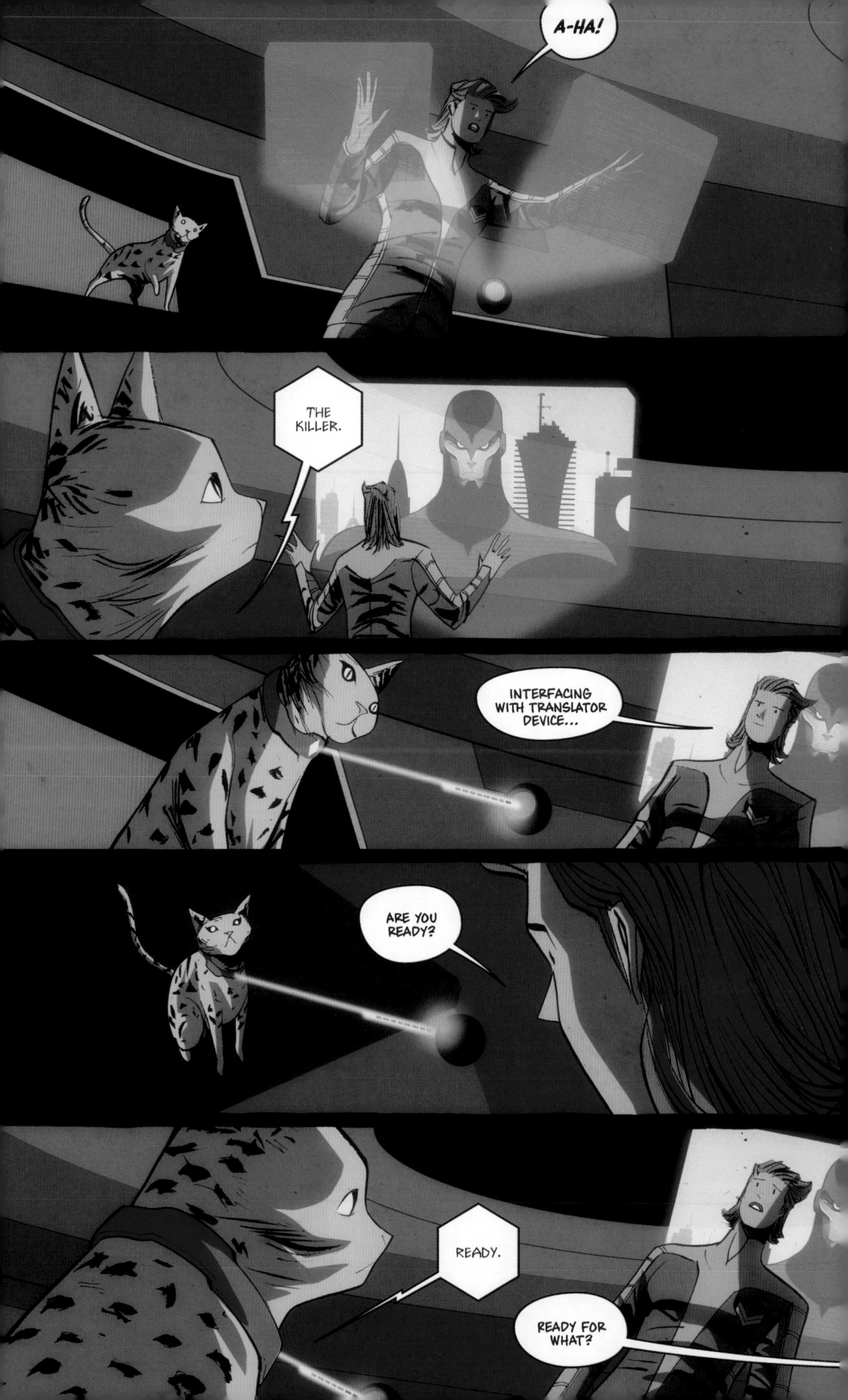
A-HA!
THE KILLER.
INTERFACING WITH TRANSLATOR DEVICE...
ARE YOU READY?
READY.
READY FOR WHAT?

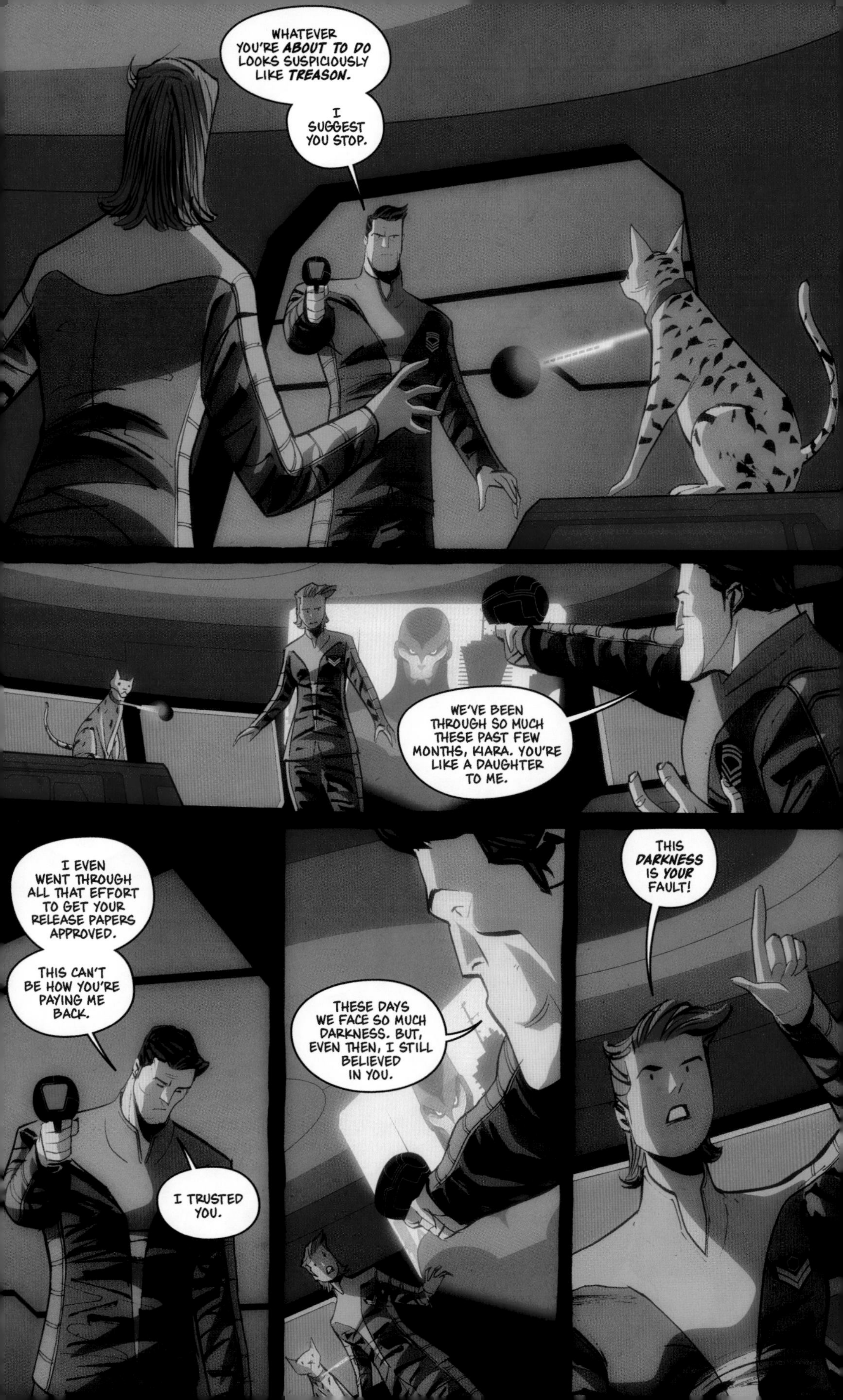
WHATEVER YOU'RE ABOUT TO DO LOOKS SUSPICIOUSLY LIKE TREASON.
I SUGGEST YOU STOP.
WE'VE BEEN THROUGH SO MUCH THESE PAST FEW MONTHS, KIARA. YOU'RE LIKE A DAUGHTER TO ME.
I EVEN WENT THROUGH ALL THAT EFFORT TO GET YOUR RELEASE PAPERS APPROVED.
THIS CAN'T BE HOW YOU'RE PAYING ME BACK.
I TRUSTED YOU.
THESE DAYS WE FACE SO MUCH DARKNESS. BUT, EVEN THEN, I STILL BELIEVED IN YOU.
THIS DARKNESS IS YOUR FAULT!

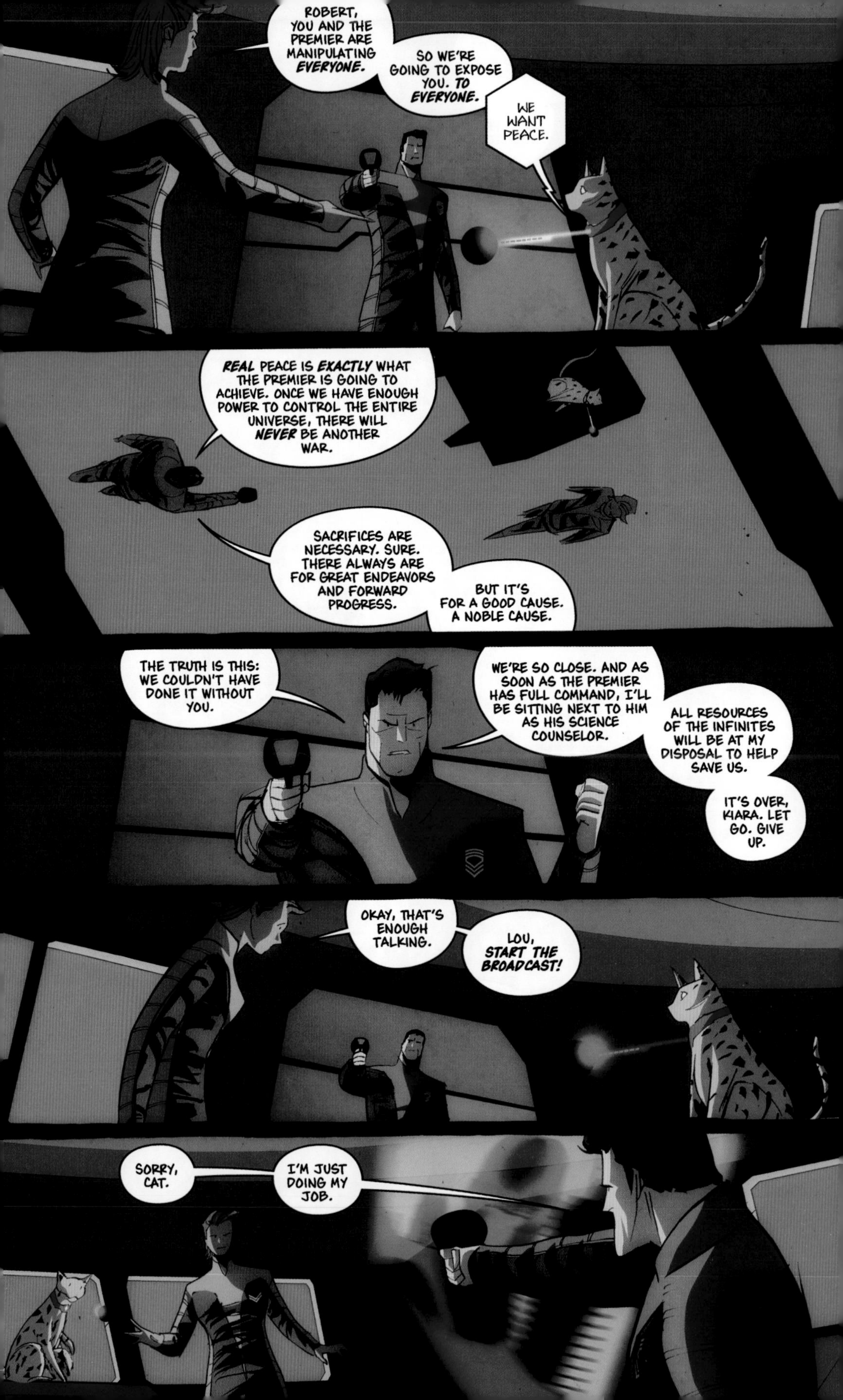
ROBERT, YOU AND THE PREMIER ARE MANIPULATING *EVERYONE.*
SO WE'RE GOING TO EXPOSE YOU. *TO EVERYONE.*
WE WANT PEACE.
REAL PEACE IS *EXACTLY* WHAT THE PREMIER IS GOING TO ACHIEVE. ONCE WE HAVE ENOUGH POWER TO CONTROL THE ENTIRE UNIVERSE, THERE WILL *NEVER* BE ANOTHER WAR.
SACRIFICES ARE NECESSARY. SURE. THERE ALWAYS ARE FOR GREAT ENDEAVORS AND FORWARD PROGRESS.
BUT IT'S FOR A GOOD CAUSE. A NOBLE CAUSE.
THE TRUTH IS THIS: WE COULDN'T HAVE DONE IT WITHOUT YOU.
WE'RE SO CLOSE. AND AS SOON AS THE PREMIER HAS FULL COMMAND, I'LL BE SITTING NEXT TO HIM AS HIS SCIENCE COUNSELOR.
ALL RESOURCES OF THE INFINITES WILL BE AT MY DISPOSAL TO HELP SAVE US.
IT'S OVER, KIARA. LET GO. GIVE UP.
OKAY, THAT'S ENOUGH TALKING.
LOU, *START THE BROADCAST!*
SORRY, CAT.
I'M JUST DOING MY JOB.

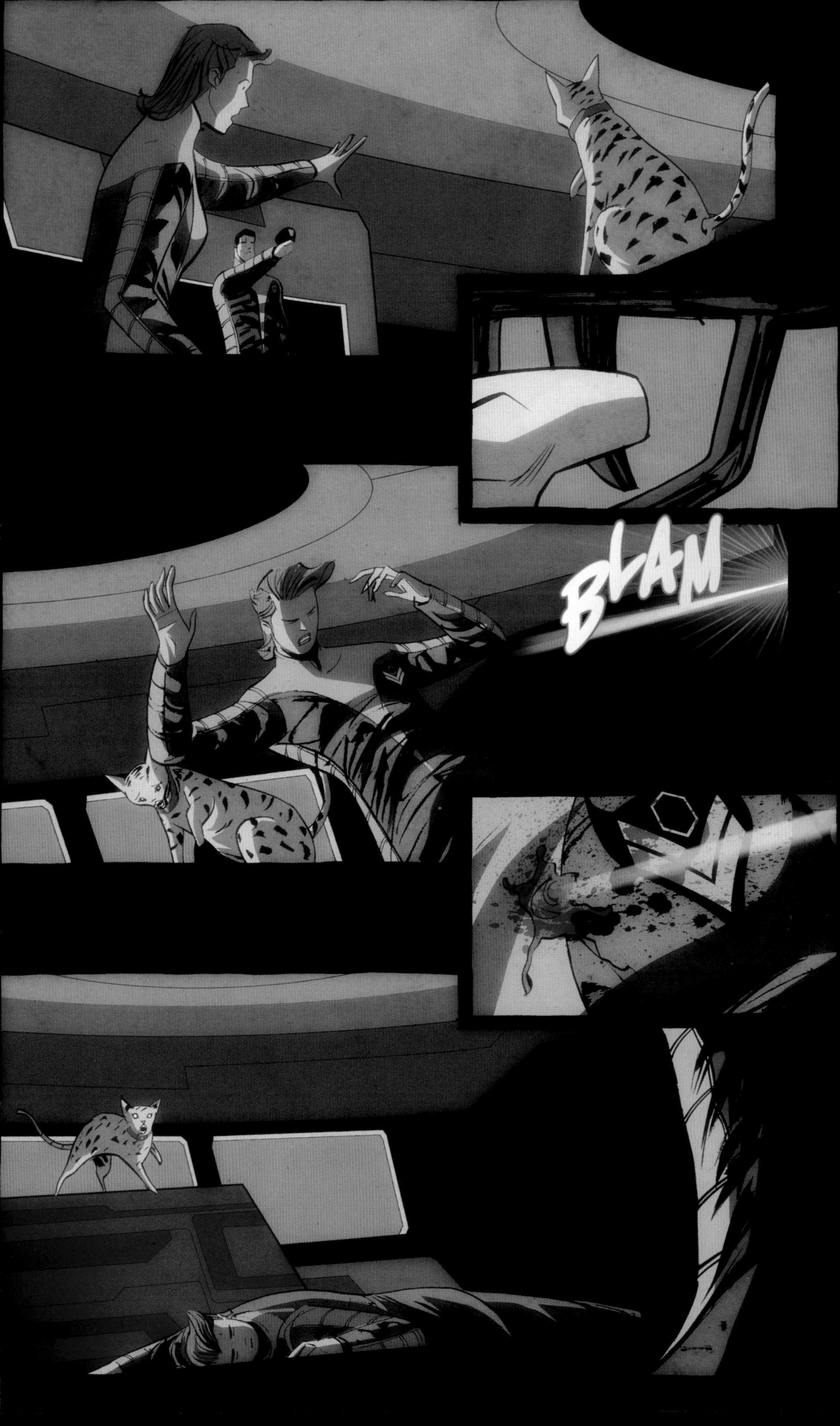
BLAM

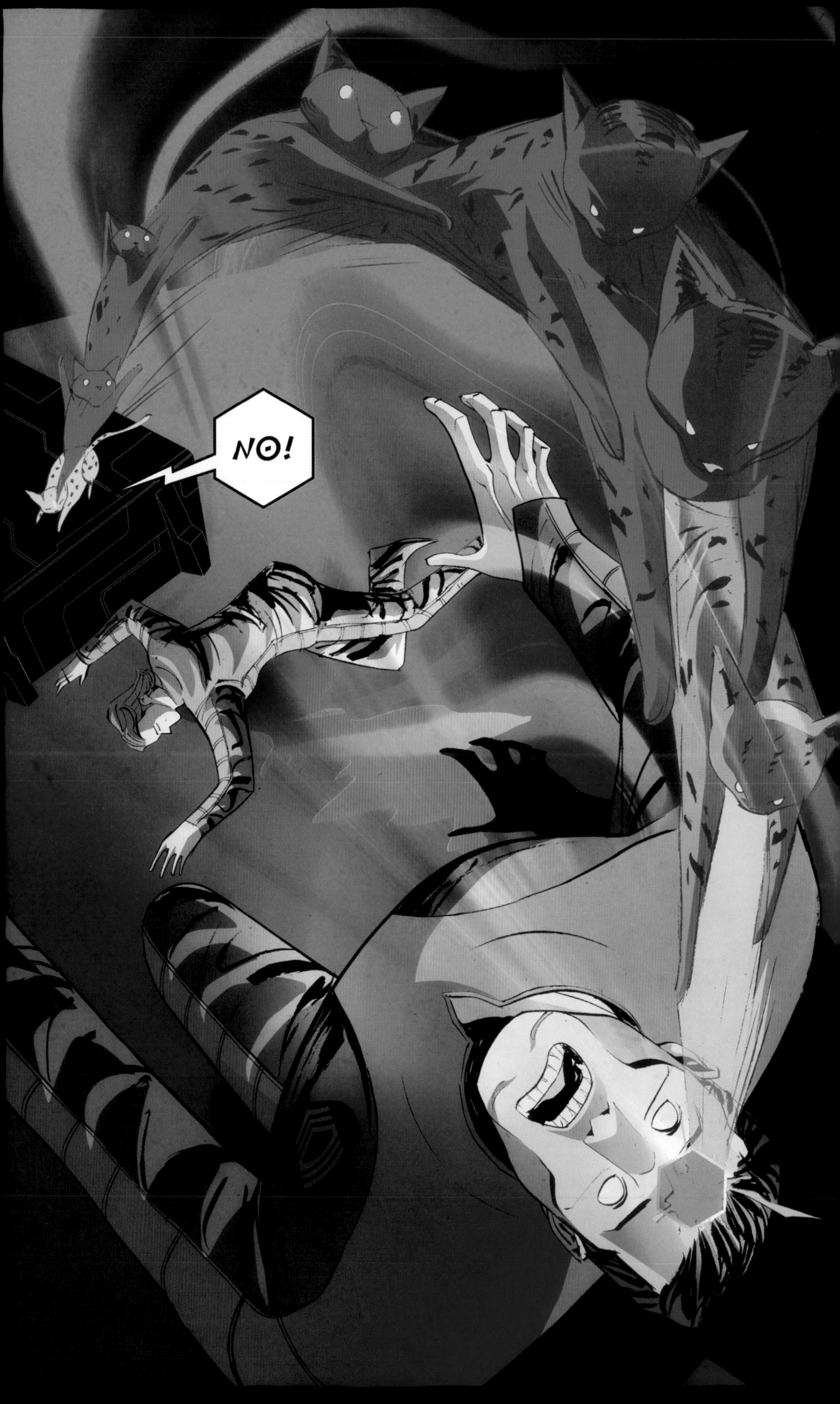
NO!

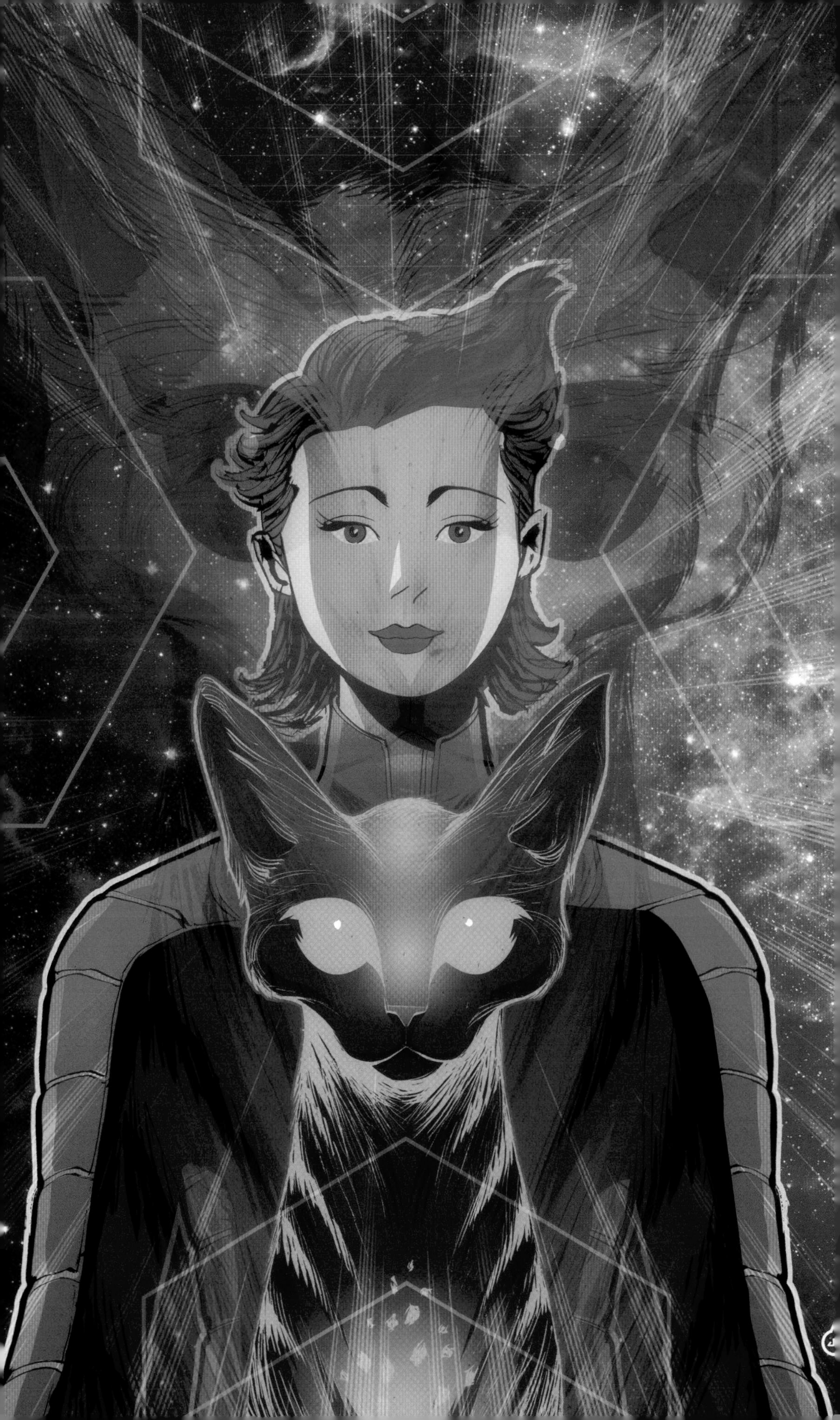

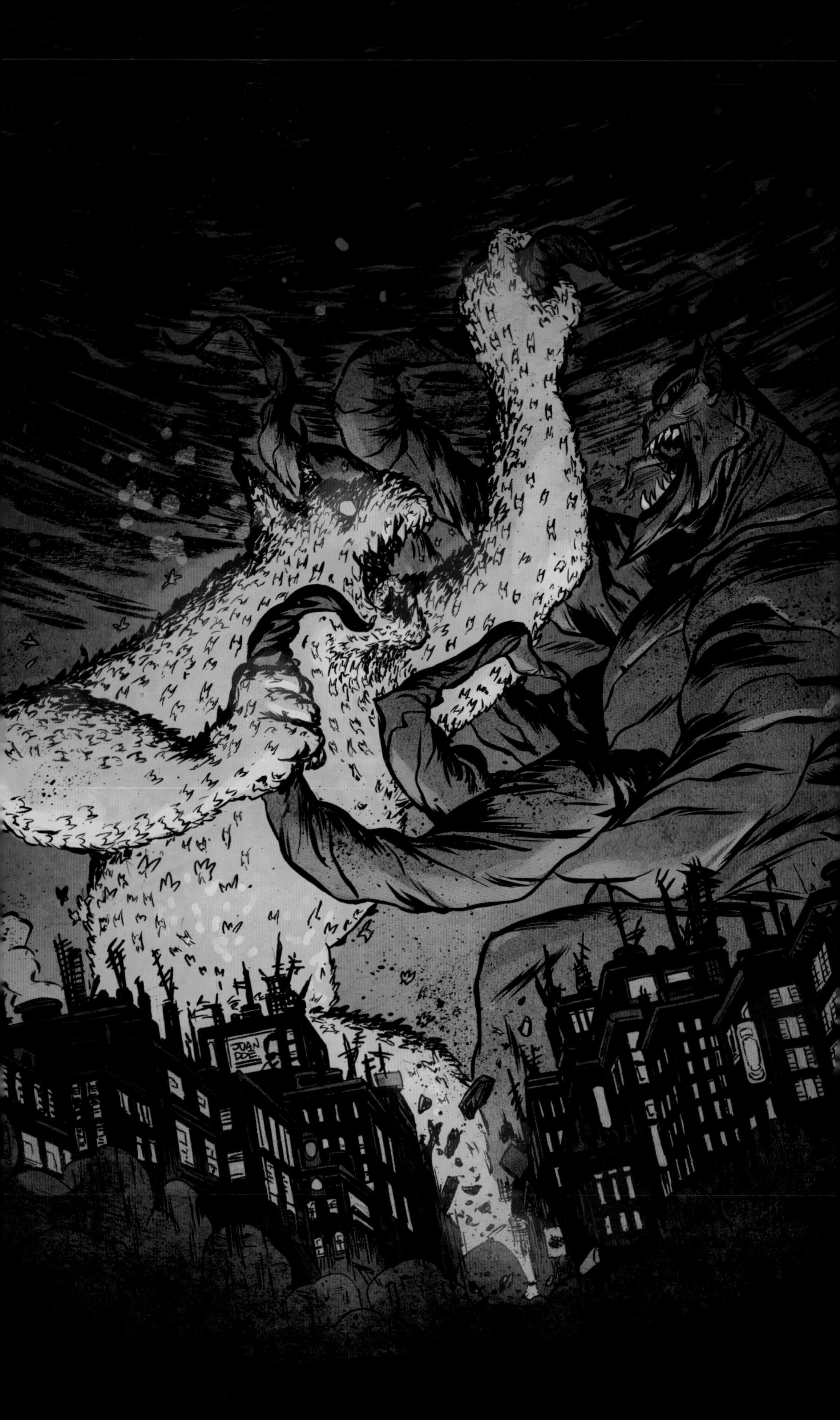

JOAN DOE

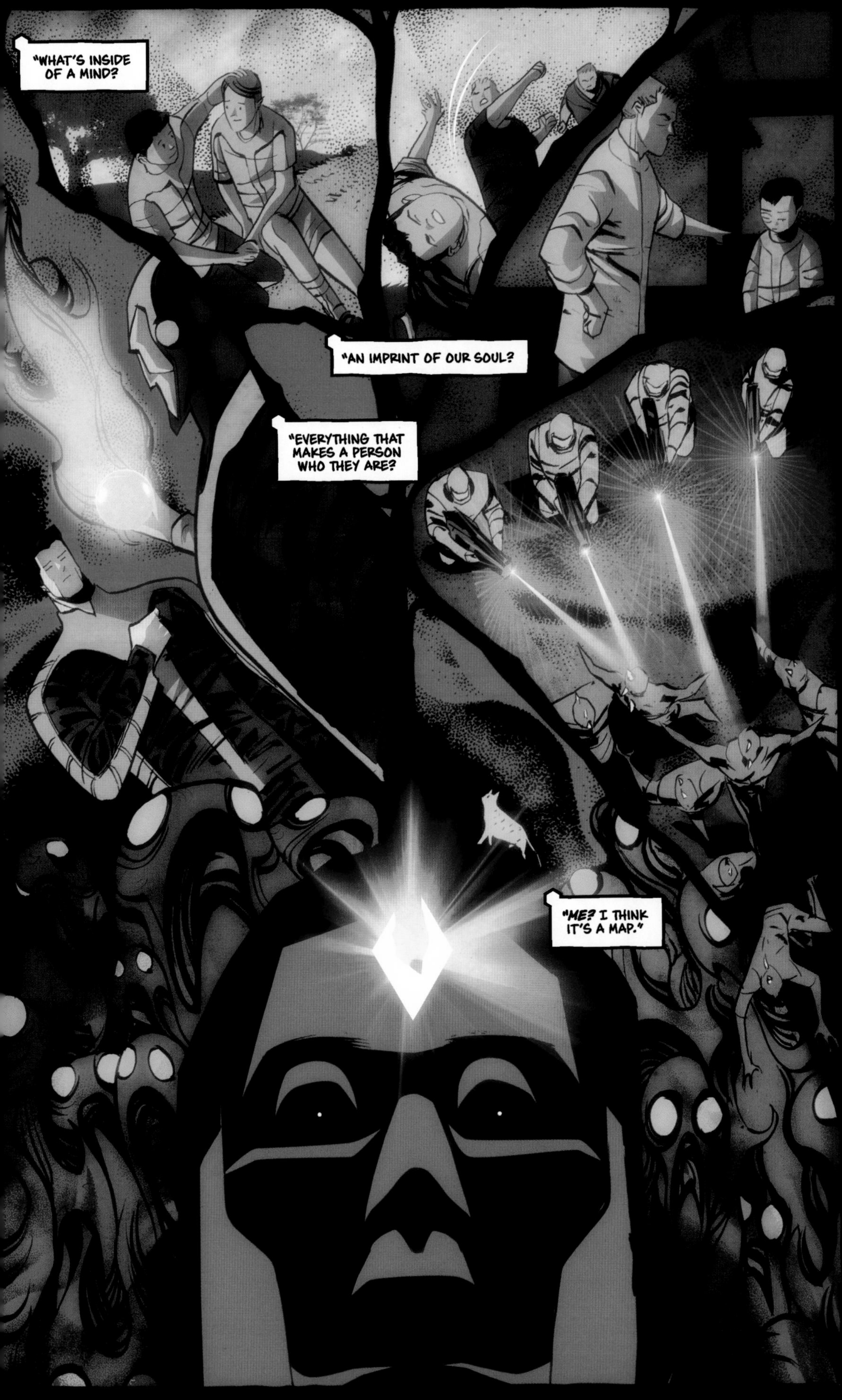
"WHAT'S INSIDE OF A MIND?
"AN IMPRINT OF OUR SOUL?
"EVERYTHING THAT MAKES A PERSON WHO THEY ARE?
"*ME?* I THINK IT'S A MAP."

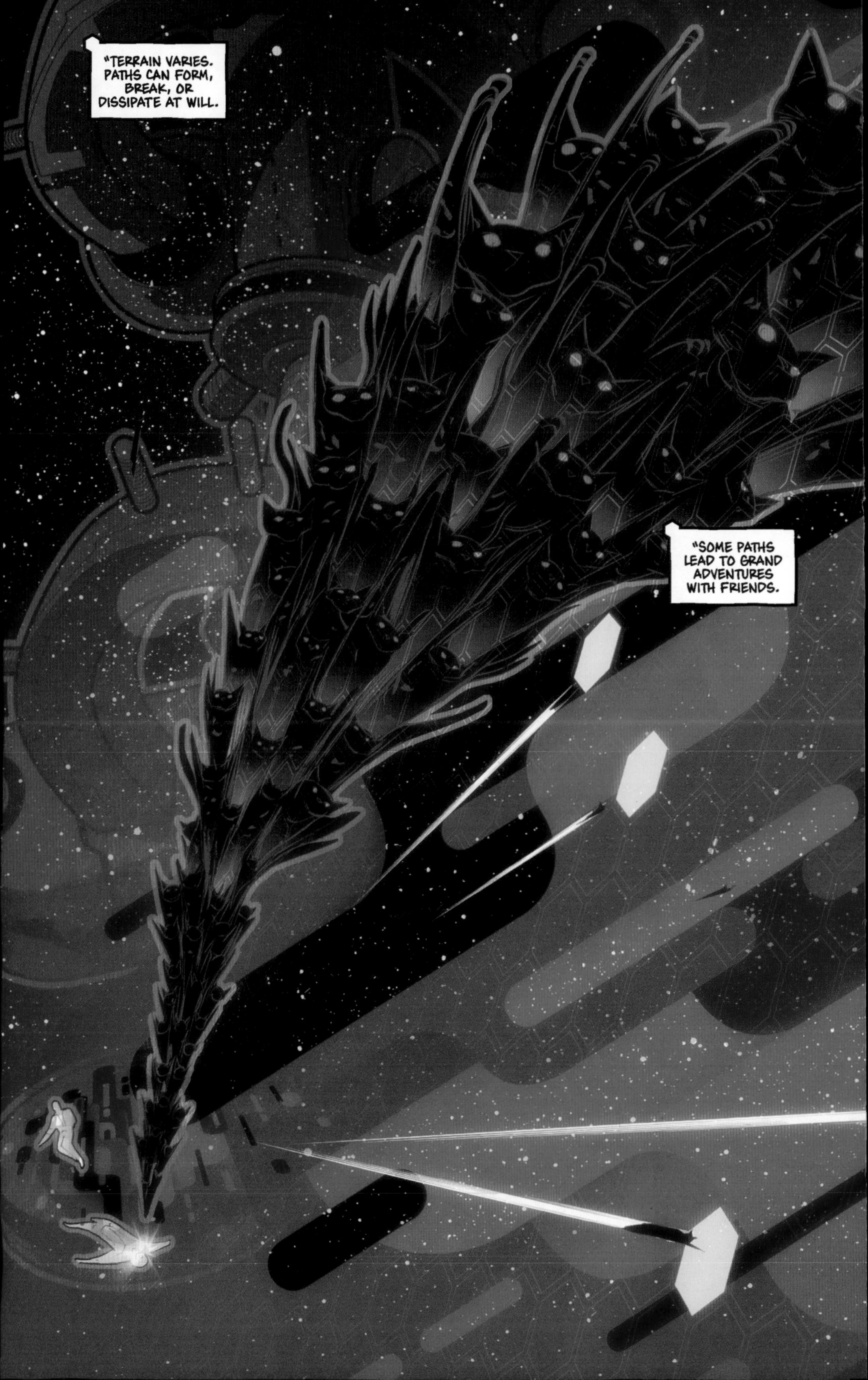
"TERRAIN VARIES. PATHS CAN FORM, BREAK, OR DISSIPATE AT WILL.
"SOME PATHS LEAD TO GRAND ADVENTURES WITH FRIENDS.

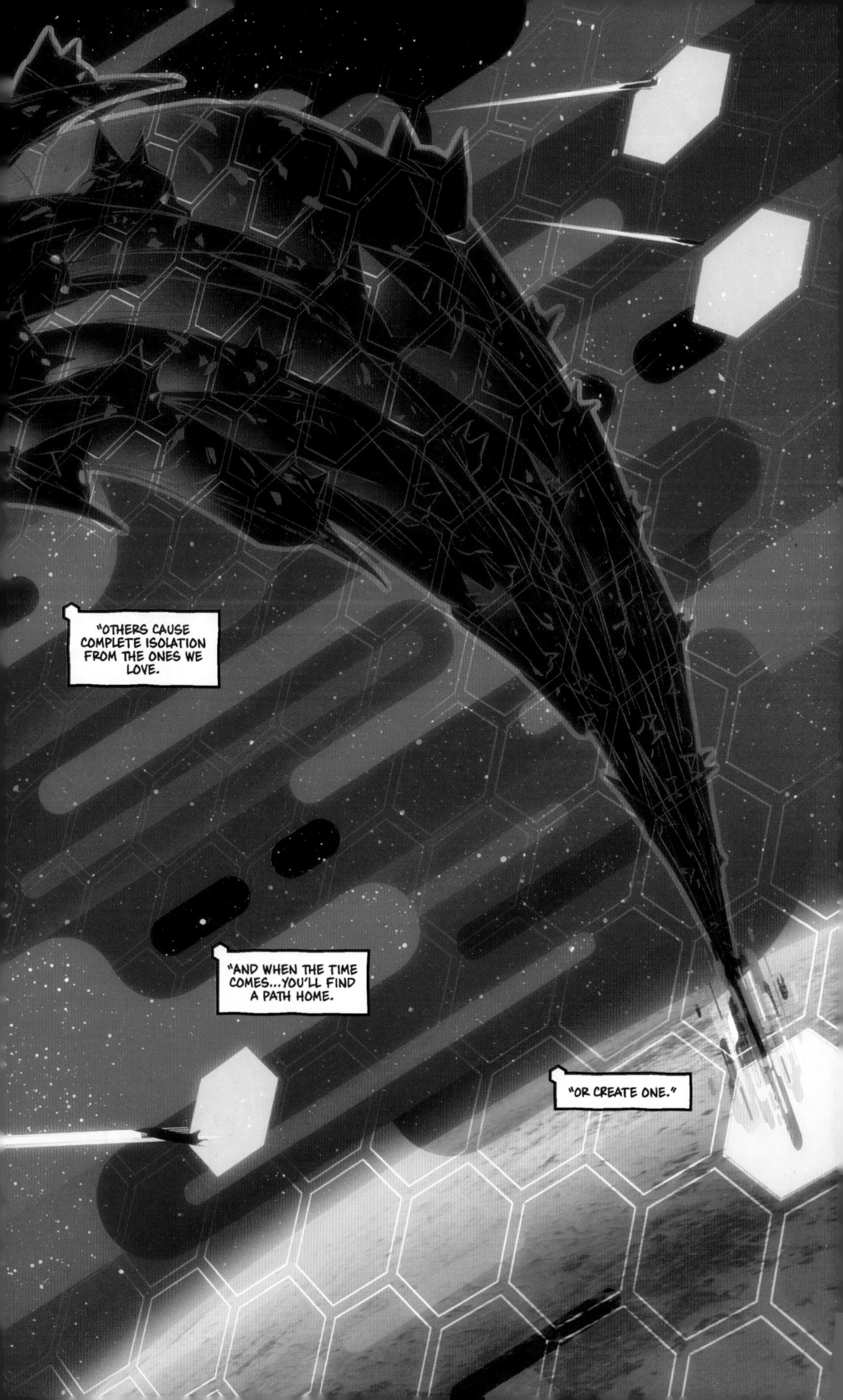
"OTHERS CAUSE COMPLETE ISOLATION FROM THE ONES WE LOVE.
"AND WHEN THE TIME COMES...YOU'LL FIND A PATH HOME.
"OR CREATE ONE."

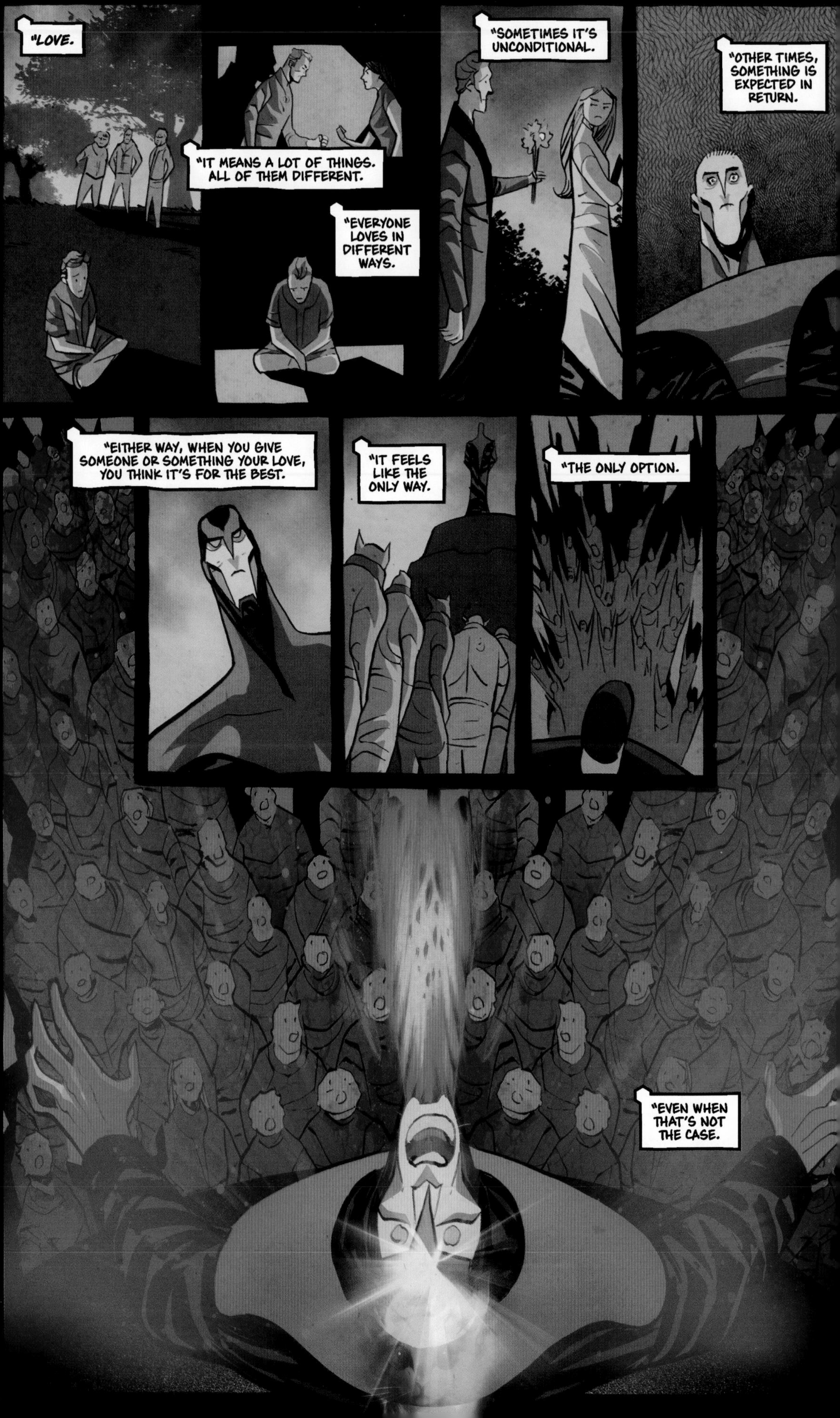
"LOVE.
"IT MEANS A LOT OF THINGS. ALL OF THEM DIFFERENT.
"EVERYONE LOVES IN DIFFERENT WAYS.
"SOMETIMES IT'S UNCONDITIONAL.
"OTHER TIMES, SOMETHING IS EXPECTED IN RETURN.
"EITHER WAY, WHEN YOU GIVE SOMEONE OR SOMETHING YOUR LOVE, YOU THINK IT'S FOR THE BEST.
"IT FEELS LIKE THE ONLY WAY.
"THE ONLY OPTION.
"EVEN WHEN THAT'S NOT THE CASE.

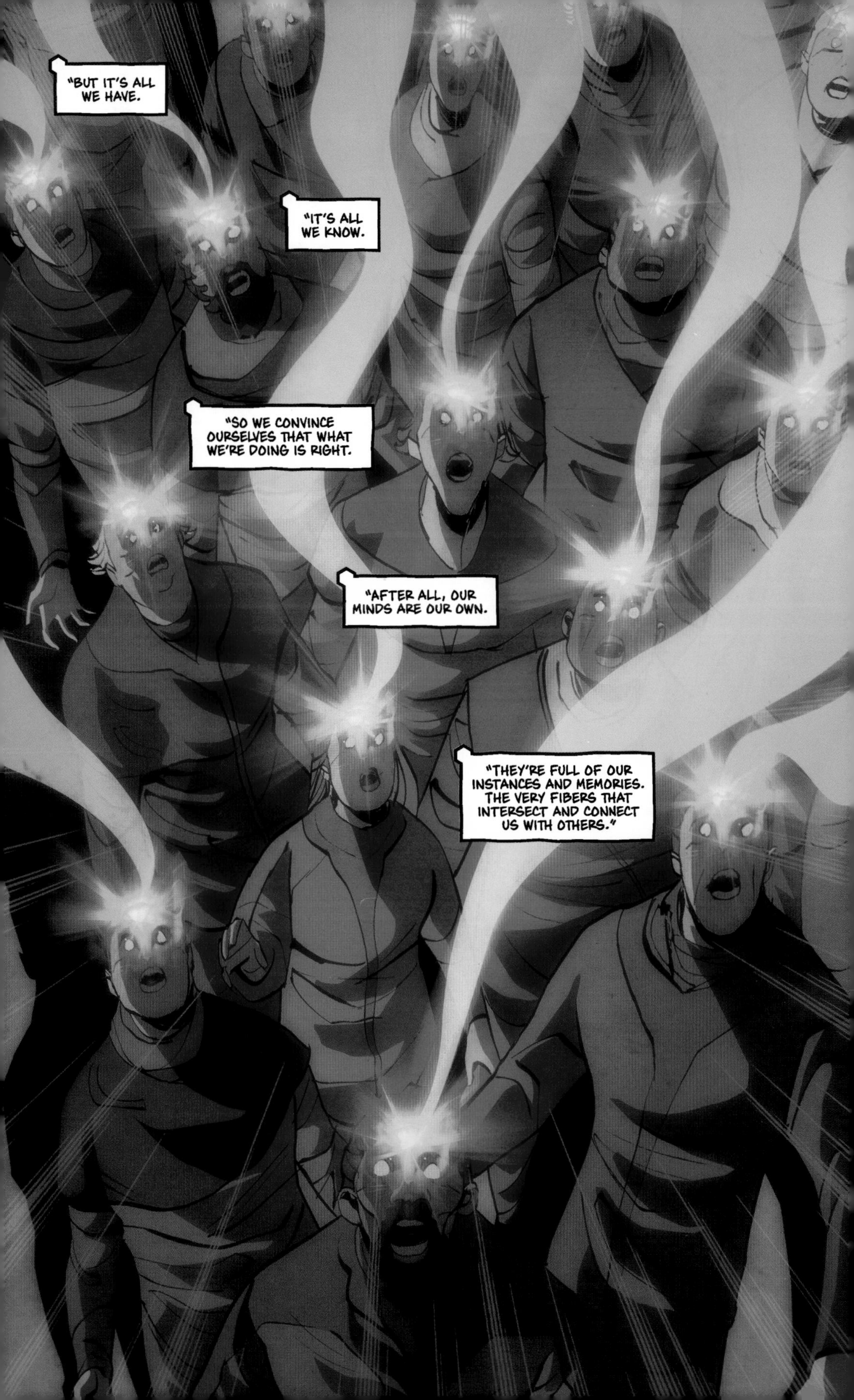
"BUT IT'S ALL WE HAVE.
"IT'S ALL WE KNOW.
"SO WE CONVINCE OURSELVES THAT WHAT WE'RE DOING IS RIGHT.
"AFTER ALL, OUR MINDS ARE OUR OWN.
"THEY'RE FULL OF OUR INSTANCES AND MEMORIES. THE VERY FIBERS THAT INTERSECT AND CONNECT US WITH OTHERS."

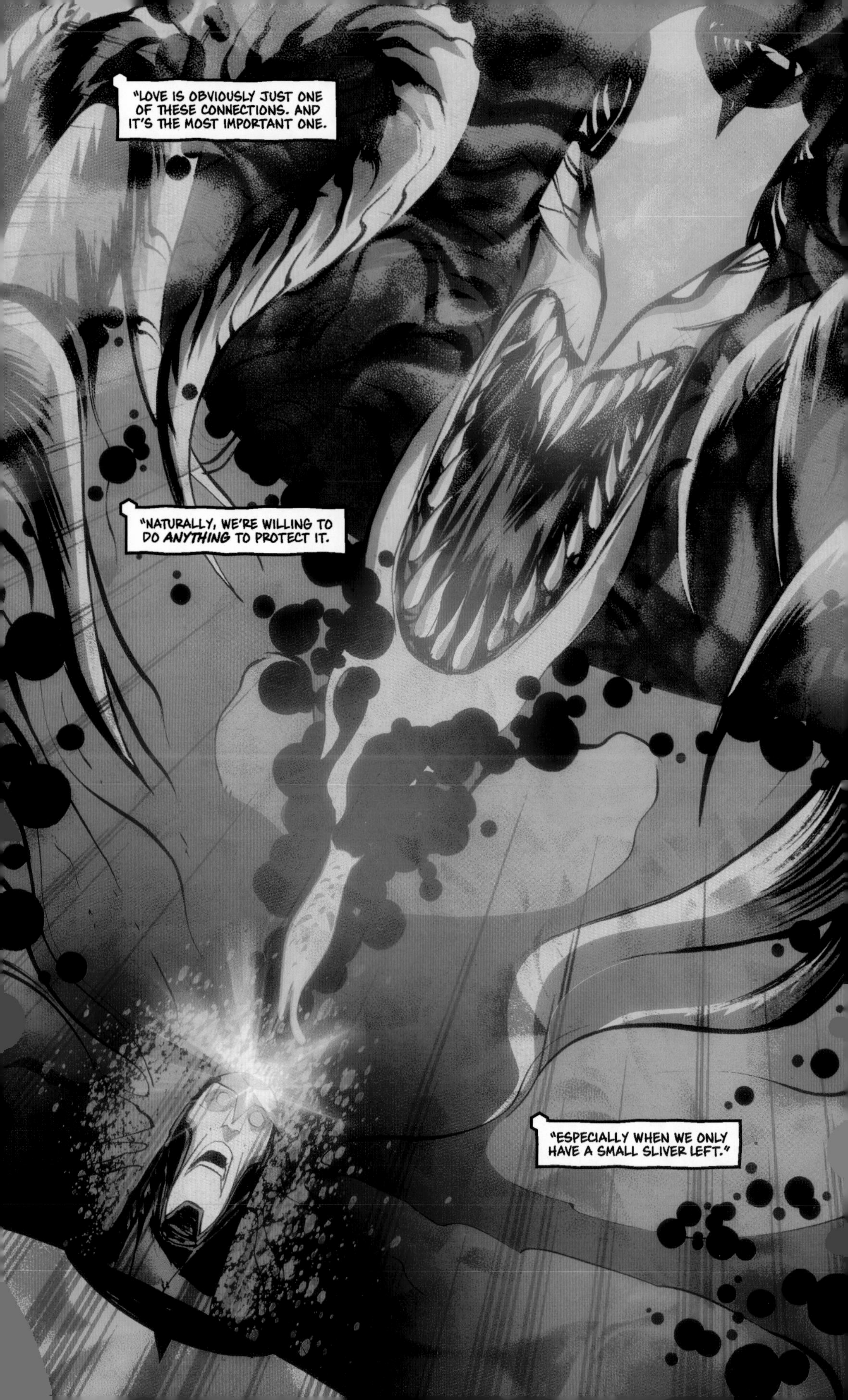
"LOVE IS OBVIOUSLY JUST ONE OF THESE CONNECTIONS. AND IT'S THE MOST IMPORTANT ONE.
"NATURALLY, WE'RE WILLING TO DO *ANYTHING* TO PROTECT IT.
"ESPECIALLY WHEN WE ONLY HAVE A SMALL SLIVER LEFT."

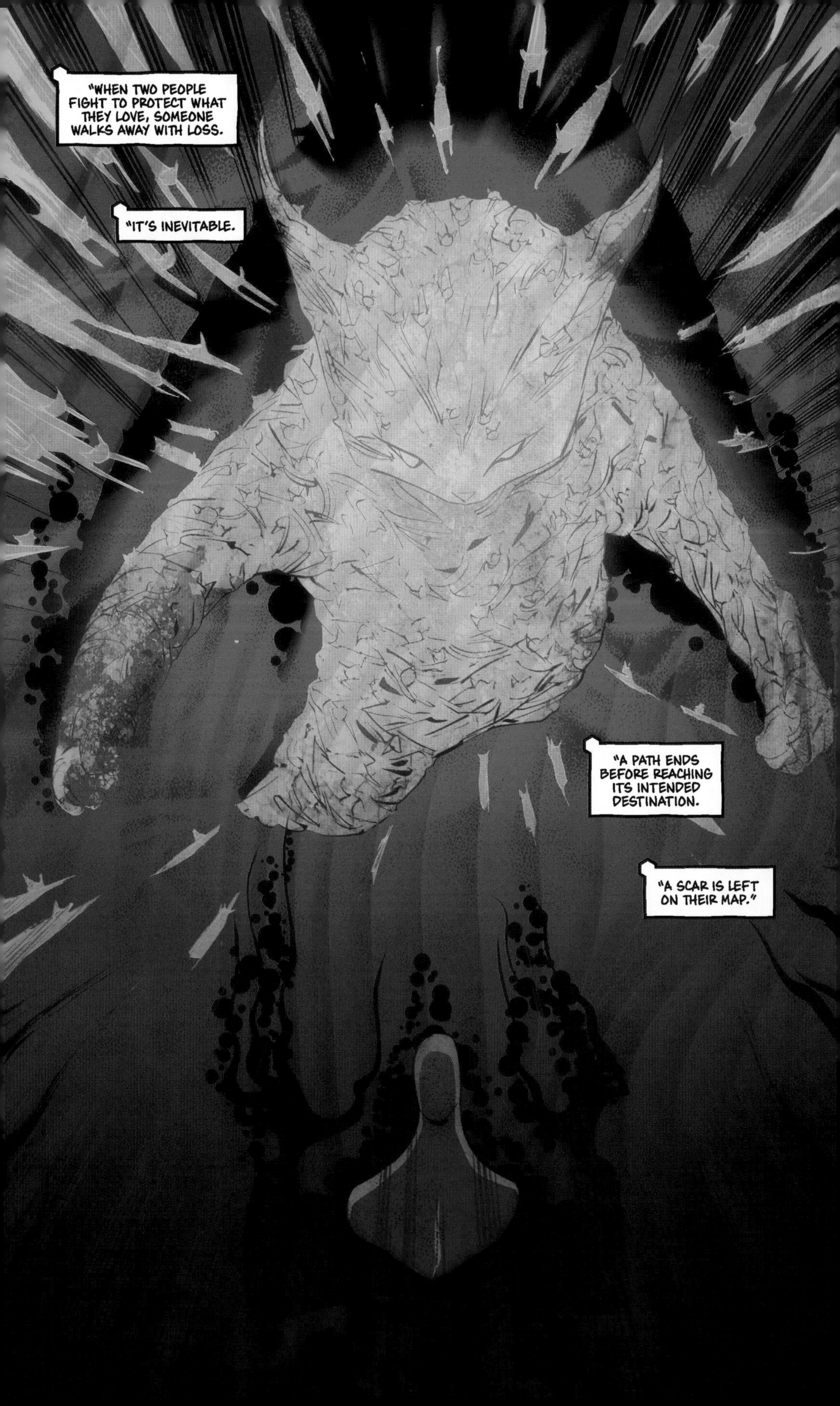
"WHEN TWO PEOPLE FIGHT TO PROTECT WHAT THEY LOVE, SOMEONE WALKS AWAY WITH LOSS.
"IT'S INEVITABLE.
"A PATH ENDS BEFORE REACHING ITS INTENDED DESTINATION.
"A SCAR IS LEFT ON THEIR MAP."

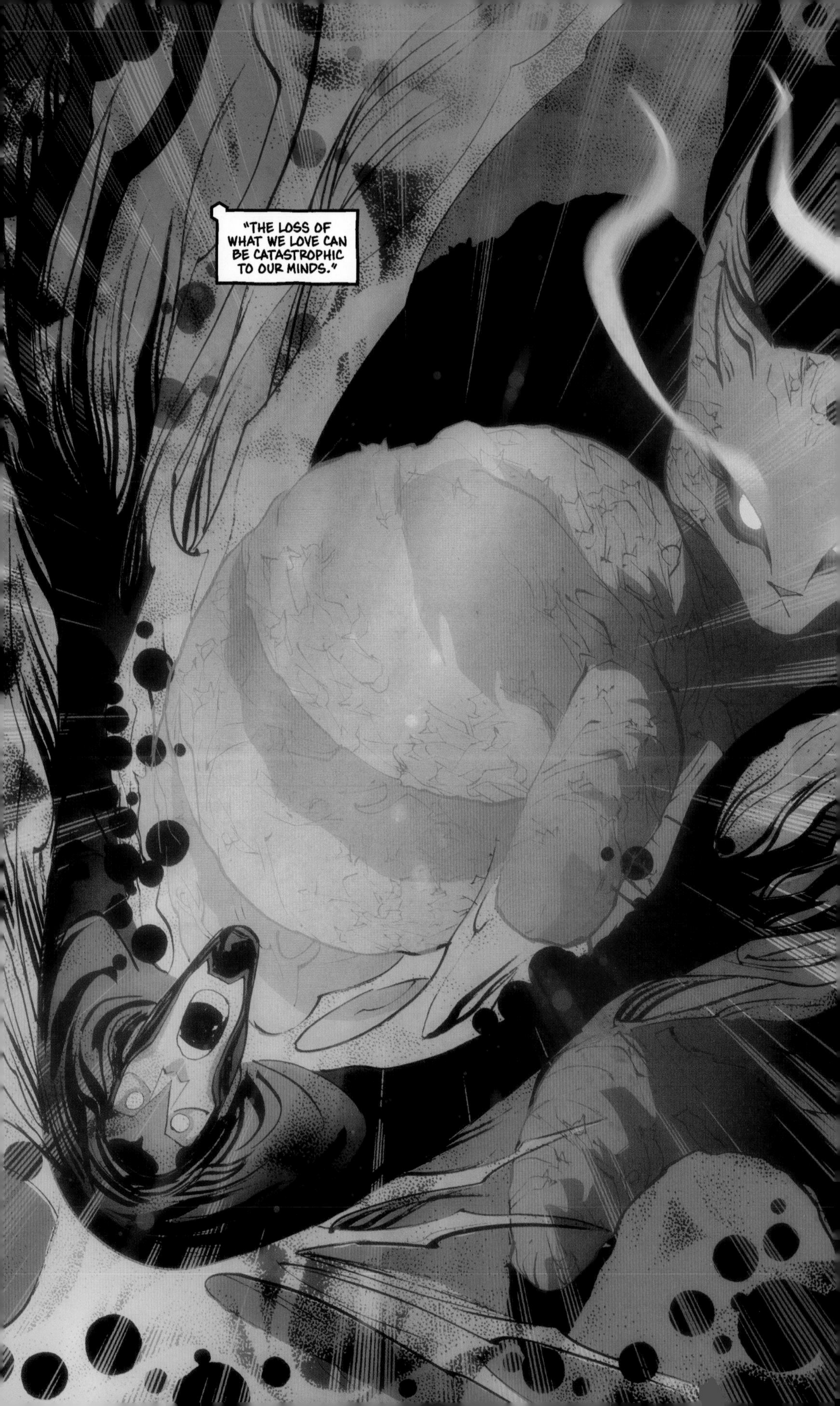
"THE LOSS OF WHAT WE LOVE CAN BE CATASTROPHIC TO OUR MINDS."

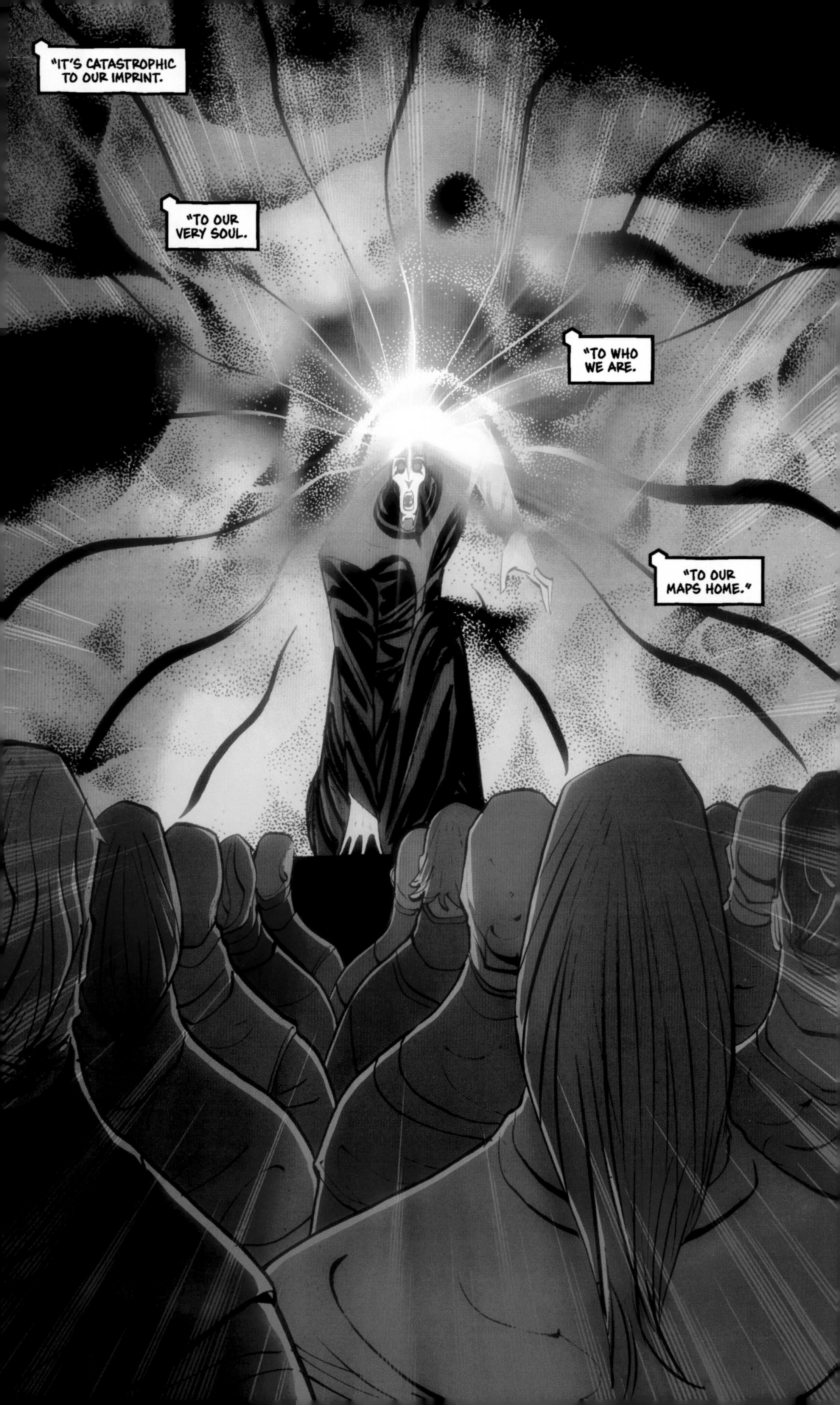
"IT'S CATASTROPHIC TO OUR IMPRINT.
"TO OUR VERY SOUL.
"TO WHO WE ARE.
"TO OUR MAPS HOME."

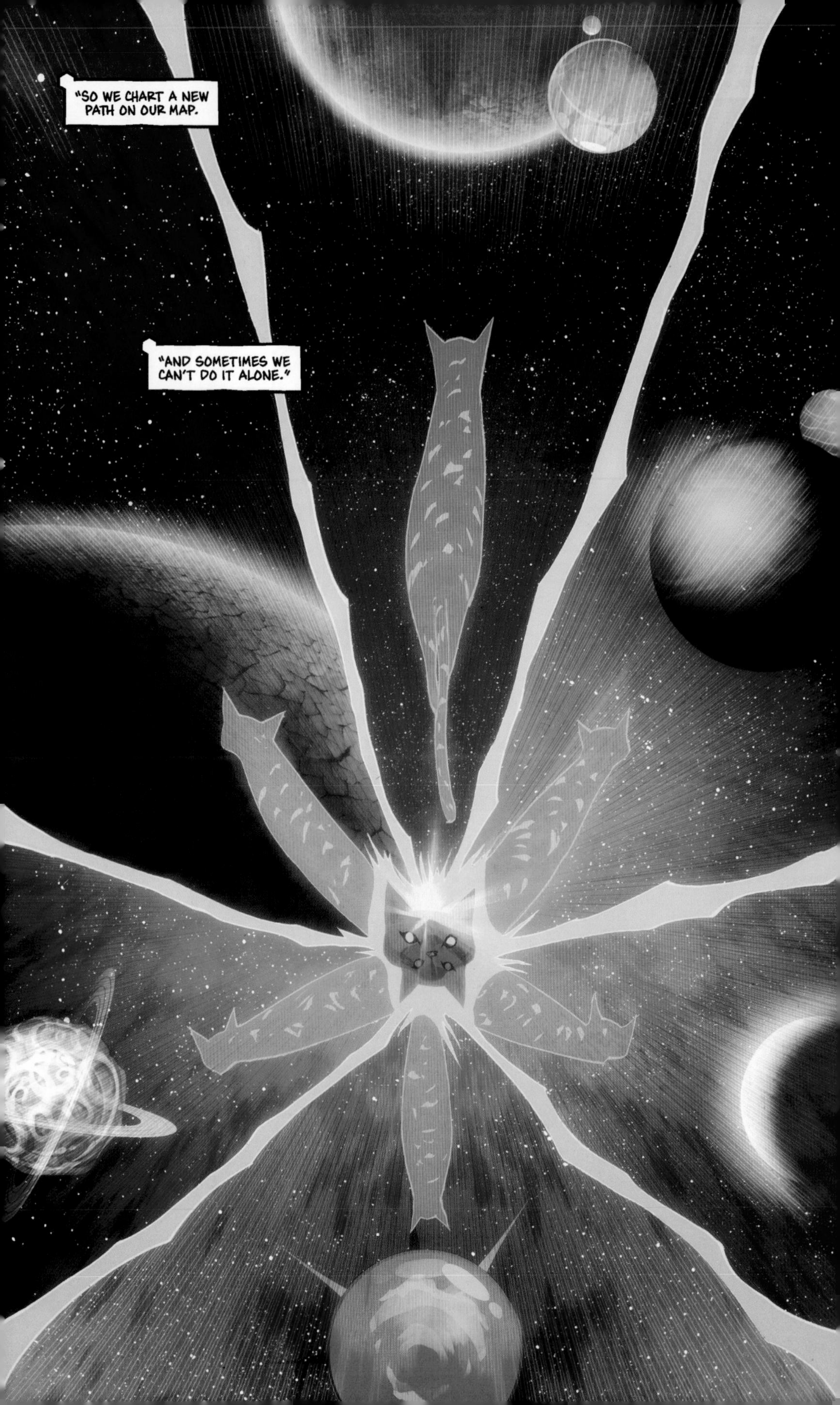
"SO WE CHART A NEW PATH ON OUR MAP.
"AND SOMETIMES WE CAN'T DO IT ALONE."

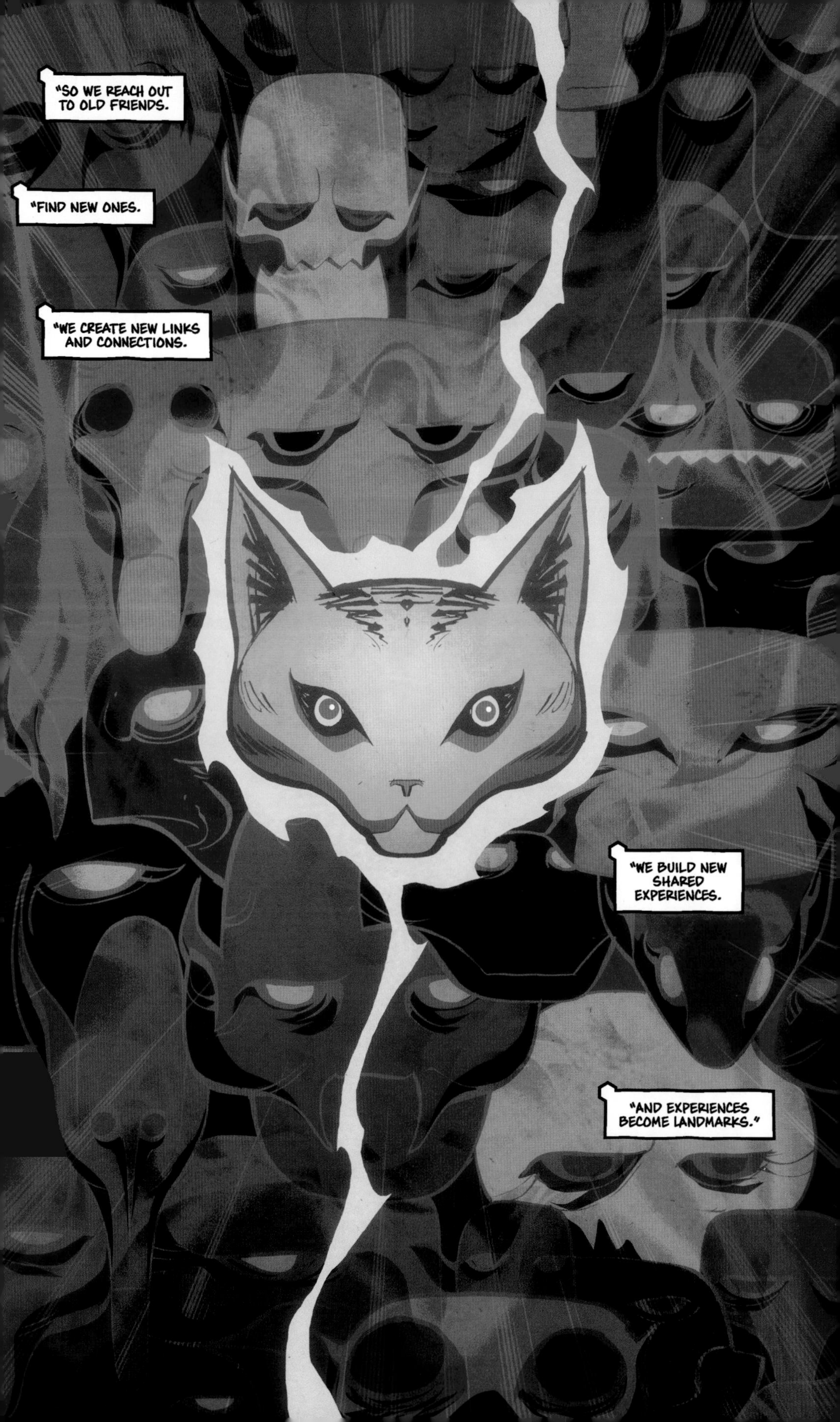
"SO WE REACH OUT TO OLD FRIENDS.
"FIND NEW ONES.
"WE CREATE NEW LINKS AND CONNECTIONS.
"WE BUILD NEW SHARED EXPERIENCES.
"AND EXPERIENCES BECOME LANDMARKS."

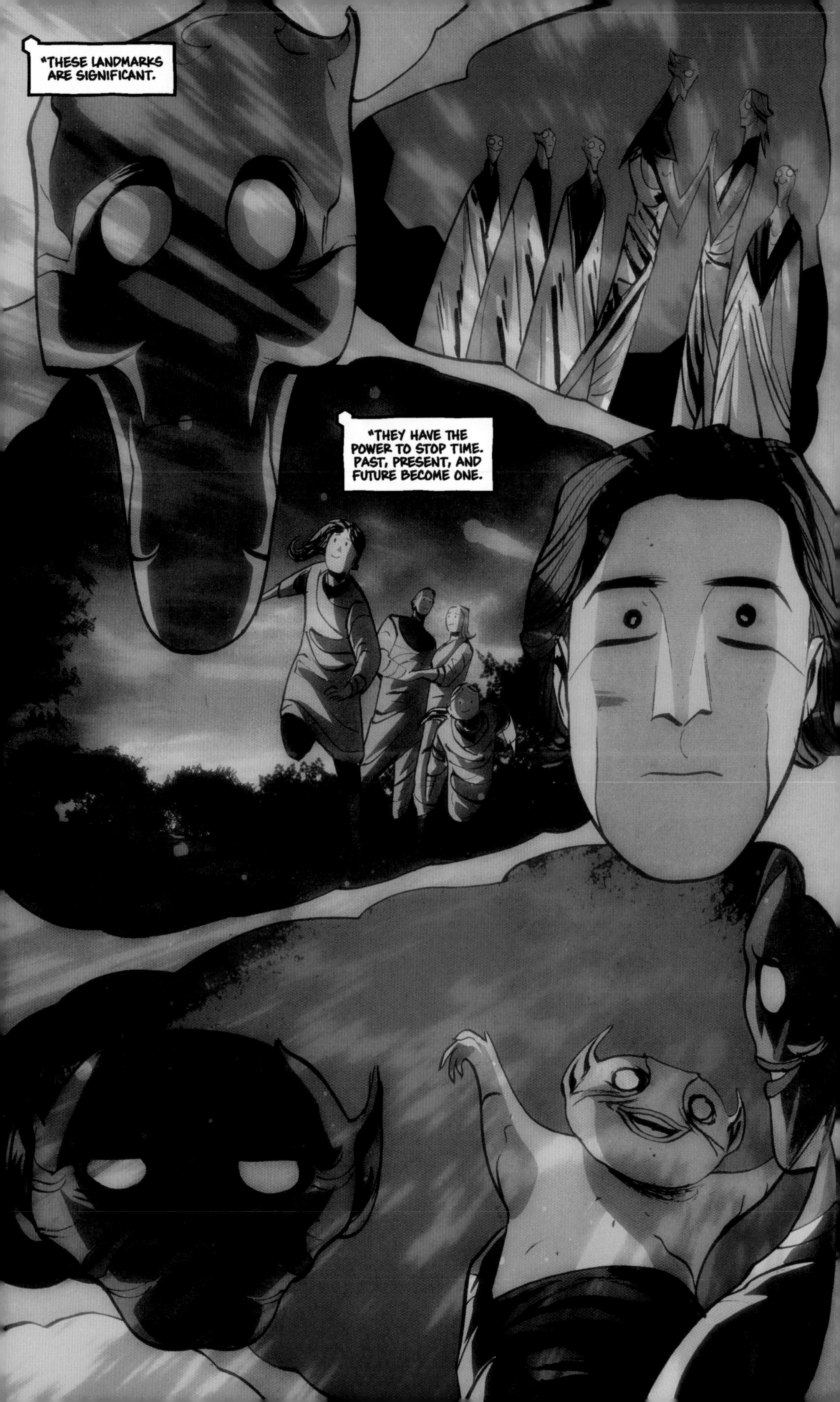
"THESE LANDMARKS ARE SIGNIFICANT.
"THEY HAVE THE POWER TO STOP TIME. PAST, PRESENT, AND FUTURE BECOME ONE.

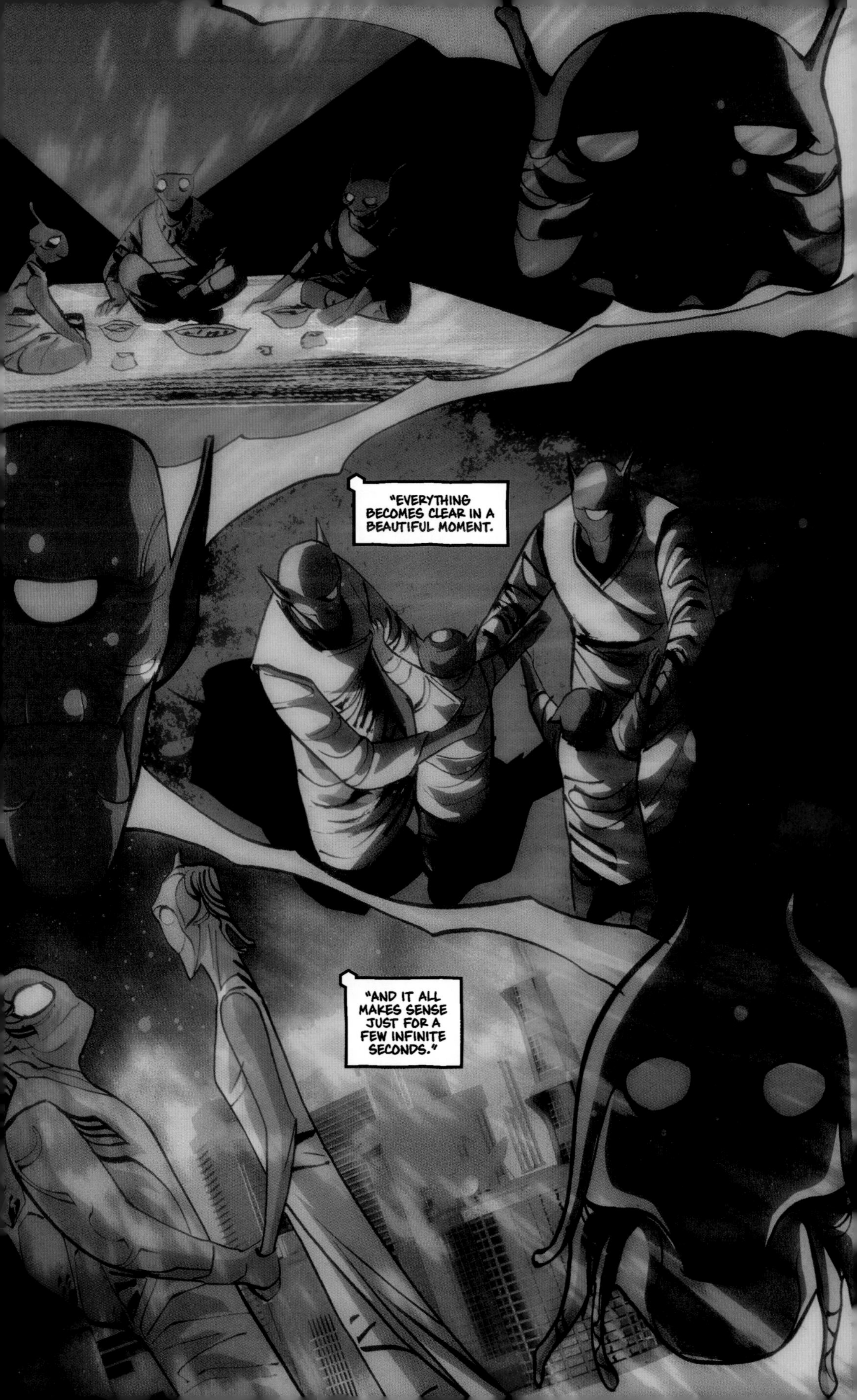
"EVERYTHING BECOMES CLEAR IN A BEAUTIFUL MOMENT.
"AND IT ALL MAKES SENSE JUST FOR A FEW INFINITE SECONDS."

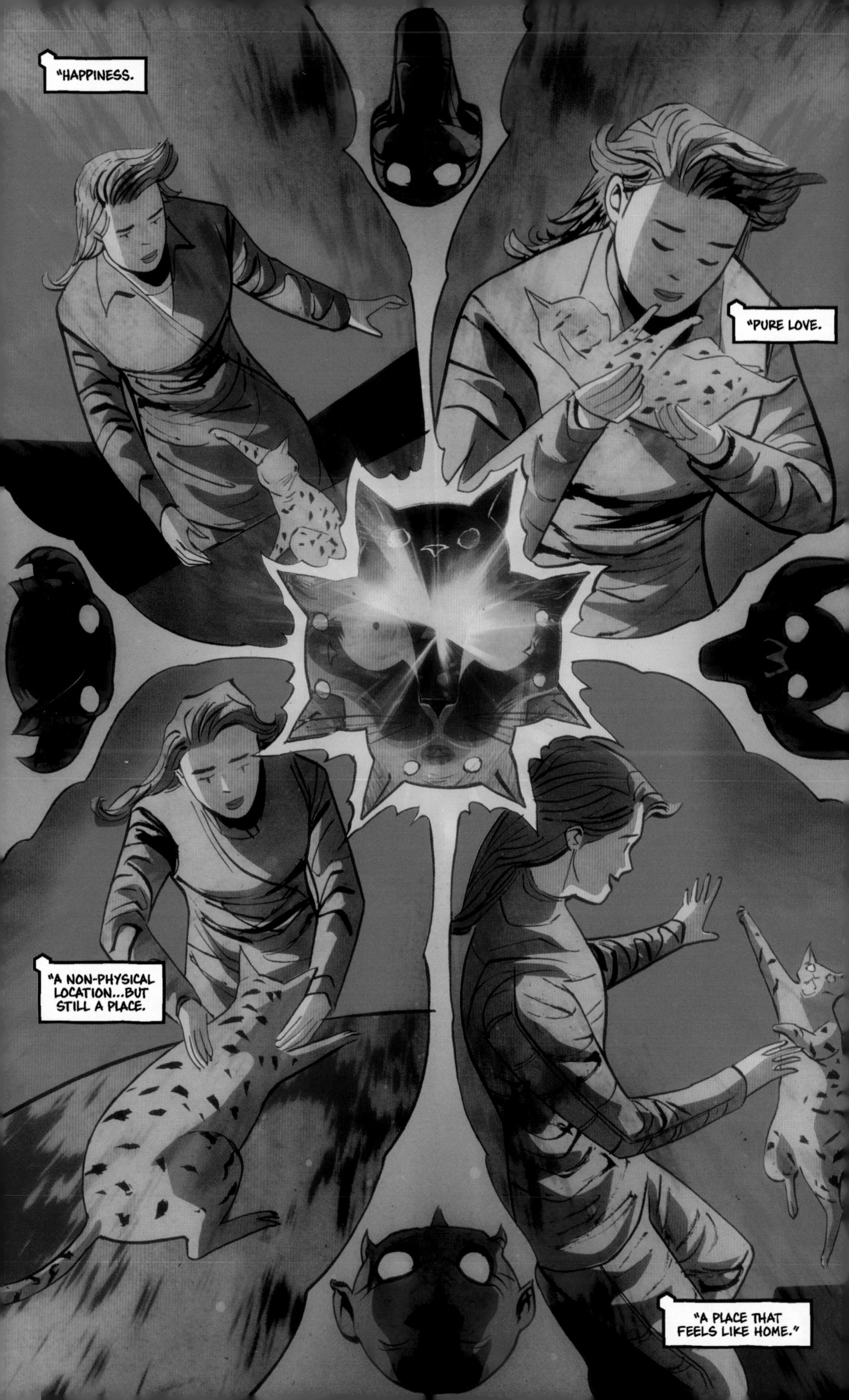
"HAPPINESS.
"PURE LOVE.
"A NON-PHYSICAL LOCATION...BUT STILL A PLACE.
"A PLACE THAT FEELS LIKE HOME."

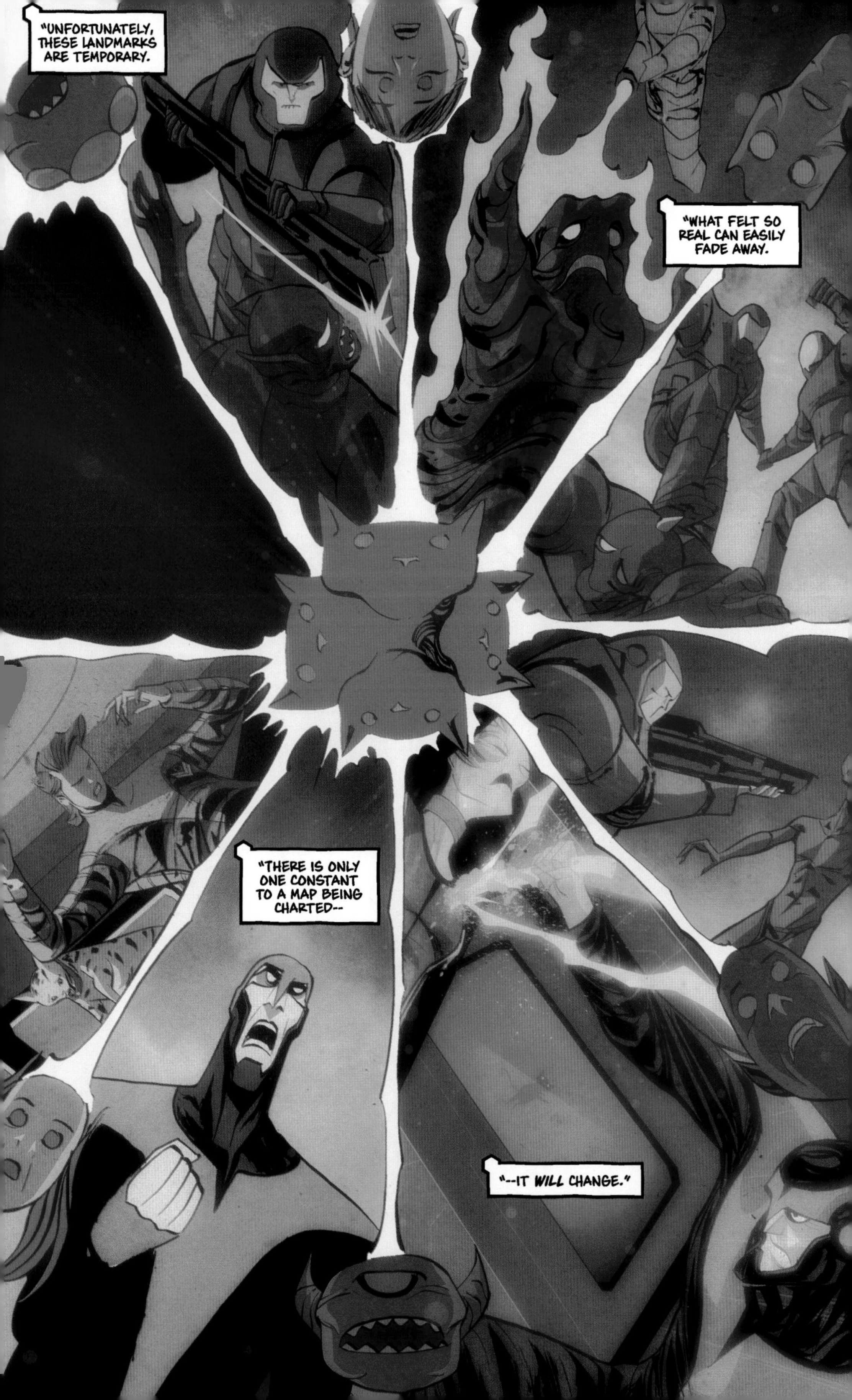
"UNFORTUNATELY, THESE LANDMARKS ARE TEMPORARY.
"WHAT FELT SO REAL CAN EASILY FADE AWAY.
"THERE IS ONLY ONE CONSTANT TO A MAP BEING CHARTED--
"--IT *WILL* CHANGE."

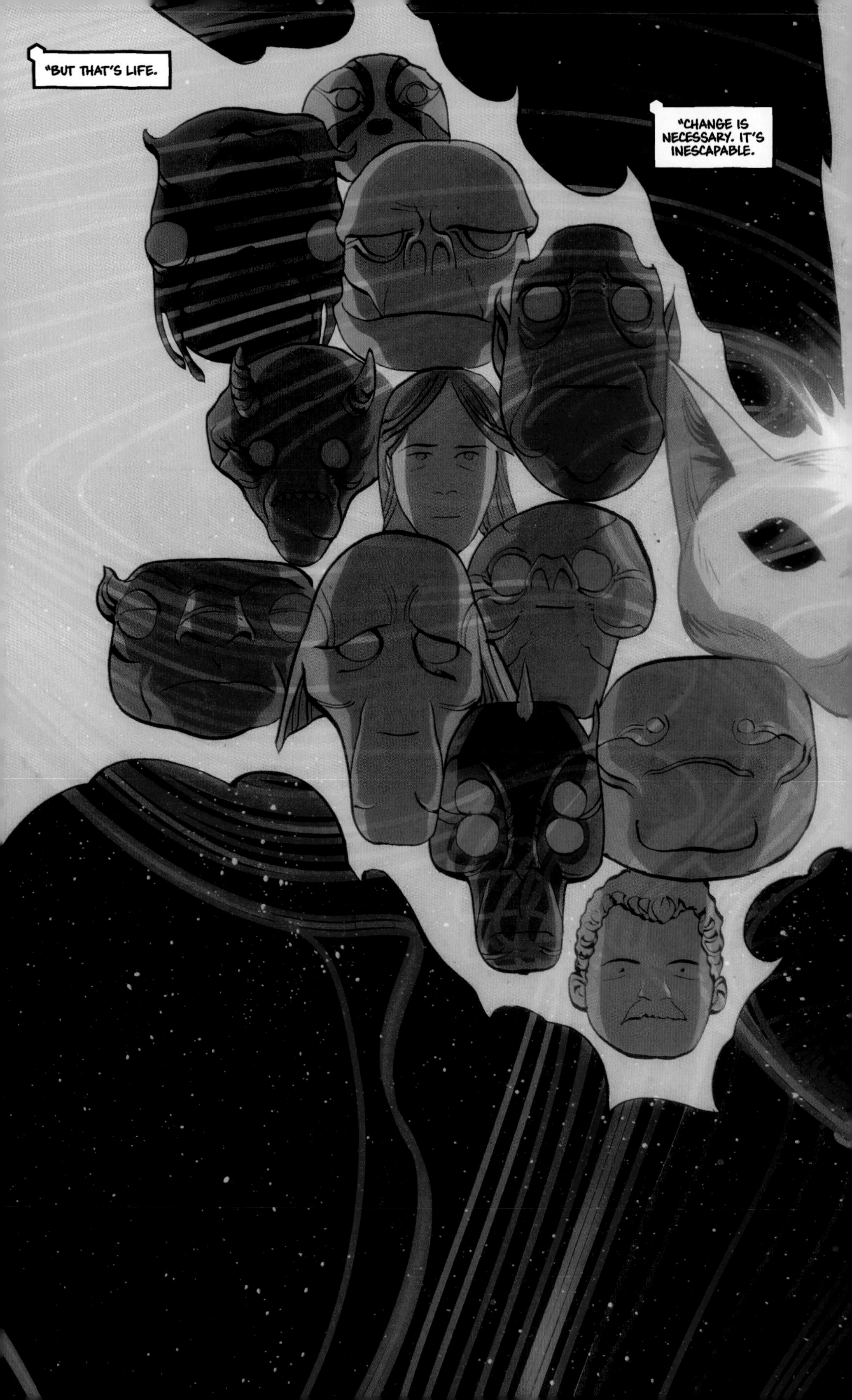
"BUT THAT'S LIFE.
"CHANGE IS NECESSARY. IT'S INESCAPABLE.

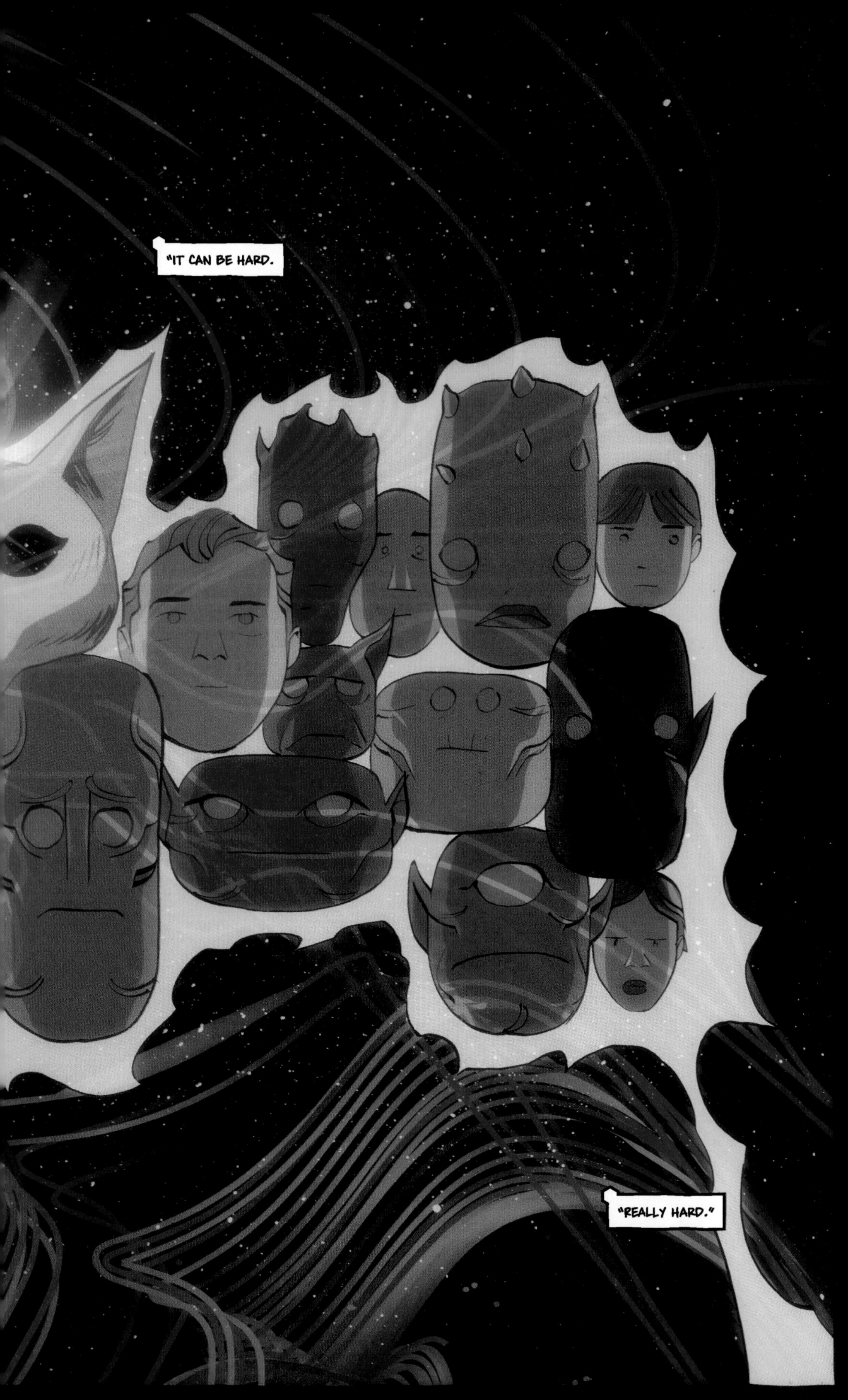
"IT CAN BE HARD.
"REALLY HARD."

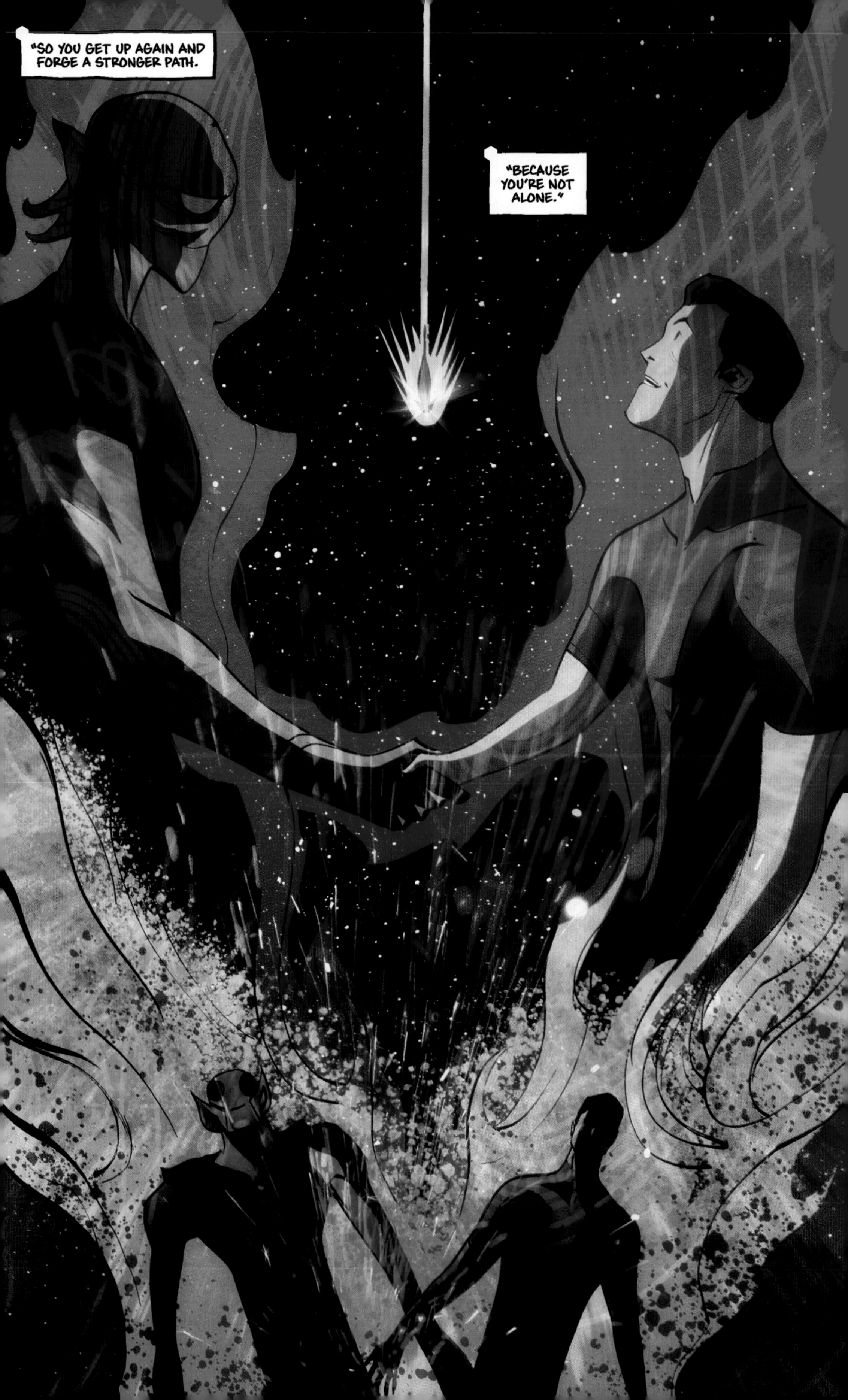
"SO YOU GET UP AGAIN AND FORGE A STRONGER PATH.
"BECAUSE YOU'RE NOT ALONE."

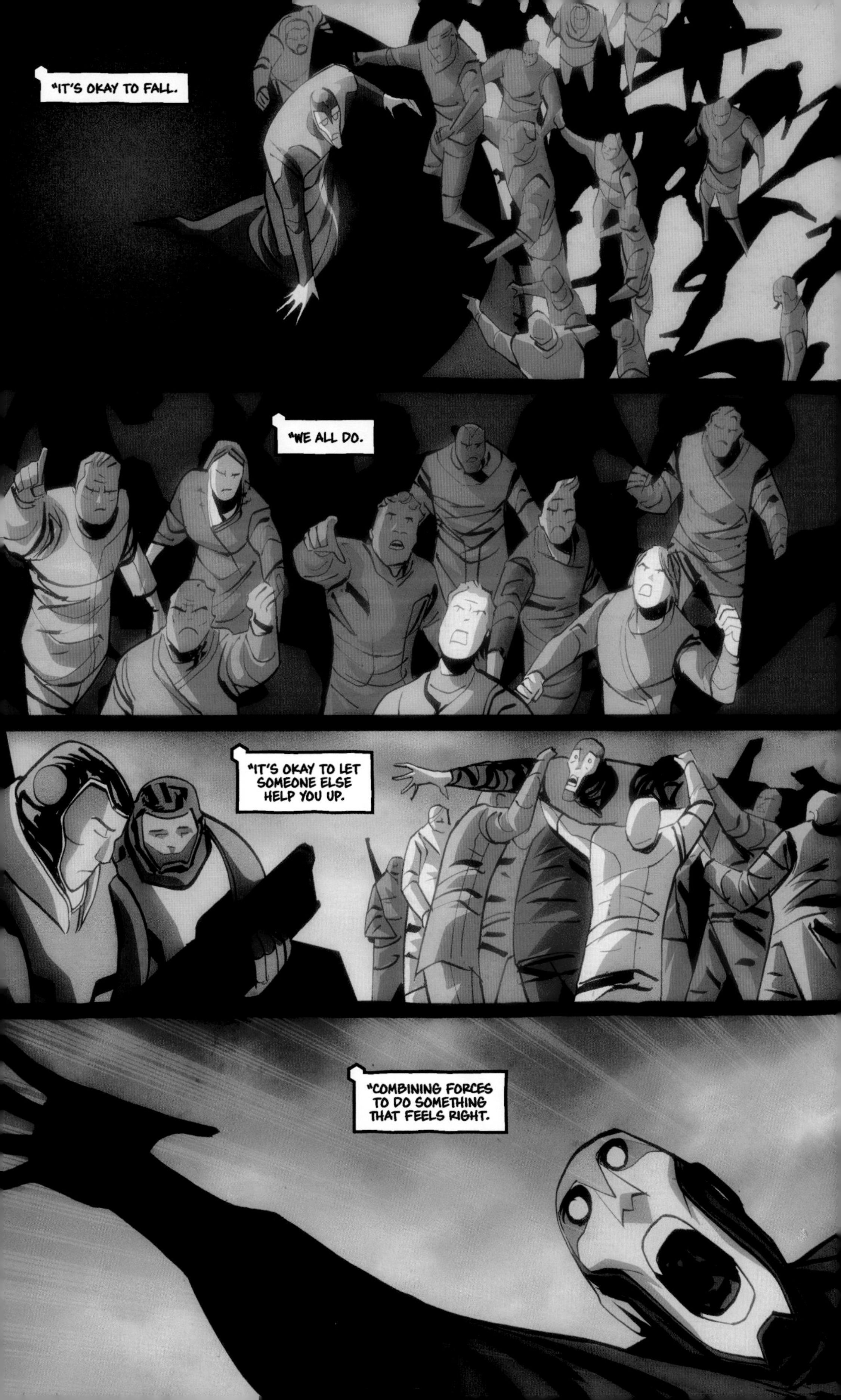
"IT'S OKAY TO FALL.
"WE ALL DO.
"IT'S OKAY TO LET SOMEONE ELSE HELP YOU UP.
"COMBINING FORCES TO DO SOMETHING THAT FEELS RIGHT.

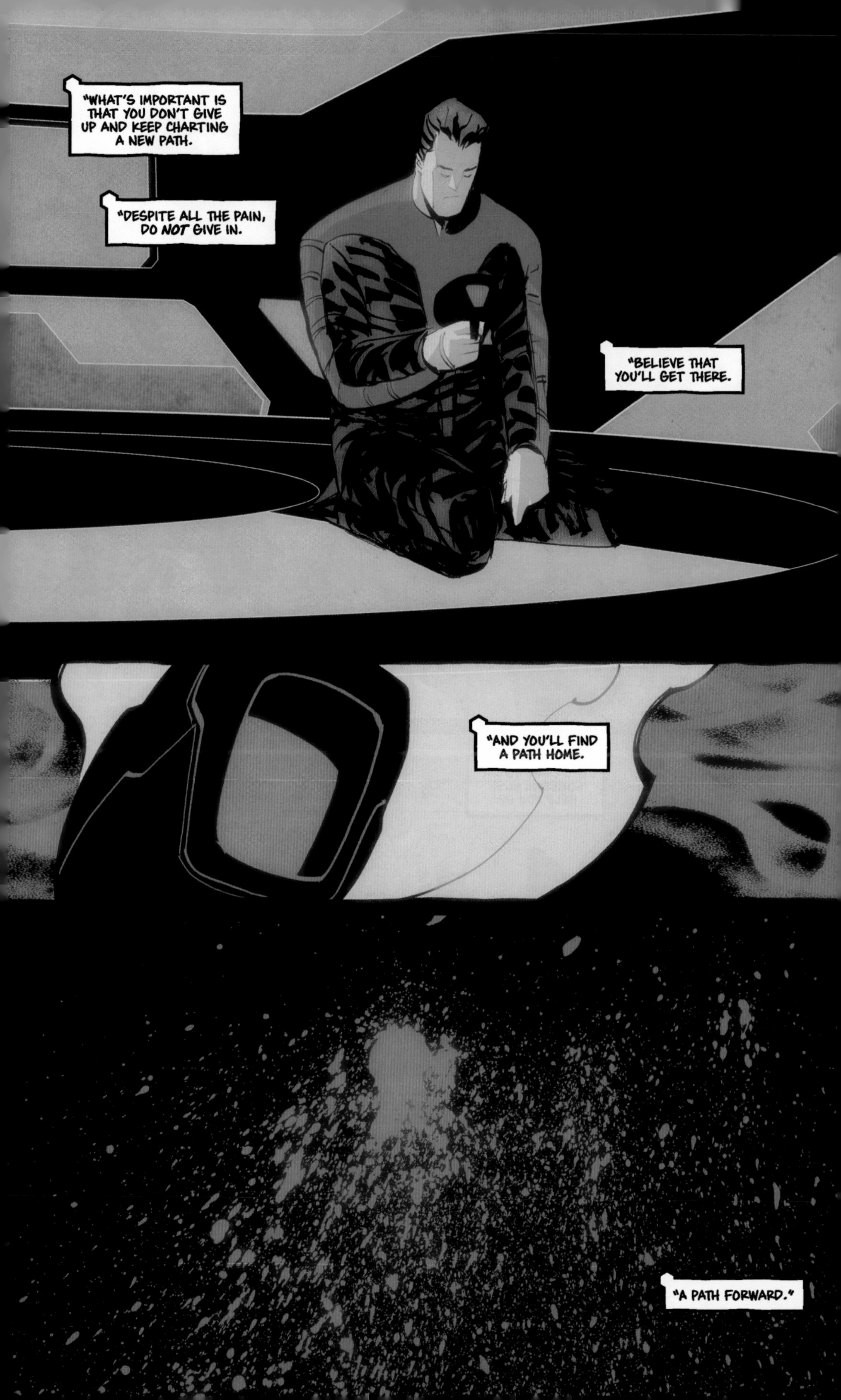
"WHAT'S IMPORTANT IS THAT YOU DON'T GIVE UP AND KEEP CHARTING A NEW PATH.
"DESPITE ALL THE PAIN, DO NOT GIVE IN.
"BELIEVE THAT YOU'LL GET THERE.
"AND YOU'LL FIND A PATH HOME.
"A PATH FORWARD."

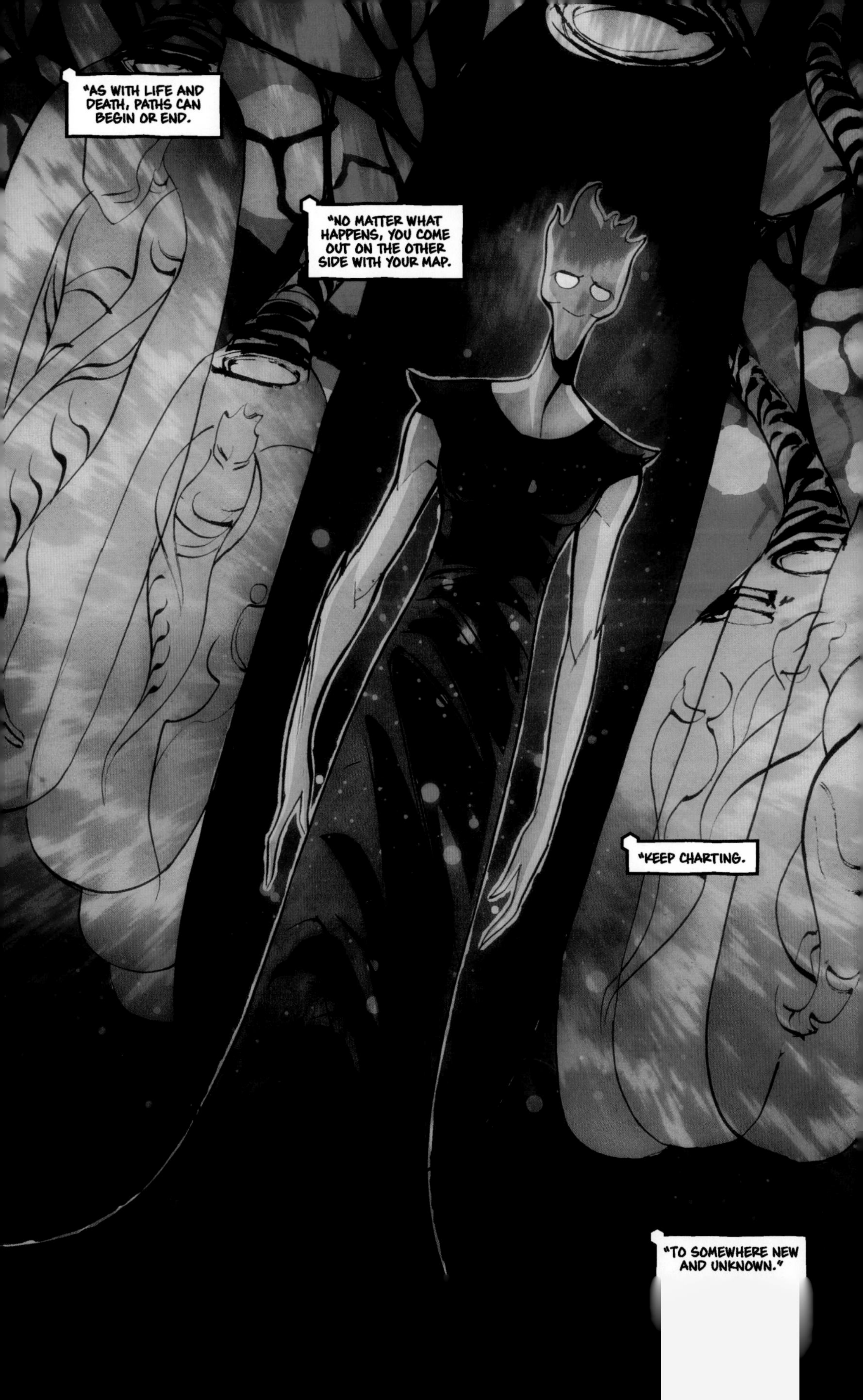
"AS WITH LIFE AND DEATH, PATHS CAN BEGIN OR END.
"NO MATTER WHAT HAPPENS, YOU COME OUT ON THE OTHER SIDE WITH YOUR MAP.
"KEEP CHARTING.
"TO SOMEWHERE NEW AND UNKNOWN."

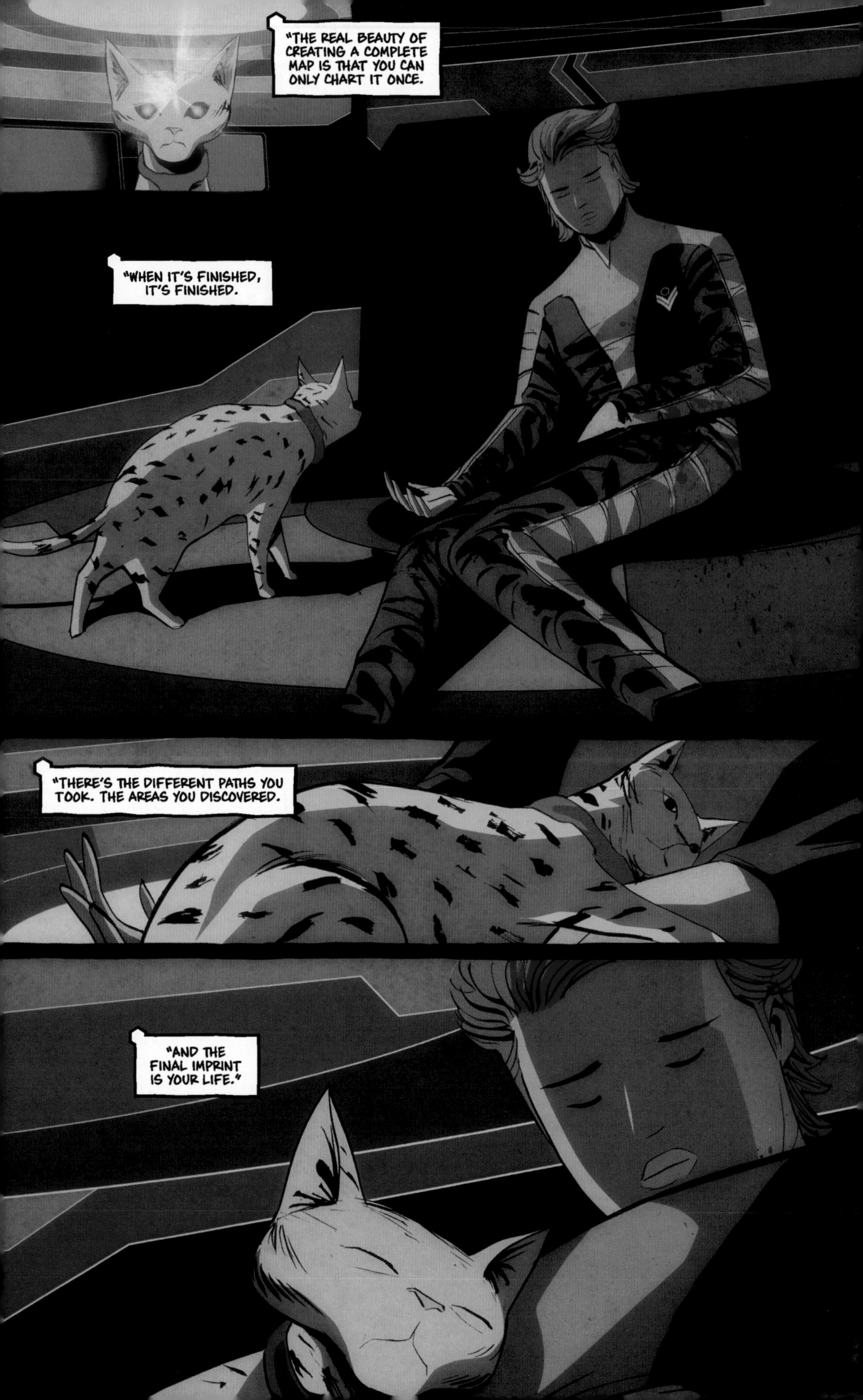
"THE REAL BEAUTY OF CREATING A COMPLETE MAP IS THAT YOU CAN ONLY CHART IT ONCE.
"WHEN IT'S FINISHED, IT'S FINISHED.
"THERE'S THE DIFFERENT PATHS YOU TOOK. THE AREAS YOU DISCOVERED.
"AND THE FINAL IMPRINT IS YOUR LIFE."

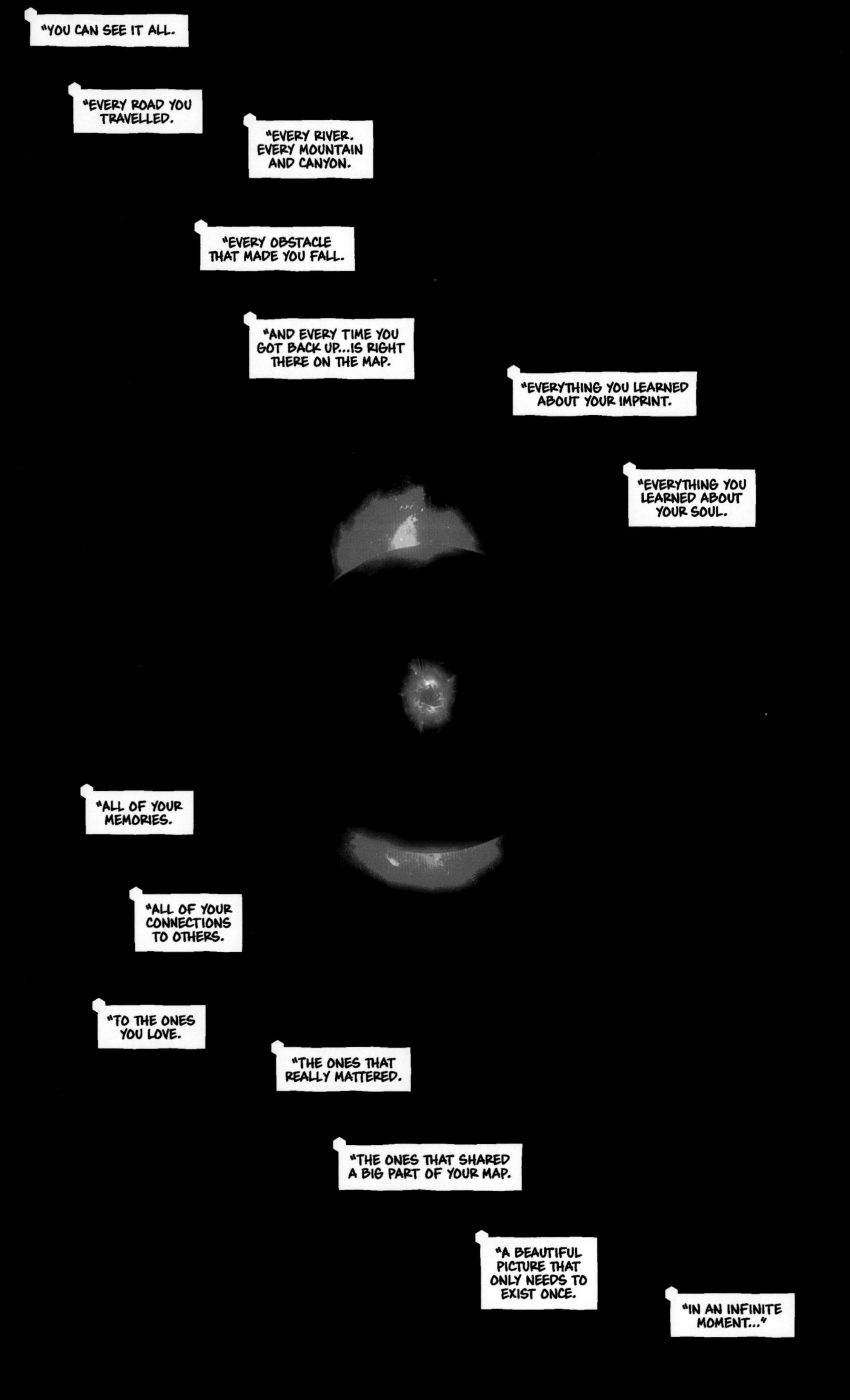
"YOU CAN SEE IT ALL.
"EVERY ROAD YOU TRAVELLED.
"EVERY RIVER. EVERY MOUNTAIN AND CANYON.
"EVERY OBSTACLE THAT MADE YOU FALL.
"AND EVERY TIME YOU GOT BACK UP...IS RIGHT THERE ON THE MAP.
"EVERYTHING YOU LEARNED ABOUT YOUR IMPRINT.
"EVERYTHING YOU LEARNED ABOUT YOUR SOUL.
"ALL OF YOUR MEMORIES.
"ALL OF YOUR CONNECTIONS TO OTHERS.
"TO THE ONES YOU LOVE.
"THE ONES THAT REALLY MATTERED.
"THE ONES THAT SHARED A BIG PART OF YOUR MAP.
"A BEAUTIFUL PICTURE THAT ONLY NEEDS TO EXIST ONCE.
"IN AN INFINITE MOMENT..."

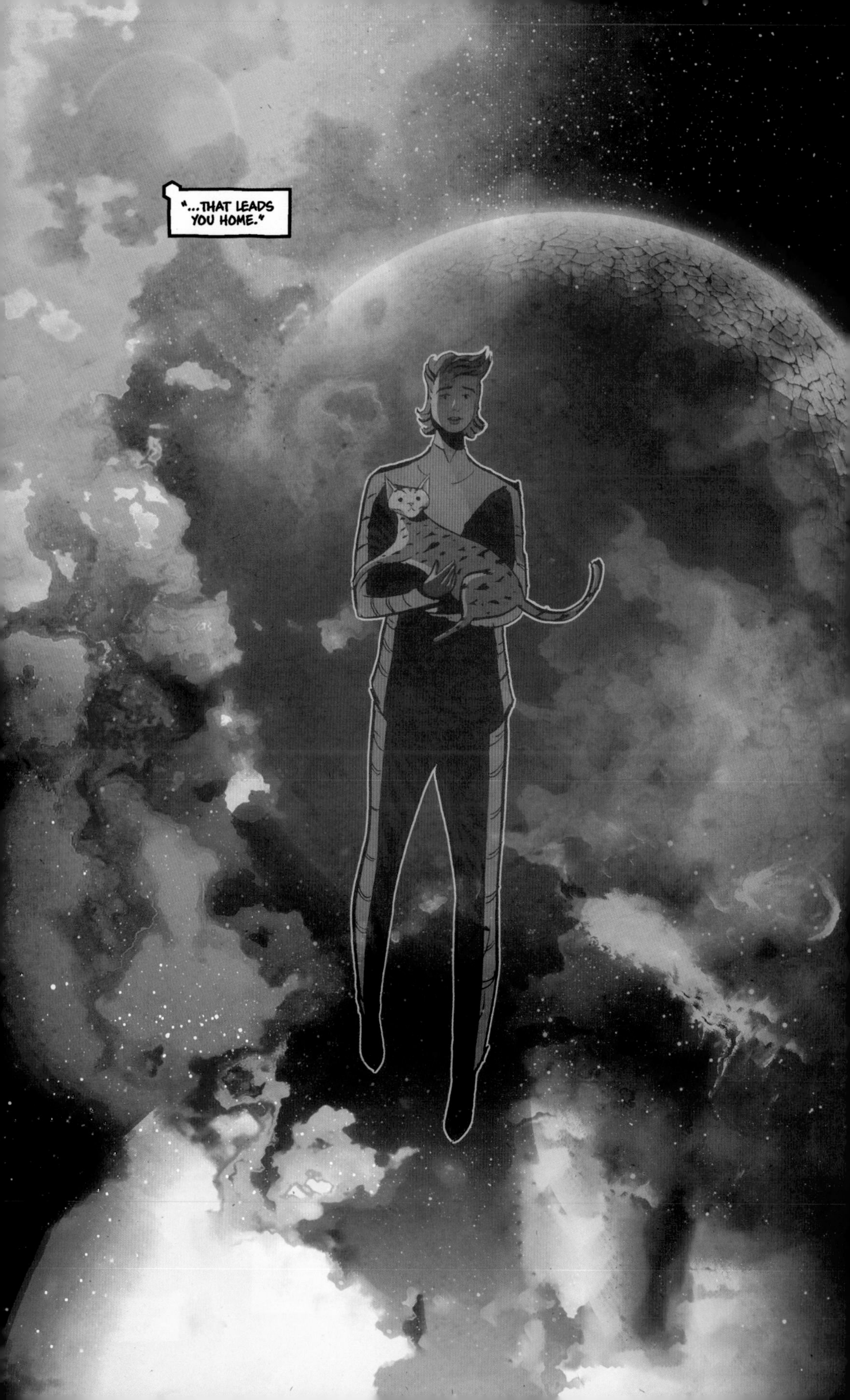
"...THAT LEADS YOU HOME."

PINUPS GALLERY

WITH ART BY

MORGAN BEEM

GAVIN SMITH

DAN HALE

JEN HICKMAN

JOHN LE

EVA REDAMONTI

CHRISTIAN WARD

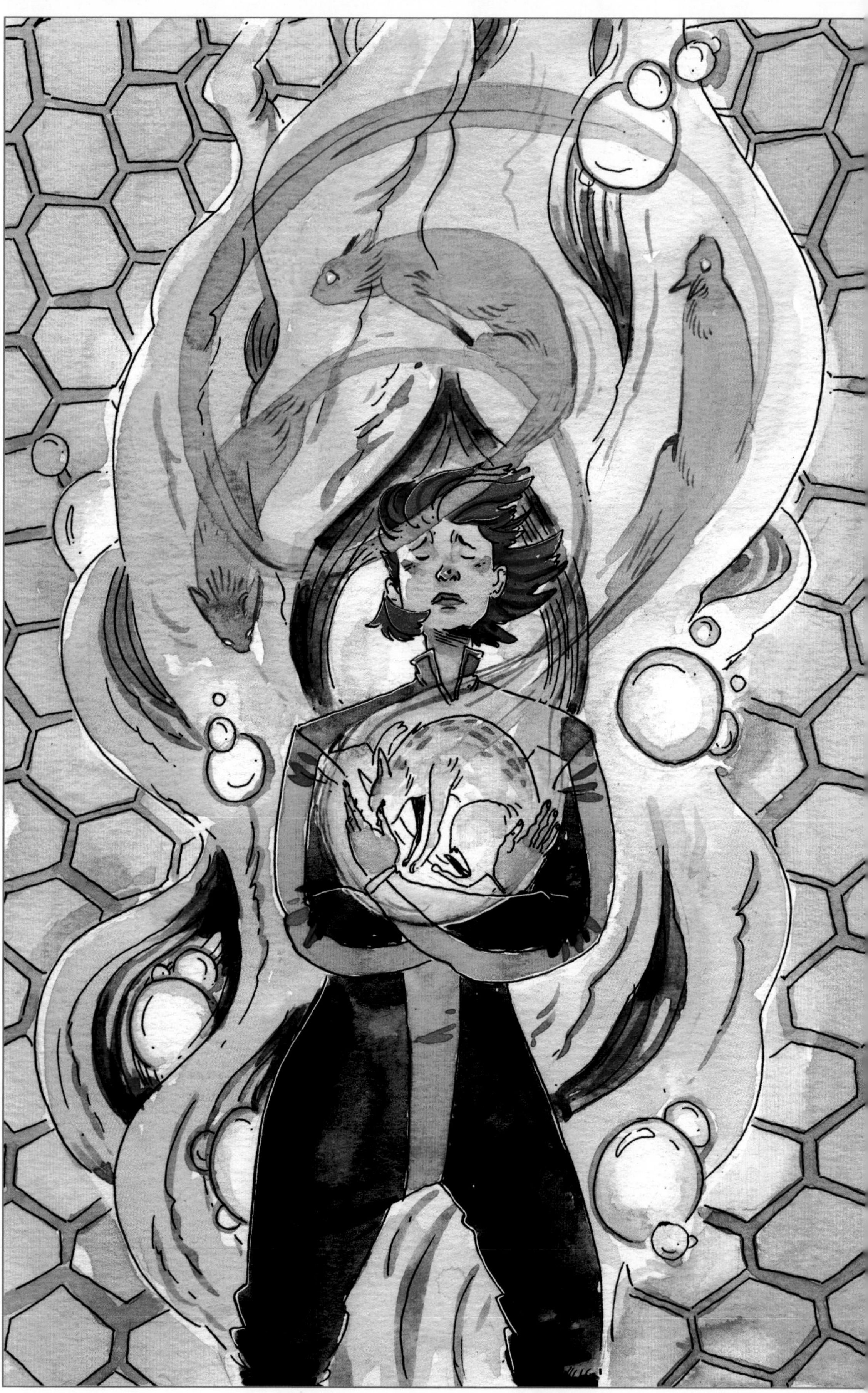

ART BY // MORGAN BEEM

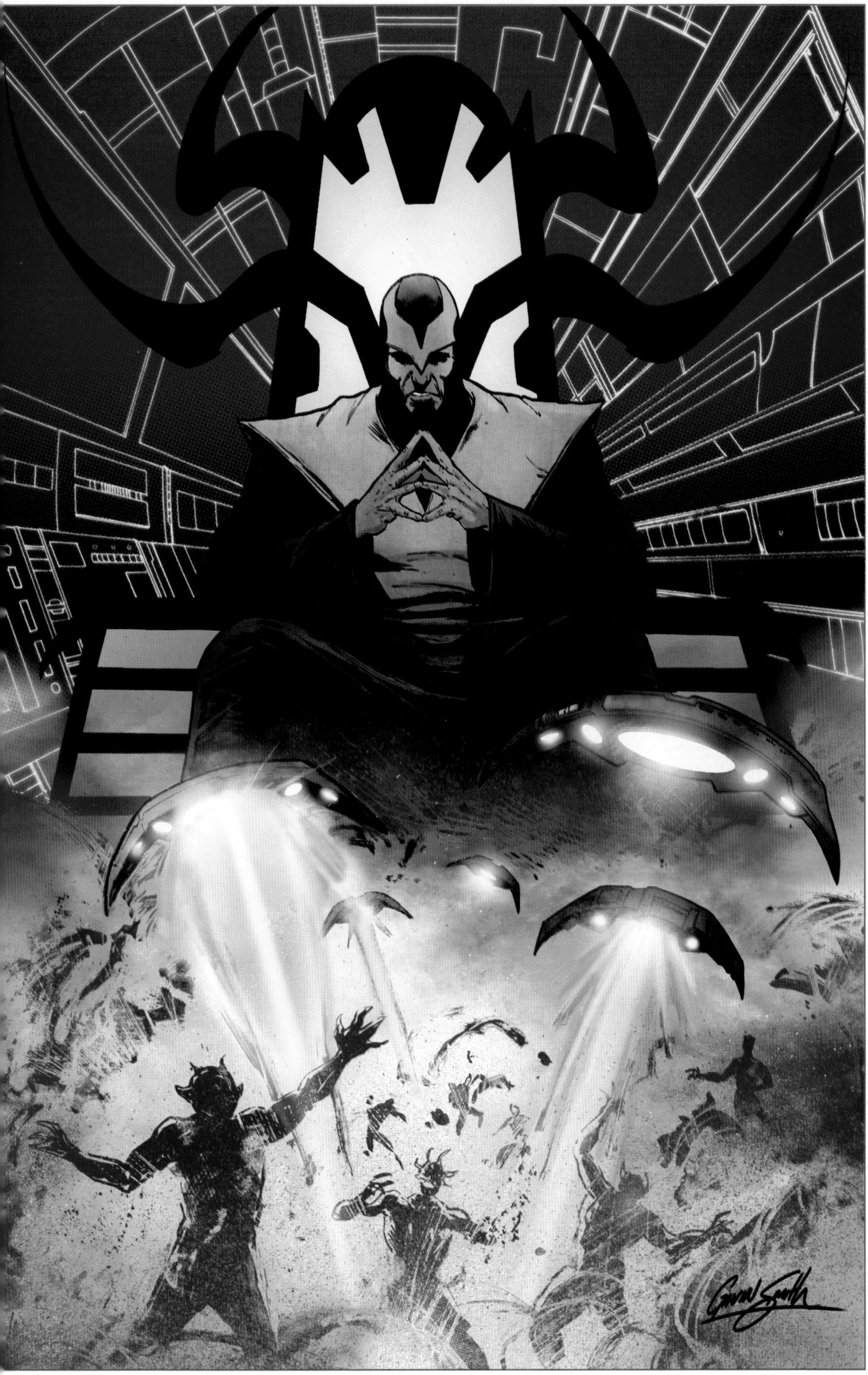

ART BY // GAVIN SMITH

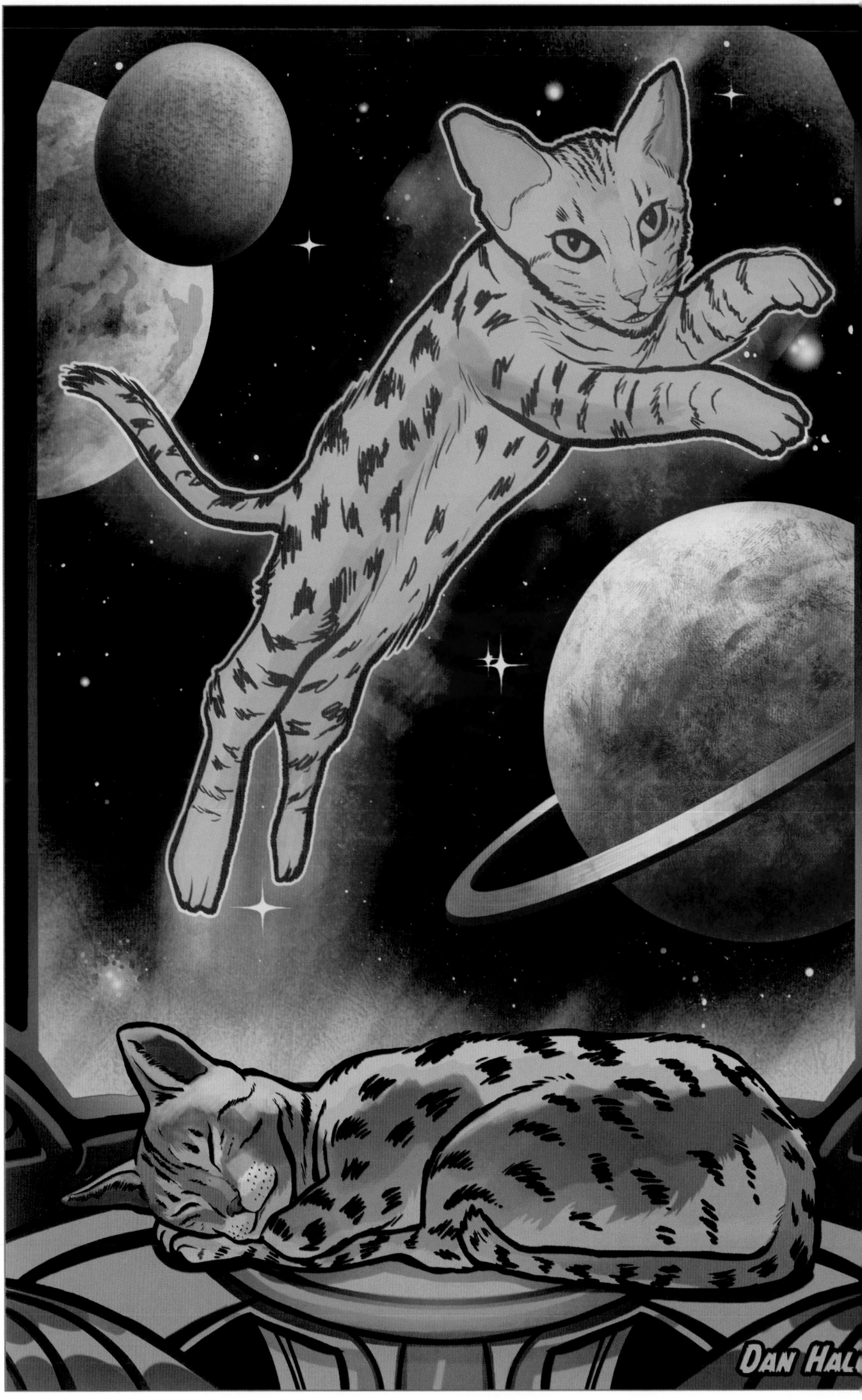
DAN HALE

ART BY // DAN HALE

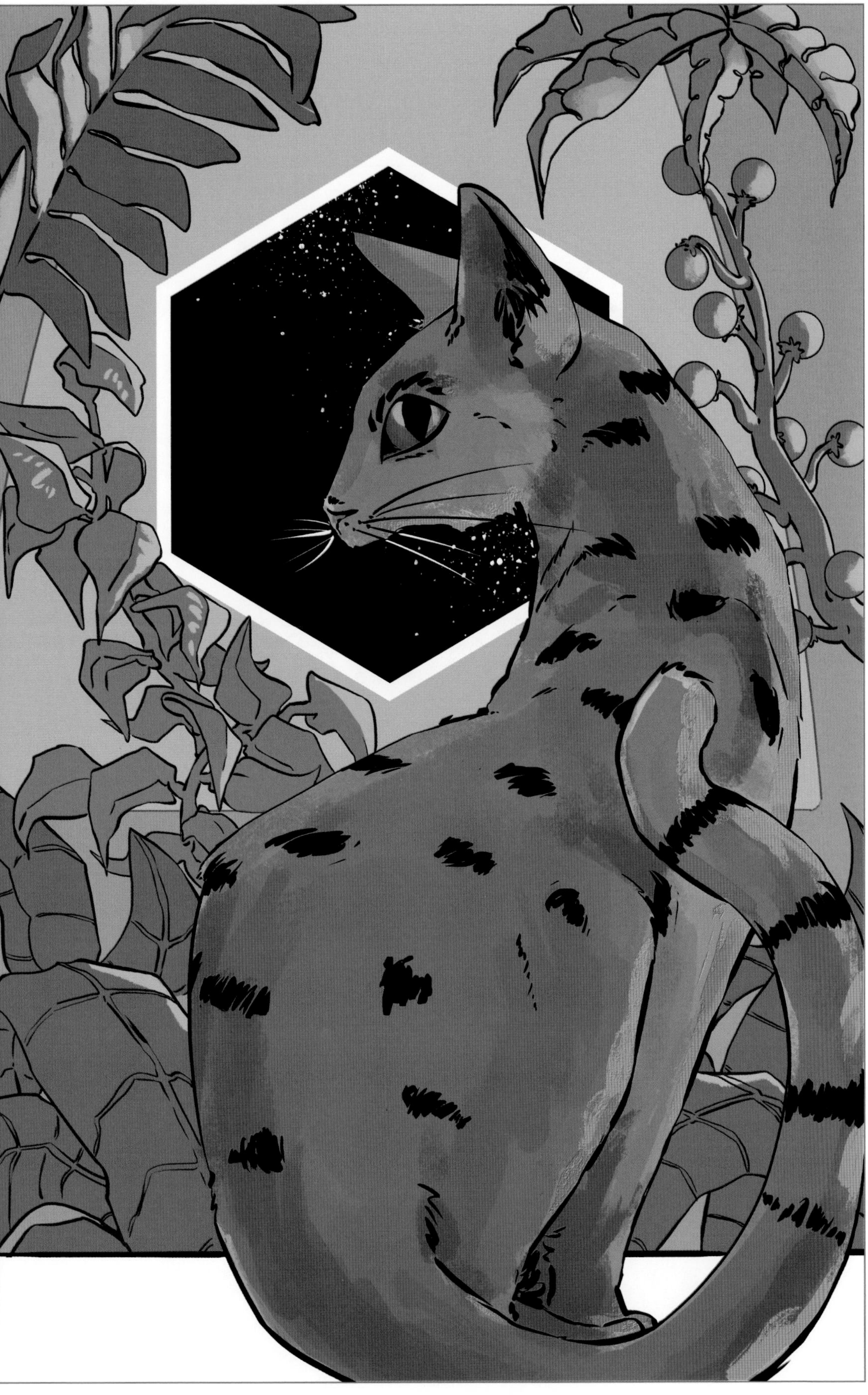

ART BY // JEN HICKMAN

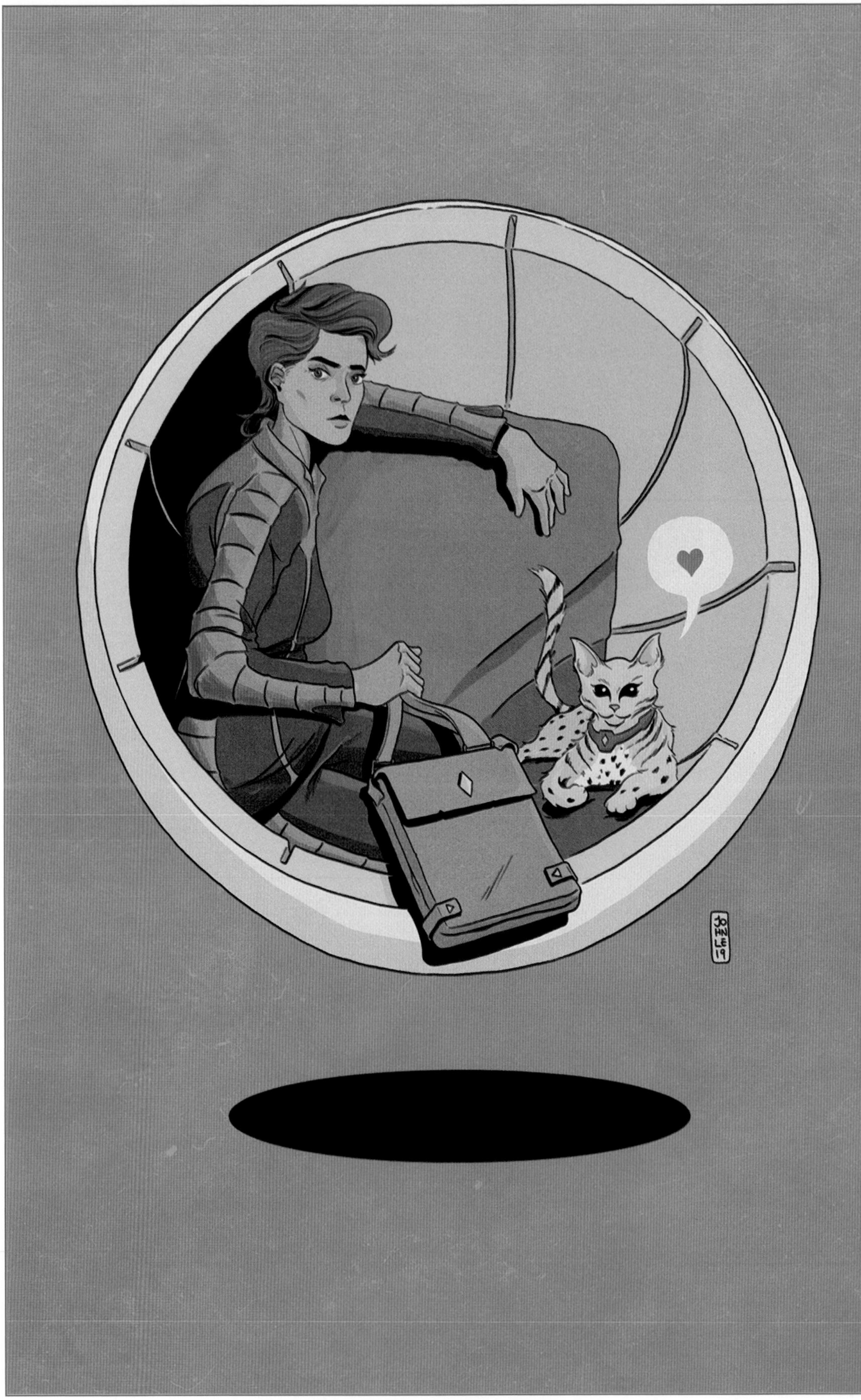
JO
HN
LE
19

ART BY // JOHN LE

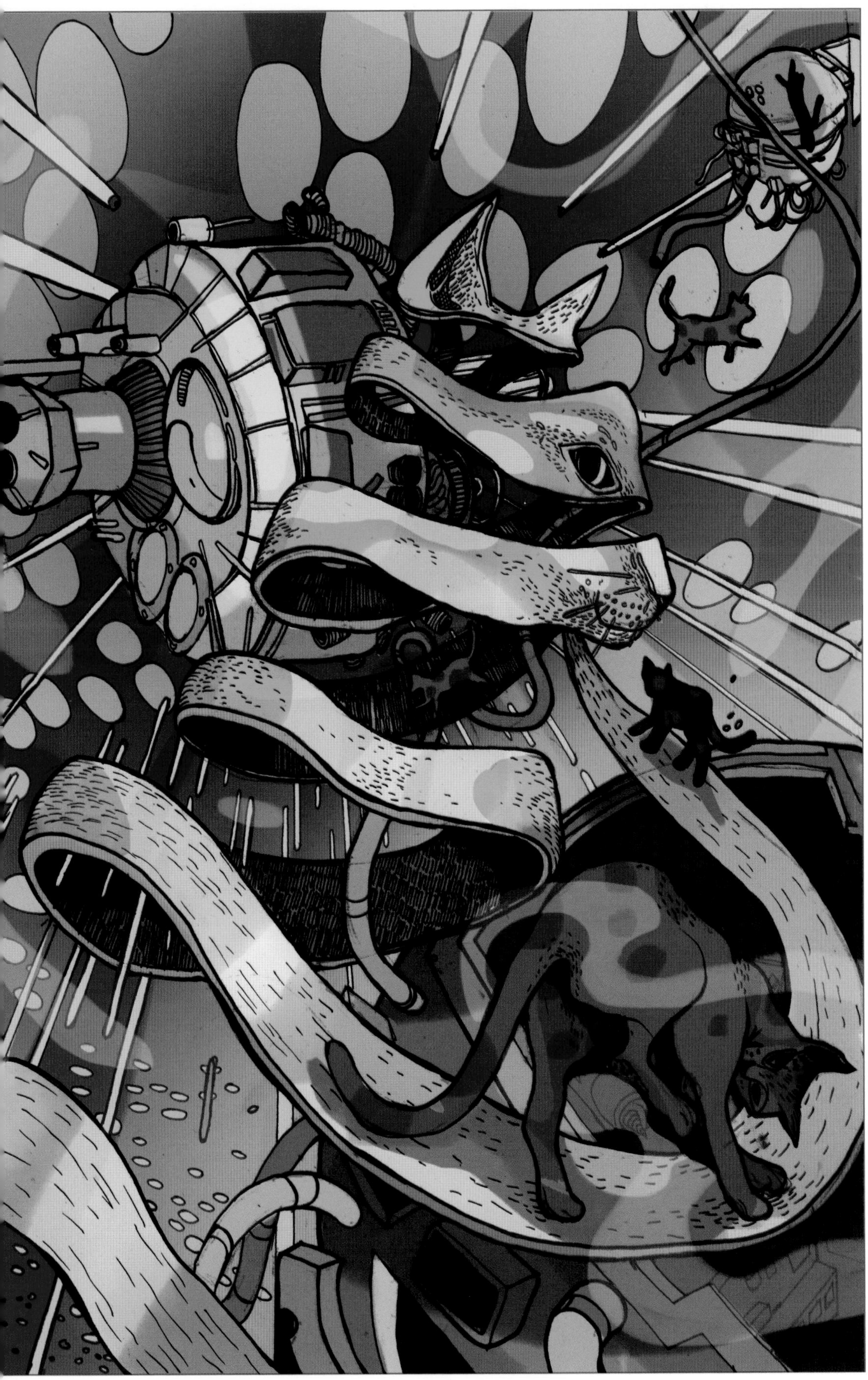

ART BY // EVA REDAMONTI

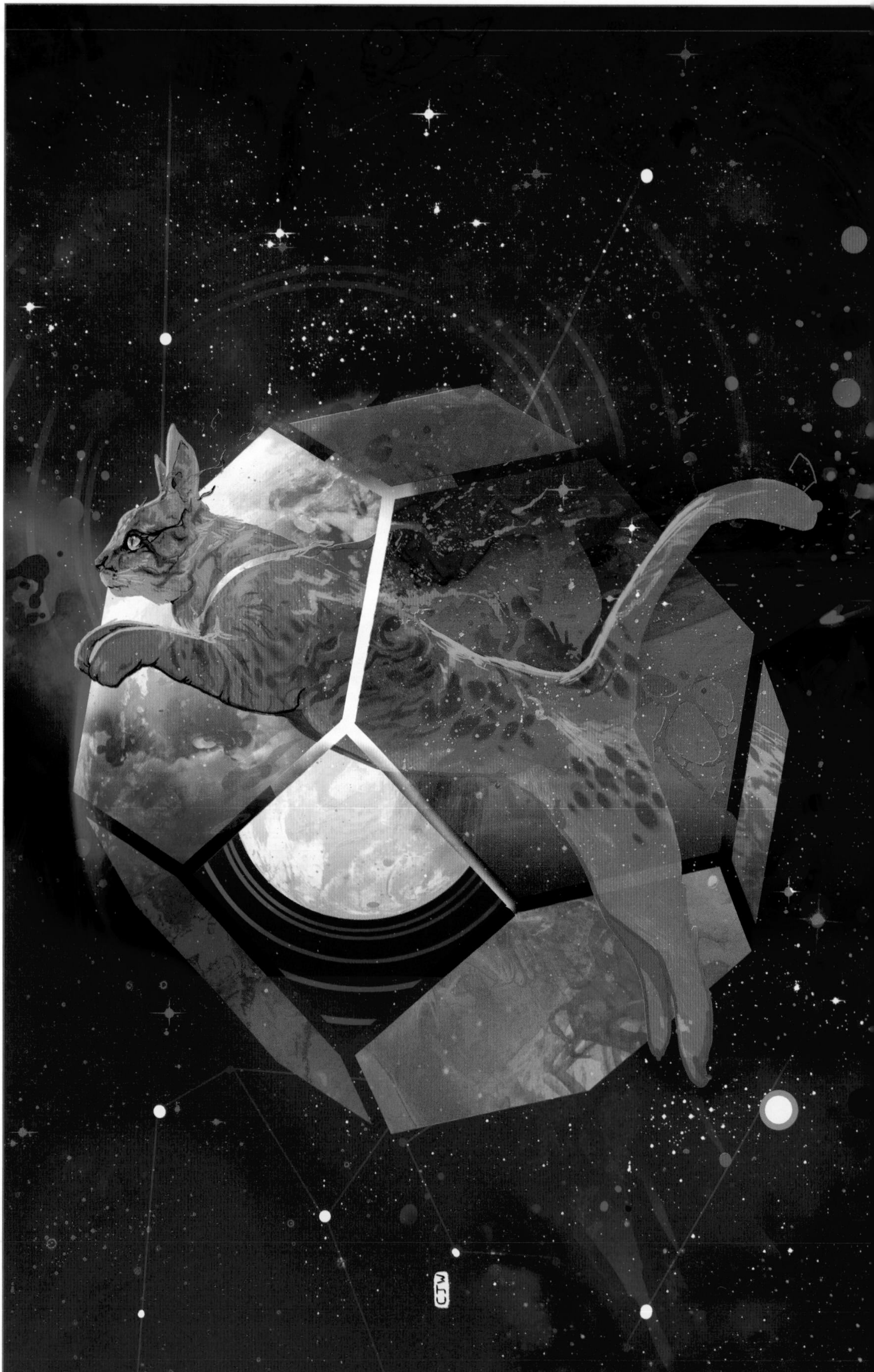

ART BY // CHRISTIAN WARD

I'D LIKE TO THANK:

The team that worked on this book, you are amazing. Thank you for coming along on this ride.

Everyone at Dark Horse, you have all been a dream to work with.

My family and friends, especially Melanie and Elaine. You are always there for me. I love you.

My two cats Viktor and Lou Reed, as well as all the pets that came before them and made my life better: Leroy, Lola, Simon, Bandido, and Ozzy.

All the readers, retailers and press that supported us.

Thank you all for believing.

—CARLOS GIFFONI

Thank you to Kylene and Ellery for their never-ending love, patience, and support. Thank you to Carlos for bringing me on this wild journey with him. Thank you to everyone who supported this book since its early stages and for all the readers (and their cats) for taking a chance on us.

—MATT KROTZER

Strayed has been an incredible experience. I can't thank Carlos enough for coming up with this trippy concept and pitching me the story. It is one of the most satisfying projects I've ever worked on. More thanks are in order for the rest of the *Strayed* team. Matt Krotzer executed the design and letters to an Eisner award-winning level, seamlessly enveloping itself within the art and words. Chas! for keeping a steady hand on the narrative all the way through and offering great notes to enhance the story. Thank you to my family for their patience and support during the long hours it took to make this puppy (kitty?) shine. A huge shout out to Dark Horse Comics for believing in *Strayed*, and publishing it for the world to see. And of course, the biggest thank you to the fans and everyone who has been engaged in this incredible story, with an astral projecting cat named Lou. Meow.

—JUAN DOE

Thank you. Yes, you. Without your support, none of this is possible.

—CHAS! PANGBURN

CREATOR BIOS

CARLOS GIFFONI is a Venezuelan writer and musician, recently working on his first creator-owned series *Strayed* for Dark Horse, and *Space Riders: Vortex of Darkness* for Black Mask. He has over 12 years of experience doing creative work in the video games industry where he has worked on projects for *League of Legends*, *South Park*, *The Daily Show*, *Ugly Americans*, and many others. As a musician, he has toured the world performing his own electronic music compositions and has also performed live improvisations with members of Sonic Youth Thurston Moore and Lee Ranaldo, Jim O'Rourke, Merzbow, and Zeena Parkins among others. He created an electronic music soundtrack for *Strayed* available at carlosgiffoni.bandcamp.com/ for free and can be reached at @carlosgiffoni on Twitter.

JUAN DOE is a writer and artist with over 15 years of experience in the comic book industry. He is currently the artist for *Strayed* with Carlos Giffoni at Dark Horse Comics and is the writer and artist for his first creator-owned comic, *Bad Reception* from Aftershock Comics. He has produced over 200 covers and some of his sequential highlights include *The Fantastic Four in Puerto Rico* trilogy with Tom Beland and *The Legion of Monsters* mini-series with Dennis Hopeless

for Marvel Comics, *Joker's Asylum: Scarecrow* with Joe Harris for DC Comics, Brian Azzarello's *American Monster*, Marguerite Bennett's *Animosity: The Rise*, *World Reader* with Jeff Loveness, and Cullen Bunn's genre-bending book *Dark Ark*, all for Aftershock Comics.

MATT KROTZER gives voices to characters and adds sound to action. As a comic book letterer and graphic designer working for powerhouses like Image, Dark Horse, and many fine independent comics around the world, he's collaborated with some of the brightest artists in comics. He is an optimist and frequent champion of lost causes, regularly found cheering for the mighty Bengals of Cincinnati. Matt lives in suburban Pennsylvania with his wife, daughter, and faithful feline companion, Teddy.

CHAS! PANGBURN puts words in balloons. (That's his all-encompassing and cheesy way of saying that he's a writer, editor, and letterer.) He lives in Northern Kentucky with a chubby corgi and two stinky ferrets. Whether you're wanting to swap pet pictures or to talk shop, he can be reached at @chasexclamation on Twitter.

STRANGER THINGS

THE NOSTALGIA-IGNITING HIT NETFLIX ORIGINAL SERIES COMES TO COMICS!

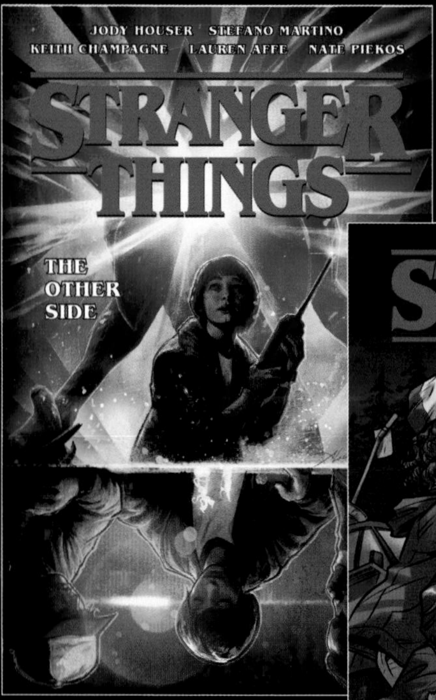
JODY HOUSER STEFANO MARTINO
KEITH CHAMPAGNE LAUREN AFFE NATE PIEKOS
STRANGER THINGS
THE OTHER SIDE

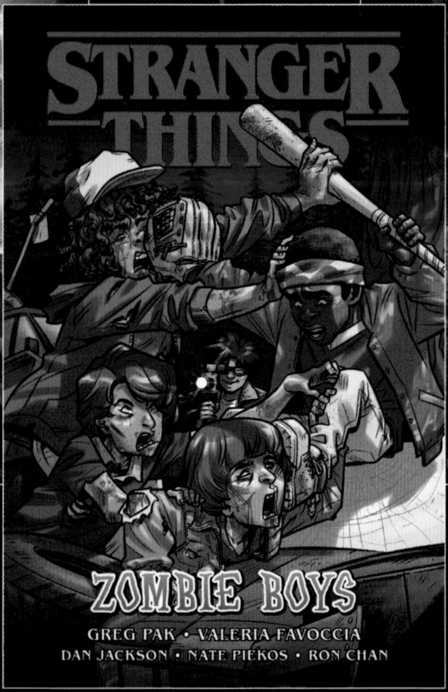
STRANGER
ZOMBIE BOYS
GREG PAK • VALERIA FAVOCCIA
DAN JACKSON • NATE PIEKOS • RON CHAN

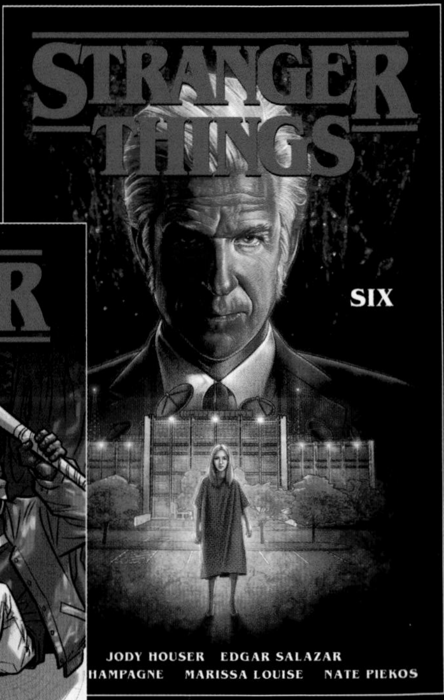
STRANGER THINGS
SIX
JODY HOUSER EDGAR SALAZAR
MARISSA LOUISE NATE PIEKOS

VOLUME 1: THE OTHER SIDE
Jody Houser, Stefano Martino, Keith Champagne, Lauren Affe
ISBN 978-1-50670-976-5
$17.99

VOLUME 2: SIX
Jody Houser, Edgar Salazar, Keith Champagne, Marissa Louise
ISBN 978-1-50671-232-1
$17.99

ZOMBIE BOYS
Greg Pak, Valeria Favoccia, Dan Jackson
ISBN 978-1-50671-309-0
$10.99

DARKHORSE.COM • AVAILABLE AT YOUR LOCAL COMICS SHOP OR BOOKSTORE
To find a comics shop near you, visit comicshoplocator.com
For more information or to order direct, visit darkhorse.com

NETFLIX